RÜDIGER LAINER

WALTER ZSCHOKKE

RÜDIGER LAINER

URBANISM · BUILDINGS · PROJECTS
STADT · BAU · WERKE · PROJEKTE
1984 – 1999

BIRKHÄUSER – PUBLISHERS FOR ARCHITECTURE
BIRKHÄUSER – VERLAG FÜR ARCHITEKTUR
BASEL · BOSTON · BERLIN

Unmarked texts: Walter Zschokke
Graphic Design: FINE LINE – Erich Monitzer, Vienna
Cover: Penthouse Seilergasse, Vienna
Cover Illustration: Margherita Spiluttini, Vienna

Translation into English: Roderick O'Donovan, Vienna
Copy-Editing: Claudia Mazanek, Vienna
Editing: Gabriele Ruff, Vienna
Picture Research: Karin Grausam, Vienna

Illustration credits
Margherita Spiluttini, Vienna pp. 10, 32, 33, 39, 41, 42, 47, 48, 50, 54, 55, 75, 76, 78, 80, 81, 82, 83, 117, 121, 122, 123
Al Eriani p. 84
Pez Hajduk, Vienna p. 160
Erich Monitzer, Vienna pp. 10, 23, 36, 56, 110, 112, 131, 134, 157, 161
Studio Paschernegg, Graz pp. 108, 109, 111, 161
Hannes Schild, Vienna pp. 30, 35, 83, 157, 158
Heinz Schmölzer, Vienna pp. 114, 131
Gert Walden, Vienna pp. 80, 161
Wolfgang Zajc, Vienna p. 165
MA 13 – Landesbildstelle BM-LV 13.088/173-1.6./95 p. 95

A CIP catalogue record for this book is available from the
Library of Congress, Washington D.C., USA.

Deutsche Bibliothek Cataloging-in-Publication Data

Lainer, Rüdiger:
[Rüdiger Lainer urbanism, buildings, projects]
Rüdiger Lainer urbanism, buildings, projects, Stadt, Bau, Werke,
Projekte : 1984 - 1999 / Walter Zschokke.
[Transl. into Engl.: Roderick O'Donovan]. –
Basel ; Boston : Berlin : Birkhäuser, 1999
ISBN 3-7643-5823-8 (Basel ...)
ISBN 0-8176-5823-8 (Boston)

This work is subject to copyright. All rights are reserved, whether the whole or part of the material is concerned, specifically the rights of translation, reprinting, re-use of illustrations, recitation, broadcasting, reproduction on microfilms or in other ways, and storage in data banks.
For any kind of use, permission of the copyright owner must be obtained.

© 1999 Birkhäuser – Publishers for Architecture/Verlag für Architektur
P.O. Box 133, CH-4010 Basel, Switzerland

Printed on acid-free paper produced from chlorine-free pulp. TCF∞
Printed in Austria, Holzhausen

ISBN 3-7643-5823-8
ISBN 0-8176-5823-8

9 8 7 6 5 4 3 2 1

CONTENTS | INHALT

Walter Zschokke
Delight in Forms – Insight into Structures | Lust an Formen – Einsicht in Strukturen   6

THE STARTER | DER EINSTIEG
Rüdiger Lainer & Ina Wagner
Open Planning | Offenes Planen   14
Housing Development | Wohnbebauung Engerthstraße, Wien–Leopoldstadt   26
Conversion | Umbau Hermanngasse, Wien–Neubau   30

FORM IS POLITICAL | FORM IST POLITISCH   36
Housing Development | Wohnbau Waidhausenstraße, Wien–Penzing   38
Housing Development | Wohnhausanlage Siegesplatz/Benjowskigasse, Aspern   44
Housing Development | Wohnhausanlage Rothenburgstraße, Wien–Altmannsdorf   50

NEUTRAL AND SPECIFIC | NEUTRAL UND SPEZIFISCH   56
Rooftop Extension | Dachaufbau Favoritenstraße, Wien–Wieden   58
Apartment Building | Wohnbau Wiedner Hauptstraße, Wien–Wieden   62
Apartment Blocks | Wohnbau Taubstummengasse, Wien–Wieden   66
Housing Development | Wohnanlage Altmannsdorfer Anger, Wien–Meidling   70
Penthouse Seilergasse, Wien–Innere Stadt   74
Conversion | Umbau Palais Equitable, Mezzanin, Wien–Innere Stadt   80

THE URBAN SCORE | DIE URBANE PARTITUR   84
Urban Guideline Project Former Aspern Airfield
Städtebauliches Leitprojekt Altes Flugfeld Aspern, Wien   86
Urban Structural Concept for the Area to the North of the Gasometers
Umfeld Gasometer, Städtebauliches Strukturkonzept, Wien–Landstraße   94
Die Wunderkammer (Chamber of Marvels)   102
Styrian Federal State Exhibition | Steirische Landesausstellung 1998   108

SHELL AND SPACE IN-BETWEEN | HÜLLE UND ZWISCHENRAUM   114
Secondary School | Hauptschule Absberggasse, Wien–Favoriten   116
Extension | Erweiterungsbau WIFI, St. Pölten   124
ZMF Center for Basic Medical Research
ZMF Zentrum für Medizinische Grundlagenforschung, Graz   128
Functions Center | Veranstaltungszentrum Kaiserbahnhof, Laxenburg   132

PICTORIAL WALL | DARSTELLENDE WAND   134
Building | Betriebsgebäude Austria Email, Wien–Favoriten   136
Eurocity Cinema Center | Kino-Center, Salzburg   140
Pleasure Dome², Wien–Landstraße   146

List of Projects | Werkverzeichnis   154
Exhibitions | Ausstellungen   163
Biography | Biografie   165
Bibliography | Bibliografie   166

LUST AN FORMEN – EINSICHT IN STRUKTUREN

Walter Zschokke

Gegenklassische Haltung als Prinzip
Eine etablierte Ordnung, eine ausformulierte Architekturströmung erreicht im Zuge ihrer Entwicklung, an der einige oder auch viele Architekten mitwirken können, eine relative Vollkommenheit, die oft als klassisch angesprochen wird. Das kollektive Arbeiten am Ausdruck von Ebenmaß, Gediegenheit und konsequenter Durchformung erfolgt in der Regel ohne Abmachung, ohne Gespräche, auch ohne dass sich die Akteure gegenseitig zu kennen brauchen. Dennoch nehmen sie die Bauten der jeweils anderen zur Kenntnis, vollziehen an ihnen die Entwurfsgedanken nach, ob am Bauwerk selbst oder anhand von Plan- und Bildmaterial in den Fachpublikationen, und messen daran ihre eigenen Arbeiten. Auf diese Weise bilden sich Tendenzen, Bewegungen und schließlich Strömungen heraus. Wenn eine derartige Strömung schon etwas breiter geworden ist, erreichen manche der ihr zuordenbaren Bauten eine alles überdeckende Glätte, aus der zwar Perfektion, zugleich aber auch Langeweile und Lustlosigkeit sprechen. Manchen mag diese Kanonisierung durchaus ein Lebensziel sein, und sie verfestigen einige Kernsätze womöglich zu Dogmen, an denen sie für einen längeren Abschnitt ihres Arbeitens festhalten. In ihren Ateliers bildet sich eine verbindliche gestalterische Sprachregelung heraus, die von den Mitarbeitern vollzogen werden kann. Bauherren wissen dann schon bei der Beauftragung, was sie ungefähr erhalten werden: Architektur wird damit irgendwie risikolos, kalkulierbar und lässt jede Spannung vermissen.

Selbst wenn dabei zahlreiche handwerklich untadelige Bauwerke entstehen mögen, gibt es immer wieder Architekten, denen Perfektion und Glätte der genannten Art – nicht in einem vordergründigen Sinn – verdächtig sind. Denn die Entstehungsgedanken verflüchtigen sich aus den eitlen Gebäudehüllen und lassen sich nicht mehr nacherleben, weil nur mehr tote Formen exekutiert wurden. Wenn man als Kritiker solche Gebilde durch Anschauung befragt, erhält man außer stereotypen Antworten keine weiteren Aussagen.

Daher wird von manchen Architekten – und zu diesen zähle ich Rüdiger Lainer – immer wieder die eine oder andere der scheinbar ewiggültigen Konventionen in Frage gestellt, ohne dass sie sogleich alles neu erfinden möchten und können. Aber sie greifen doch soweit ein, dass der vorher glatte Spiegel gestört ist. Oft ist es nur etwas mehr als ein Hauch, knapp über der Wahrnehmungsschwelle, manchmal ist es ein kräftiger Windstoß, aber immer wird mit einem derartigen Entwurf die alles dämpfende, prästabilisierte Harmonie verabschiedet. Diese Haltung wird gemeinhin gegenklassisch genannt. Sie muss nicht umstürzlerisch, nicht zerstörerisch sein, das stünde dem Architektsein, das bauen, aufbauen will, entgegen. Aber sie lässt sich

DELIGHT IN FORMS – INSIGHT INTO STRUCTURES
Walter Zschokke

The Counter-Classical Approach as a Principle
An established order, a formulated architectural tendency, achieves in the course of its development – in which one or a number of architects can participate – a relative completeness often referred to as classical. Collective work on the expression of harmony, quality and consistent development generally takes place without prior agreement or discussion and without it being necessary for the protagonists to know each other. Nevertheless they register each other's buildings, trace the design concepts behind them, whether by viewing the buildings themselves or on the basis of plans and photographic material in the specialist publications, and assess their own work accordingly. In this way, tendencies, movements and ultimately directions are established. When such a direction becomes broader many of the buildings that can be ascribed to it develop a smoothness which covers everything, demonstrating perfection but at the same time a certain boredom and joylessness. It may well be the goal of some architects to have their works numbered in such a canon, to achieve this they consolidate certain basic statements into firm dogmas by which, for a long part of their working lives, they abide. In their ateliers a binding design language develops which can be applied by their staff. Clients know when placing a commission more or less what they will get. In this way architecture becomes somehow less free, calculable and lacking in any tension.

Although such an approach may lead to numerous buildings that are irreproachable in terms of craftsmanship there always remain architects who find perfection and smoothness of the kind referred to – not in a superficial sense – suspicious. The original ideas disappear from the vain building shells and cannot be retraced because the forms erected are dead. If, as a critic, one questions such formations on looking at them one receives no reply other than stereotypical responses.

Therefore many architects, among whom I number Rüdiger Lainer, repeatedly question one or other of those conventions which apparently have an eternal validity while neither wishing nor being in a position to create everything anew. But they intervene in such a manner that the previously smooth surface is destroyed. Often it is barely more than a breath just within our range of perception, at times it is a powerful gust but in every case a design based on such an approach departs from the pre-established harmony and its dampening effect. This approach is generally described as counter-classical. It must not be revolutionary or destructive as this would not be in accordance with the nature of an architect whose aim it is to build and build up. But it refuses to be forced into established tracks without making an – appropriate – independent contribution and, above all, insists on delight in new

LUST AN FORMEN – EINSICHT IN STRUKTUREN

nicht in vorgegebene Spuren drängen, ohne mit einem – angemessenen – Beitrag Eigenständigkeit und vor allem Lust an offenen, neuartigen Formen, Materialwirkungen und Kombinationen zu entwickeln und mit soziokulturellem Engagement auch politische Gedankenfreiheit zu beweisen.

Bei Rüdiger Lainers Arbeiten drängt die gegenklassische Haltung von innen heraus immer wieder an die Oberfläche und macht sich an seinen Bauwerken bemerkbar. Auch wenn er vielleicht an mehreren aufeinanderfolgenden Projekten ein ähnliches Konzept verfolgt, sind immer wieder offene oder ungeregelte Komponenten enthalten, die das Ganze in eine spezielle Drehung versetzen, die spezifische Aspekte in den Vordergrund rücken und dem Bauwerk einen eigenen Charakter verleihen. Seine Arbeiten wecken daher immer wieder Neugier und befriedigen den Hunger nach gegenklassischen Antworten. Natürlich sind sie manchmal etwas trendig, denn Rüdiger Lainer wäre nicht Rüdiger Lainer, ohne dieses affirmative Bewegen im Zeitstrom; seine Eingriffe erfolgen jedoch nie unreflektiert, sondern in bewusster Auswahl, mit Neugier, Einfühlungsvermögen und mit Spielwitz.

Lernen von der Stadt

Das Wesen der Stadt zeichnet sich unter anderem dadurch aus, dass es für ihr Funktionieren zwar diverse Regeln gibt, dass sich im Lauf der Entwicklung eines städtischen Organismus und seiner Materialisierung in gebauter Substanz immer auch Ausnahmen, Mehrfachlösungen, doppelte Wahrheiten und unerwartete Widersprüche ergeben. Stadt ist daher an sich gegenklassisch, immer schon gewesen. Sie verweigert sich dem Dirigismus und lässt sich nicht absolut beherrschen. Die Beschäftigung mit der Stadt, mit sozialen, kulturellen und allgemeinmenschlichen Fragen hat Rüdiger Lainer früh dahin geführt, Lebensprozesse nicht abschließend definieren zu wollen, sondern Enwicklungsfreiräume vorauszusehen oder zumindest mitzudenken. Seine Architektur ist daher geprägt vom Wissen um die Stadt, um ihre Lebendigkeit, Vielschichtigkeit und Zufallsabhängigkeit.

Die Natur der Stadt bringt es mit sich, dass der Architekt zu ihr eher in ein spielerisches Verhältnis treten kann, als dass er einen Herrschaftsanspruch durchzusetzen vermöchte. Denn dem Wesen Stadt lässt sich nicht befehlen. Immerhin können bei klugem Einfühlungsvermögen Verdichtungen in einem sich entmischenden Gefüge erzielt und lokale, oft sogar geviertgroße Erneuerungen der Urbanität initiiert werden, die auf ihre Umgebung ausstrahlen.

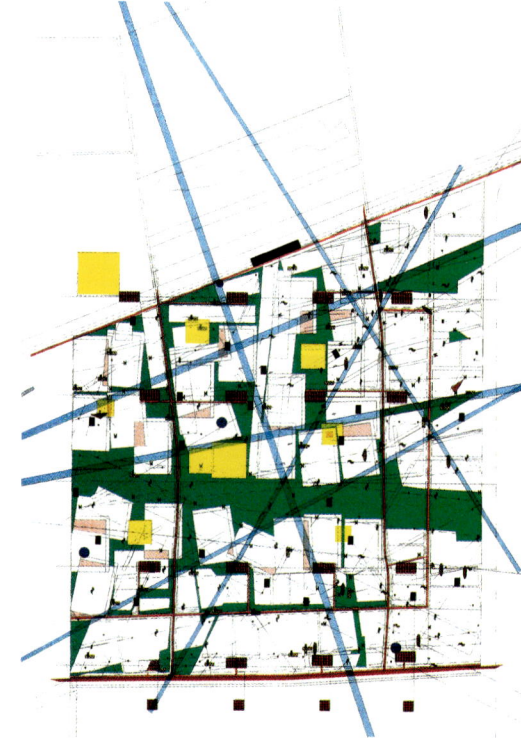

Bei fast allen Bauten von Rüdiger Lainer lässt sich diese Grundhaltung feststellen, da seine Konzepte immer auch die umgebende Stadt mitdenken. Ob es sich um die stark plastischen, im Inneren differenzierten Wohnhausanlagen aus den späten achtziger Jahren handelt oder um seine in Bereiche, Zonen, Schichten und Screens strukturierten Gebäudekonzepte aus den neunziger Jahren, der Komplex „Stadt" ist jeweils innen und außen präsent.

Wie nur wenige Architekten seiner Generation pflegt Rüdiger Lainer beim Umgang mit Prozessen soziokultureller Natur einen offenen, dynamischen Stil. Er sieht das Nebeneinander verschiedener Lebensauffassungen, er anerkennt die Schwierigkeiten, die aus sozialen Verwerfungen, Migrationsproblemen und dergleichen resultieren, aber er sucht den positiven Ansatz, der vieles aufnimmt, Nötiges vorkehrt, aber vor allem nach vorne offen bleibt.

DELIGHT IN FORMS – INSIGHT INTO STRUCTURES

open forms, in developing material effects and combinations and in proving political freedom of thought through socio-cultural involvement.

In Rüdiger Lainer's work the counter-classical approach forces its way from the inside to the surface, making itself evident in his buildings. Although he may well pursue a similar concept in several consecutive buildings they always contain open, unregulated components which set the entire project in a special rotation moving specific aspects into the foreground and giving the building its individual character. Thus his buildings always excite curiosity and satisfy the hunger for counter-classical responses. Naturally they are, at times, somewhat trendy. Rüdiger Lainer would not be Rüdiger Lainer without his affirmative agility in moving with the tendencies of our times. However his interventions are never unthinking but reflect a considered choice, curiosity, sensitivity and wit.

Learning from the City
The essence of the city is revealed in the fact that, although there are various rules governing the way it functions, in the course of the development of an urban organisation and its materialisation as built substance, there are always exceptions, multiple solutions, double truths and unexpected contradictions. Thus the city is, and always has been, essentially counter-classical, it refuses to accept a planned system and does not allow itself to be dominated. His investigations of the city and socio-cultural and general human questions lead Rüdiger Lainer, at an early stage, to wish to avoid making final definitions of life processes but to foresee, or at least conceptually include, open spaces for development. Consequently his architecture is marked by his knowledge of the city, its life, variety and dependence on chance.

The nature of the city means that it is far easier for the architect to enter into a playful relationship with it than to succeed in dominating it. The essence of the city does not allow itself to be commanded. With intelligent sensitivity increases in density, even within a disintegrating mix, can be achieved and local renewal, often up to the scale of a district, of the urban quality initiated which then exerts an impact on the surroundings.

This basic approach can be discerned in almost all of Rüdiger Lainer's buildings as his concepts always include the surrounding city. Whether we refer to the strongly sculptural, internally differentiated housing developments that date from the late eighties or his building concepts from the nineties that are structured in terms of areas, zones, layers and screens, the complex of the city is always present, externally and internally.

Like only few architects of his generation Rüdiger Lainer cultivates an open, dynamic style in his handling of the processes of socio-cultural development. He sees the coexistence of different understandings of life, recognises the difficulties which result from social rejection, migration problems and such like but always looks for a positive starting point, that can absorb much, make essential provisions and, above all, remain open towards the future.

LUST AN FORMEN – EINSICHT IN STRUKTUREN

Bewegtheit im Raum

Das Wissen um Veränderbarkeit und Dynamik mancher gesellschaftlicher und individueller Lebensprozesse provozierte Rüdiger Lainer in den achtziger Jahren zu Formen, die dieser Dynamik Ausdruck zu geben versuchten. Stark plastisch, hier aufbrechend, dort ineinander übergehend, mal bandartig schlingend, mal schildartig schirmend, definieren seine architektonischen Elemente, Räume und Raumzonen, Orte und Übergänge, Schleusen und Beschleunigungsstrecken. Dieses abbildende Prinzip sieht das Bauwerk in virtueller Bewegung: Seitentrakte stoßen gerundet in Gangräume vor, Großräume ecken über die Fassadenebene hinaus, Hochgestemmtes lastet, scheint aber an anderer Stelle gleichsam zu schweben, und einzelne Fassadenteile wirken, als würden sie atmen.

Manchmal, wie beim Dachaufbau Seilergasse, am Freizeitklassentrakt der Schule oder an der Stirnseite des Dachaufbaus Favoritenstraße, erfasst die Bewegung die Fläche einer Glas- oder Leichtbaufassade, staucht und faltet, ja zerknittert sie und belässt das Endprodukt den Bewohnern als irritierende Störung der benachbarten Glätte, als gegenklassischen Denkanstoß. Aus allem spricht die Lust an Formen, die Freude an Bewegung und die Neigung zum Spiel. Diese Lebendigkeit fand eine Entsprechung in den konkreten Farbkonzepten von Oskar Putz, die mit der Plastizität interpretatorisch umgehen, einmal den Formen folgend, dann ebendiese Formen wieder konterkarierend.

In seinen Wohnbauprojekten der neunziger Jahre verlässt Rüdiger Lainer diese Art der Interpretation und bietet vermehrt neutrale Räume an sowie alternative Möglichkeiten, das Bad zu platzieren oder die Küche zu organisieren. Das Vorläufige, Unfertige überlässt den künftigen Bewohnern die definitive Interpretation ihrer Raumzonen, schafft unterschiedliche Außenraumbereiche und legt Wert auf differenzierte Arten des Zugangs, wie etwa in der Wiedner Hauptstraße, wo vorgeschaltete Stege mit gondelartigen Ausweitungen für eine individuell-private Nutzung des Wohnungszugangs vorgesehen sind.

Alpine Tektonik hinter schleierartigen Screens

Eine Vorliebe für ungeregelte Ordnungen oder geregelte Unordnungen findet sich in der Folge bei größeren Anlagen, wie den Multiplex-Kinos, dem Cluster für das WIFI St. Pölten und anderen Projekten. Die Volumen von Großräumen werden wie riesige Felsblöcke behandelt, die, zu geologischen Formationen gestapelt, extrem unregelmäßige Zwischenräume erzeugen: Schluchten, Tunnelgewölbe, Galerien, Deckendurchbrüche und Stege wechseln mit Terrassen und Kanzeln, wo Blicke in die Höhe und in die Tiefe den Gleichgewichtssinn ansprechen.

Die Lust an Formen springt hier im Maßstab, ist nicht mehr sanft wellig und verlässt das flache Relief. Sorgfältig differenzierte Gestaltung weicht schroffer Wildheit und einer rohbaumäßigen Oberfläche, was aber durchaus kalkuliert ist und im weiteren Projektfortschritt als kräftiger Grundton gegenüber differenzierten Interventionen auf der Detailebene dient.

Parallel zu dieser Entwicklung verlief eine andere, die den äußeren Ausdruck betrifft. Die plastische Durchformung im flachen Relief führte bei den Fassaden zu einer ausgeprägten Gebäudephysiognomie, was etwa an den Wohnbauten Waidhausenstraße, Benjowskigasse und vielleicht am ausgeprägtesten an der Straßenfront zur Rothenburgstraße in Wien-Altmannsdorf zu sehen ist. Eine vergleichbare Wirkung hat die hohe Schildwand mit dem Schriftornament von Erich Monitzer beim Haupteingang zur Schule Absberggasse.

DELIGHT IN FORMS – INSIGHT INTO STRUCTURES

Animation in Space

His awareness of the changeable nature and dynamics of many social and individual life processes provoked Rüdiger Lainer in the eighties to create forms which attempt to give this dynamic force expression. Strongly sculptural, at points bursting out, at others interpenetrating, sometimes extending ribbon-like or shimmering like a shield, his architectonic elements define spaces and spatial zones, places and transitions, sluices and acceleration strips. This depictive principle envisages the building in virtual movement. Side wings, rounded-off, intrude into a corridor space, major spaces extend beyond the facade plane, supported elements transfer their load while appearing at other points to hover, individual parts of the facade seem to breathe. In some cases, such as the rooftop conversion in Seilergasse, the free-time classroom wing of the school building or the end elevation of the Favoritenstrasse attic conversion, the movement captures the surface of a facade made of glass or in light-weight construction, concentrates and folds or even crumples it, leaving the final product for the residents as an irritant that disturbs the neighbouring smoothness, a counter-classical provocation to think. All this illustrates delight in forms, joy in movement and a tendency towards playfulness. This liveliness is matched by Oskar Putz' colour concepts which deal with the plasticity in an interpretative way, at times following the forms and then again counterbalancing them.

In his housing projects in the nineties Rüdiger Lainer departs from this manner of interpretation and increasingly offers neutral spaces and different possibilities of placing the bathroom or organising the kitchen. The provisional, incomplete nature leaves the definitive interpretation of the spaces up to the residents themselves, creates various outdoor areas and lays emphasis on differentiated ways of approaching the building. One example is the Wiedner Hauptstrasse project where footbridges with gondola-like expansions are planned to allow an individual, private use of the approach to the apartment.

Alpine Tectonics behind Veil-like Screens

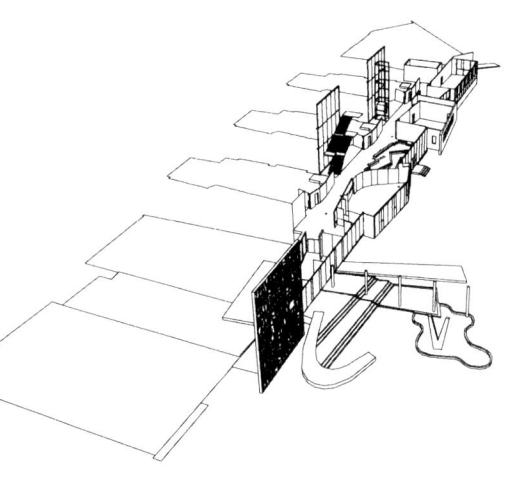

A fondness for unregulated order or regulated disorder is to be found in the larger projects such as the Multiplex cinemas, the cluster for the WIFI in St. Pölten and other schemes. The volumes of these major spaces are treated like gigantic crags which are stacked up to create geological formations and extremely irregular spaces in between: canyons, vaulted tunnels, openings in floor slabs and footbridges alternate with terraces and pulpits where views upwards and into the depths test one's sense of balance.

The delight in forms here makes a jump in scale, it is no longer gently wavy, abandons the flat relief. Carefully differentiated design is replaced by a rugged wildness and untreated surfaces which are, however, completely intentional and serve in the further development of the project as a powerful basic tone against which the differentiated interventions on the level of detail design take place.

Another development which occurs parallel to this affects the external expression. Sculptural formation in low relief led in the case of the facades to a marked physiognomy of the building as, for example, in Waidhausenstrasse, Benjowskigasse and, perhaps most strikingly, in the street front to Rothenburgstrasse in Vienna–Altmannsdorf. The tall screen with lettering by Erich Monitzer at the main entrance to the Absberggasse school has a comparable effect.

LUST AN FORMEN – EINSICHT IN STRUKTUREN

An den neuen Großstrukturen, den Multiplex-Kinos, aber auch bei einigen Wohnbauten der zweiten Generation schlägt Rüdiger Lainer eine äußere Haut aus gebäudehohen Screens oder flächigen Pflanzenbewuchs vor, die, fallweise mit Informationen und Bildern bespielbar, sich von der dahinterliegenden Gebäudestruktur absetzen. Temporär kam ein solcher Screen in roter Farbe bei der Ausstellung „YOUgend" in Bad Radkersburg zum Einsatz, wo spielerisch mit der „Verpackung" von Gebäuden, wie sie im Zuge von Umbauten oder Renovationen üblich ist, umgegangen wurde. Eine schleierartige Wirkung drückt sich auch in einer Begrünung oder in einer begrünten Raumschicht aus. Wo dem Entwerfer Screen oder Schleier zu weich wären, kann der untere Teil der Fassadenschicht den Charakter einer Schürze oder Blende annehmen, wie beim Projekt Pleasure Dome[2] in Wien–Landstraße, wo diese mit den geböschten und begrünten Sockeln der Gasometer konkurrieren muss. In allen Fällen löst sich die Umfassung der Großbauten von der inneren Struktur und entwickelt ein Eigenleben.

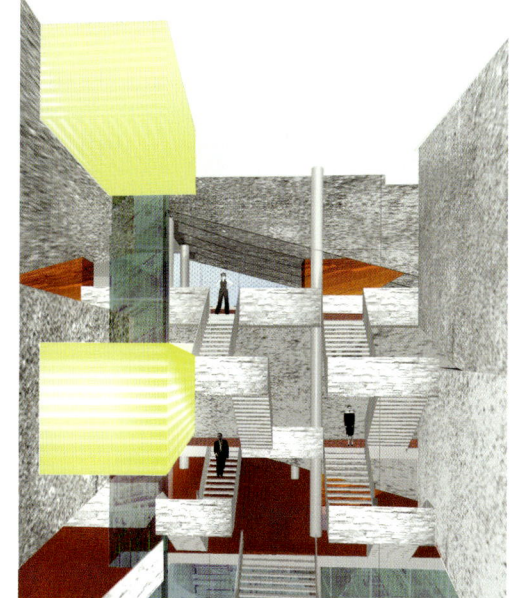

Industrialisierung und Vorfertigung – Teamarbeit

Der Kostendruck zwang auch beim Bauwesen im vergangenen Jahrzehnt zum Umdenken. Waren die Wohnbauten der achtziger Jahre damaligen Verhältnissen entsprechend, konventionell errichtet, was der individuell konkreten Plastizität entgegenkam, stellt die Schule an der Absberggasse insofern einen Wendepunkt dar, als dort aus Kostengründen anstelle einer Ortsbetonskelettkonstruktion eine aus vorgefertigten Stahlbetonelementen zum Zug kam. Die neue Erfahrung mit der Vorfabrikation und ihre problemlose Integration in architektonischer Hinsicht weckten die Neugier. Entscheidend ist, dass heute seitens der Bauindustrie kompetente Gesprächspartner zur Verfügung stehen, die sich in den Möglichkeiten ihrer Systeme auskennen und sich mehr zu wagen trauen, sodass der Architekt seinerseits die Grenzen auszuloten vermag. Mag sein, dass in Ostösterreich diese Entwicklung etwas später einsetzte, nicht zuletzt aber auch deshalb, weil es den Architekten darum ging, die architektonischen Chancen zu wahren. Hier fand die Neugier und Offenheit von Rüdiger Lainer und seinem inzwischen eingespielten Team ein neues Arbeitsfeld. Die Entwürfe aus den neunziger Jahren weisen alle diesen Zug auf, Alternativen der Vorfertigung schon beim Entwurfskonzept zu berücksichtigen und die Vorteile von Leichtbauweisen und Montagetechnik zu nützen. Das in die Breite gewachsene Wissen zeigte sich schon am Dachaufbau Seilergasse und wird auch an den jüngsten Wohnbauprojekten sichtbar. Mit den neuesten Entwürfen weitet Rüdiger Lainer diese Praxis auch auf den Bereich des Holzbaus aus, wo mit neuartigen Holzwerkstoffen und innovativen Konzepten noch ein weites Feld der Bearbeitung und Erschließung harrt.

Trotz dieser Entwicklung, die eine Entfernung von der form- und detailversessenen Wiener Szene bedeutet, zu deren Nachfolgegeneration auch Rüdiger Lainer gezählt werden darf, bleibt er der guten Wiener Tradition einer differenzierten Herangehensweise, der Einbeziehung zahlreicher, auch unerwarteter und nebensächlicher Faktoren in die Entwurfsarbeit weiterhin treu. Dem entspricht eine differenzierte Ausdrucksweise, die jedoch mit neuen Mitteln und Materialkombinationen angestrebt wird.

Die Arbeit im Team, als Anreger, Partner und seit kurzem als Lehrender für eine Meisterschule an der Akademie der bildenden Künste zeigt Rüdiger Lainer als unverbrauchten Menschen, der sich die Zuversicht und seine Fröhlichkeit bewahren konnte. Dies in einem Beruf, in dem manch anderer ob der Belastungen zum Zyniker wurde. Für eine Architektur, die sich an einem gesellschaftsorientierten, undogmatischen Menschenbild orientiert, leistet er damit nicht wenig.

DELIGHT IN FORMS – INSIGHT INTO STRUCTURES

In the new major structures, the Multiplex cinemas but also in the case of several second generation housing blocks, Rüdiger Lainer suggests an external skin in the form of a flat layer of planting or of screens the full height of the building which, in some cases, can be projected with images and information and distance themselves from the building structure behind. Such a screen, coloured red, was used temporarily in the "YOUgend" exhibition in Bad Radkersburg where a playful approach was taken to "wrapping" a building as is often done when a structure is being converted or renovated. Planting or a planted spatial layer can also have a veil-like effect. Where a screen or veil seem to weak to the designer the lower part of the facade layer can adopt the character of an apron or shield as in the Pleasure Dome[2] project in Vienna–Landstrasse where this feature must compete with the sloping grassy base of the gasometers. In each case the container of the large buildings detaches itself from the inner structure and develops a life of its own.

Industrialisation and Prefabrication – Teamwork

The pressure of costs has lead in the last decade to rethinking in the building industry. Whereas the housing blocks from the eighties were, in accordance with the prevailing situation, built in a conventional manner, a fact which facilitated the individual concrete plasticity, the school in Absberggasse represents a turning point in so far as there, for reasons of cost, prefabricated concrete elements were employed instead of an in situ concrete skeletal frame. The newly acquired experience with prefabrication and its unproblematic architectural integration awakened curiosity. The decisive thing is that today there are competent partners in the building industry familiar with the possibilities of their particular system and with a more adventurous approach so that the architect for his part is enabled to explore the limits. It may well be the case that in eastern Austria this development occurred somewhat later, not least of all due to the fact that the architects were primarily interested in safeguarding the architectural chances. Rüdiger Lainer and his by now experienced team here found a new area in which to apply their curiosity and openness. The designs from the nineties all demonstrate that the option of prefabrication was already considered at the outline design stage, and exploit the advantages of lightweight construction and assembly technology. This expanding knowledge was illustrated in the Seilergasse rooftop project and can also be seen in the most recent housing schemes. In the latest designs Rüdiger Lainer expands this practice to the area of timber construction where, with the use of new timber products and innovative conceptions, a further area awaits opening up and processing.

Despite this development, which means that he distances himself from the form- and detail-obsessed Viennese scene (Rüdiger Lainer can be numbered among the next generation in this scene), he remains true to the positive Viennese tradition of taking a differentiated approach and incorporating numerous, sometimes unexpected and secondary factors in the design process. This is reflected in a differentiated form of expression which is, however, aimed at by using new means and combinations of materials.

His work as part of a team, as a "mover," partner and, since recently, as a teacher of a master class at the Academy of Fine Arts reveals Rüdiger Lainer as a person who is not burnt out and has been able to preserve his confidence and cheerfulness within a profession in which many grow cynical as a result of the pressure. Consequently he makes a considerable contribution to creating an architecture that is socially oriented on an undogmatic image of mankind.

OFFENES PLANEN
Rüdiger Lainer & Ina Wagner

Offenes Planen, das Entwickeln von Strategien anstelle von rein subjektiven Idealentwürfen, ist eine Anforderung, um zukunftsfähig zu planen und die Architektur aus der Sackgasse des Formalistischen zu führen. Möglichkeiten komplexen Planens sollen deshalb zur Diskussion gestellt werden. Im Zentrum offenen Planens steht die Vorstellung, sich nicht frühzeitig auf fixierte Lösungen hinzubewegen, sondern das architektonische Entwerfen im offenen Raum möglicher Annäherungen erfolgen zu lassen. Als Leitidee für die Entwicklung einer Entwurfsmethodik sollten Wege aufgezeigt werden, die Stärken und die konzeptuelle Integrität eines Entwurfskonzepts zu bewahren und gleichzeitig Offenheit gegenüber sich verändernden und im Planungsverlauf sich erst konkretisierenden Anforderungen zu ermöglichen.

Offenes Planen entspricht einem morphologischen Konzept des Entwurfsprozesses und geht über das Arbeiten mit Fakten einerseits und die rein subjektiv-intuitive Interpretation von Raumerlebnissen andererseits hinaus. Es erfordert die Konzeptualisierung von Vorstellungen auf der Ebene von Bildern, Metaphern und Analogien, ihre Konfrontation mit den Gegebenheiten und den Umgang mit Gegensätzlichkeiten. Dabei soll vom Denken in spezifischen Lösungen zu einem mit Platzhaltern übergegangen werden, wobei notwendige Spezifikationen als partiell und vorläufig zu betrachten sind. Offenes Planen beruht auf einer Dynamik des Ausweitens, Mobilisierens, vorläufigen Festlegens und erneuten Öffnens. Entwurfsverfahren wie diese laden zum Experimentieren mit offenen Formen der Raumorganisation ein.

Im folgenden werden die spezifischen Qualitäten der Praxis offenen Planens anhand einiger Planungsprojekte beschrieben:

- das Mobilisieren vielfältiger Ressourcen
- das Arbeiten mit Themen
- das Offenhalten und Erweitern der Lösungsräume
- die Offenheit der Raumorganisation

Mobilisieren vielfältiger Ressourcen

Wir verwenden den Begriff Ressourcen für die vielfältigen inspirativen Objekte und für konkrete Fakten, die Architekten im Planungsprozess unterstützen. Im Kino-Projekt Eurocity waren dies vor allem die Kenntnis von Ort und Kontext, eine Vorstellung der Anforderungen (einschließlich jener, das neue Objekt mit einem Altbau zu „verbinden") sowie die Alltagserfahrung von Kino.

Während Ort, Kontext und Anforderungen zunächst unscharf und im Hintergrund bleiben, wird eine Vielzahl von Bildern und Metaphern aktiviert. Eines dieser Bilder waren etwa Stapel komprimierten Altpapiers, in der Flüchtigkeit des Vorbeifahrens peripher wahrgenommen und als Metapher für das Stapeln von Volumina aufgefangen. Jede dieser Ressourcen – Pläne, Fotos, Texte, Bilder, Metaphern etc. – mobilisiert den Entwurfsprozess, hilft Ideen zu formieren und Qualitäten auszudrücken: Raumqualitäten

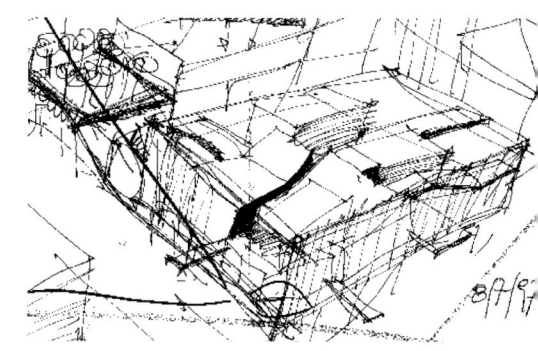

OPEN PLANNING
Rüdiger Lainer & Ina Wagner

Open planning, the development of strategies instead of purely subjective ideal designs, represents a requirement to plan in a future-oriented way and to lead architecture out of the dead-end represented by formalism. With this aim in mind the possibilities of complex planning are presented here for discussion. At the heart of the open planning process lies the idea of not moving too quickly towards fixed solutions but rather of allowing architectural design to take place within the open space of possible approaches. Directions should be indicated as a guiding idea for the development of a design method in order to preserve the strengths and conceptual integrity of a design concept while, at the same time, allowing an openness towards those changing demands that first become concrete in the course of planning.

Open planning represents a morphological understanding of the design process that extends, on the one hand, beyond working with facts and, on the other, beyond a purely subjective and intuitive interpretation of spatial experiences. It requires a conceptualisation of ideas on the level of images, metaphors and analogies, it means confronting them with the given situation and dealing with contradictions. It is necessary that a transition from thinking in terms of specific solutions to an approach involving place markers should take place whereby any requisite specifications should be seen as both partial and provisional. Open planning is based on a dynamic of expansion, mobilisation, provisional definition and renewed opening. Design processes such as these invite experimentation with open forms of spatial organisation.

In the following article the specific qualities of the practice of open planning will be described with reference to several planning projects:
- the mobilisation of varied resources
- working with themes
- keeping options for solution spaces open and expanding them
- the openness of spatial organisation

The Mobilisation of Varied Resources

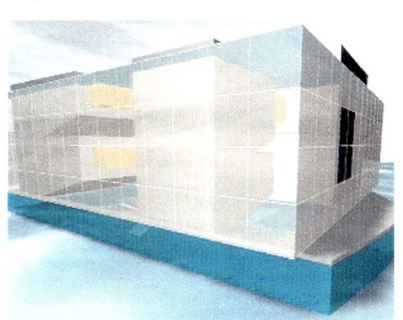

We employ the term resources to describe the variety of inspirational objects and those concrete facts that support architects in the planning process. In the Eurocity cinema project these were primarily a familiarity with place and context, a conception of the requirements (including those involved in "connecting" the new object with an old building) as well as the everyday experience of cinema.

Whereas place, context and requirements are at first unclear and remain in the background, a variety of images and metaphors is activated. One of these images was that of stacks of compressed waste paper, marginally registered while hastily passing by, as a metaphor for the stacking of volumes.

OFFENES PLANEN

(großes Volumen, hermetisch, monolithisch, knappe Berührung, Raumstapelung, transluzente Hülle), Textualität (felsig, steinig, gestockt, rauh) und Licht (flutend, als schimmernde Fläche).

Die Kunst des Entwerfens besteht darin, mit einer Fülle von Parametern zu jonglieren, sie allmählich in ein Konzept zu fügen, ohne ihre Beziehungen vorab zu verfestigen. Dieses Konzept muss in der Schwebe gehalten und mit immer neuen Eindrücken und Fakten konfrontiert werden. Dabei ist die bildlich-metaphorische Sprache ein wichtiges Element des Verständigungsprozesses der an der Planung Beteiligten. Um andere von einer Entwurfsidee, einer konstruktiven Lösung zu überzeugen und dazu zu bewegen, sich auf die eigene Perspektive einzulassen, ist es notwendig, Objekte zu erfinden, die sich für Dialoge in vielen Stimmen und von unterschiedlichen Orten aus eignen.

In der Gasometer Studie wurden viele solcher Kommunikationsfaktoren zu einer reichhaltigen Erzählung zusammengefügt, wie beispielsweise das Konzept eines Kunstraums zeigt.

Der Prozess des Mobilisierens inspirativer Objekte ist in mehrfacher Hinsicht relevant: ein Entwurfskonzept besser (be)greifbar zu machen, es zu externalisieren, in Bildern, Metaphern zu beschreiben, die Vielfalt der Parameter und Einflüsse über Prozesse des Filterns, Kontextualisierens, In-Verbindung-Bringens handhabbarer zu machen und damit neue Wege der Wahrnehmung und Interpretation von „constraints" zu eröffnen. Dies gilt nicht nur für das Architektenteam im engeren Sinne, sondern für alle Kooperationen in einem komplexen Umfeld multipler Akteure.

Das Arbeiten mit Themen

Der nächste Schritt besteht darin, Projektpläne anzufertigen, um den Gedankenansatz zu detaillieren und erste Bearbeitungen zu ermöglichen. Die noch schwebende Entwurfsidee muss mit den Gegebenheiten konfrontiert und weitergedacht werden. Problemstellungen treten in der Arbeit an Details, in der sukzessiven Konfrontation mit den Gegebenheiten, in Arbeitssitzungen mit wechselnden Gesprächspartnern oder in Verhandlungen mit Behörden auf.

Themen unterstützen ein Entwurfskonzept in der Sprache von Bildern und Metaphern. Sie definieren jene Grundgestaltungsprinzipien eines Objekts, die es im Prozess des Erarbeitens spezifischer technischer Lösungen zu überblicken gilt. Themen betonen unterschiedliche Qualitäten eines Gebäudes oder Raums. Während einige dessen Erscheinungsbild beschreiben, charakterisieren andere die Eigenschaften spezifischer Elemente oder Strukturen. Themenbezogenes Arbeiten strukturiert gleichzeitig das zu entwerfende Objekt und den Planungsprozess selbst.

Thema 1 behandelt im Kino-Projekt Eurocity die transluzente, stofflich wirkende, das Licht differenziert filternde Hülle des Gebäudes, die eine fast unmerkliche Metamorphose bewirkt: morgens hermetisch schimmernd, abends als Projektionsfläche zur Inszenierung von Lichtbildern eingesetzt oder als Schleier, der Menschen, Bewegungen und Volumina zart verbirgt.

Thema 2 ist jenes des Inneren, eines einzigen hermetischen, monolithischen Raums, in dem die massiven Volumina der Kinosäle gestapelt werden, felsig, steinig, mit einer gestockten, sandgestrahlten Oberfläche (eine Art Felsenreitschule des 20. Jhs.). Der Zugang, der Aufstieg zu diesen Felsen muss offen und transparent sein.

Thema 3 betrifft die Beziehung dieses großen Volumens zum Altbestand – sich annähernd, aber nicht berührend – und damit eine Spannung zwischen Autonomie und kontextueller Referentialität erzeugen.

OPEN PLANNING

Each of these resources – plans, photos, texts, images, metaphors, etc. – mobilises the design process, helping both to form ideas and express qualities: spatial qualities (large volumes, hermetic, monolithic, barely touching, stacked space, translucent shell), texture (craggy, stony, bush-hammered, raw), and light (flooding, as a shimmering surface).

The art of design consists of juggling with a number of parameters and gradually arranging them in a concept without at first cementing the relationship between them. This concept must be kept floating and continually confronted with new impressions and facts. A language of images and metaphors is an important element in the process of informing those involved in planning. In order to convince others of a design idea or a structural solution and to animate them to adopt their own perspective it is necessary to invent objects suitable for dialogues with various voices and from different places.

In the gasometer study many such communication factors were combined to form a rich narrative as indicated, for example, by the concept of a Kunstraum.

This process of mobilising inspirational objects is relevant in a variety of ways: it can be used to make a design concept easier to grasp, to externalise it, to describe it in images, metaphors, to make the variety of parameters and influences more tangible through the processes of filtering, contextualising and establishing connections and thus opening new ways of perceiving and interpreting constraints. This applies not only to the team of architects in the strict sense but to all forms of co-operation within the complex environment with multiple protagonists.

Working with Themes

The next step consists of preparing the plans for the project in order to detail the initial idea and allow the first developments. The design idea, which is not yet concrete, must be confronted with the existing situation and worked out further. Problematic areas emerge while working on the details, during successive confrontations with the given situation and in the course of meetings with changing partners or during negotiations with the authorities

Themes support a design concept using the language of images and metaphors. They define those basic design principles of an object which must be kept in view during the process of working out specific technical solutions. Themes emphasise the different qualities of a building or space. Whereas some of them define its appearance others characterise the qualities of specific elements or structures. Working in a theme-related way structures, at one and the same time, the object to be designed and the planning process itself.

Theme 1 deals in the Eurocity cinema project with the translucent, material-like shell of the building which filters light in a differentiated way, effecting an almost unnoticed metamorphosis: in the morning it shimmers hermetically, in the evening it is a projection surface employed to stage light images or a veil that gently conceals people, movements and volumes.

Theme 2 is that of the interior, of a single, hermetic, monolithic space in which the massive volumes of the cinemas are stacked: craggy, stony, with a bush-hammered, sand-blasted surface (a kind of 20th century Felsenreitschule). The approach, the ascent to these cliffs must be open and transparent.

Theme 3 deals with the relationship of these large volumes to the existing old building, which it approaches but does not touch, thus producing a tension lying somewhere between autonomy and contextual referentialism.

OFFENES PLANEN

Thema 4 schließlich ist die Dramaturgie des Raums, erzeugt durch die Kombination von Material und Licht, einerseits sowie die Gestaltung der Foyers, Stiegen und Gangways als Zwischenräume andererseits.

Diese vier Themen orientieren den Planungsprozess und helfen, ihn auf das konzeptuell-gestalterisch Wesentliche zu fokussieren. Beispiele sind etwa die Konstruktion, Textur und Beleuchtung der Fassade sowie die dramaturgische Gestaltung des Innenraumes. Hier spielt das Licht eine große Rolle, das einerseits als flutend und strahlend gedacht wird, andererseits als eine ruhige Oberfläche oder Membran, auf die sich Bilder projezieren lassen.

Der themenbezogene Zugang zum Beleuchtungsdesign ist für die Materialrecherche und das Einkreisen technischer Lösungen wichtig. Die Vorstellung des Lichts als modulierbare Oberfläche beeinflusst die Interpretation und Diskussion von Parametern. Sie wird realisiert als eine Kombination von indirekter Beleuchtung des Innenraumes (Lichtstreifen an den Decken der Foyers), mit Projektionskabinen als Lichtboxen, Farbschimmern auf den felsigen Kinosälen und weißen Decken, flächiger und unterschiedlich dichter Verteilung der Lichtquellen in der Fassade usw. Im Gespräch mit dem Team und externen Beratern werden neue, das Thema präzisierende Metaphern, wie das spannende Licht, erarbeitet.

Die themenbezogene Sprache hilft Lösungen zu fokussieren und den Bezug zwischen technischem Detail und Entwurfskonzept aufrechtzuerhalten. Sie unterstützt das Pendeln zwischen Detail und Ganzem, Präzision und Unschärfe.

Offenhalten und Erweitern der Lösungsräume

Die Metapher des Mäanderns beschreibt das kunstvoll fließende Oszillieren zwischen Vor-Schreiben und Be-Schreiben, Festlegen und Öffnen. Für die Praxis offenen Planens bedeutet dies zum einen, dass es möglich sein sollte, zu einem früheren Projektstadium zurückzukehren, Bilder, Assoziationen und Lösungswege zu mobilisieren, die zu diesem Zeitpunkt nicht weiter verfolgt, gleichsam in Reserve gehalten wurden. Zum anderen geht es darum, Entscheidungen über Material und Produkte (einschließlich der durch diese geprägten Entwurfsparameter) möglichst lange für weitere Veränderungen offenzuhalten.

Oft ergibt sich der Druck, eine bereits getroffene Entwurfsentscheidung aus einer veränderten Anforderung oder unerwarteten Einschränkung wieder zu öffnen. So entstand etwa im Projekt Eurocity mit der Notwendigkeit, eines der wuchtigen Volumina hinauszuschieben, ein zuvor nicht gedachter Platz für eine (konstruktiv erforderliche) Säule. Deren Vertikalität, verstärkt durch die konische Form, reflektiert und verstärkt das Konzept des Monolithischen und doch Schwebenden in dramatischer Weise.

Ein Ansatz dazu, dieses Mäandern von Entscheidungen vorwegnehmend mitzudenken, ist das Arbeiten mit Platzhaltern, in die austauschbare Elemente eingefüllt und auf ihre Implikationen hin überprüft werden können. Ein Platzhalter steht für eine noch offene Entwurfsentscheidung, er besetzt einen spezifischen Platz innerhalb eines relationalen Raums. Was als Platzhalter definiert und offengehalten werden kann, hängt von den Inhalten und dem Kontext eines Projekts ab. Das Prinzip Fassade für das Kino-Center Eurocity entwickelt sich aus einer Kombination vorläufiger und unvollständiger (eben offener) Spezifikationen von Material (eine unregelmäßige, textile Struktur, die das Licht in differenzierter Weise filtert), Konstruktion und thermischem Konzept. Unterschiedliche Gläser und Verarbeitungstechniken stellen Annäherungen an das Thema dar, die erst schrittweise und bezugnehmend auf eine Vielzahl von Parametern zu einer konkreten Lösung der Fassade verdichtet werden.

OPEN PLANNING

Finally, theme 4 which is the dramaturgy of the space produced by the combination of materials and light and the design of the foyers, staircases and gangways as spaces in-between.

These four themes orient the planning process, helping to focus it on the important conceptual and design aspects. Examples include construction, texture and lighting of the facade as well as the dramaturgic design of the interior. Light plays an important role here. On the one hand, it is conceived of as flooding and radiant, on the other, as a calm surface or membrane onto which images can be projected. The theme-related approach to the lighting design is important for both material research and the definition of technical solutions. The idea of light as a surface which can be modulated influences the interpretation and discussion of parameters. This idea is realised as a combination of indirect lighting of the interior (strips of light on the ceilings of the foyer) with projection booths as light boxes, shimmering colour on the rocky cinemas and white ceilings, the planar distribution, in varying degrees of concentration, of light sources in the facade, etc. In discussion with the team and consultants and experts brought in from outside new metaphors, which make the theme more precise, such as the excitement of light are worked out.

The theme-related language helps to focus solutions and preserve the relationship between technical detail and the design concept. It supports the movement back and forth between the detail and the whole, between precision and lack of sharpness.

Keeping the Options for Solution Spaces Open, and Expanding Them

The metaphor of meandering describes an oscillation artificially flowing between prescribing and describing, defining and opening. For the practice of open planning this means, firstly, that it should be possible to return to an earlier phase of the project in order to mobilise images, associations and the specific directions of solutions which, at that previous stage, were not further pursued but kept in reserve. On the other hand, the issue is to keep decisions on materials and products (including the design parameters determined by these) open as long as possible to allow for further alterations.

Often the pressure to reconsider a decision already made results from a change in the brief or from unexpected restrictions. For example, in the Eurocity project the necessity to slide one of the massive volumes outwards created a place not previously considered for a (structurally necessary) column. Its verticality, emphasised by its tapering form, reflects and strengthens in a dramatic manner the concept of a monolithic and yet hovering quality.

An initial point in including, from the very start, this meandering of decisions is working with place markers in which interchangeable elements can be placed and where their implications can be examined. A place marker represents a design decision that is still open, it occupies a specific place within a relational space. What can be defined and kept open as a place marker depends on the contents and context of a project. The principle of the facade for the Eurocity cinema center developed from a combination of provisional and incomplete (i.e. open) specifications of materials (an irregular, textual structure, which filters light in a differentiated manner), construction and thermal concept. Different kinds of glass and methods of using them represent approaches to the theme which only gradually, referring to a variety of parameters, could be intensified to create a concrete facade solution.

OFFENES PLANEN

Die Entwurfsarbeiten zum Gasometerareal machen in systematischer Weise von Platzhaltern Gebrauch. Der Entwurf definiert unterschiedliche Raumqualitäten statt spezifische Objekte. Eine dieser Raumqualitäten ist die der Vitrine. Deren Bedeutungsschichten werden durch eine spezifische Kombination von Metaphern und Bildern beschrieben. Als osmotische Wand vermittelt die Vitrine zwischen innen und außen, zwischen öffentlichem Raum, Konsum- und Unterhaltungswelt. Die Vitrine kann begangen, durchschritten oder als Ausstellungsraum genutzt werden (wie im Projekt Austria Email). Arbeiten mit Platzhaltern heißt, die Vitrine oder die vorläufige Spezifikation des Prinzips Fassade als eine Hypothese zu betrachten.

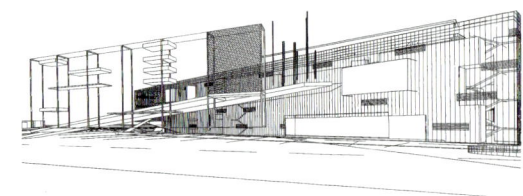

Offene Raumorganisation – Evolvierende Nutzungen

Als eine Form der Annäherung an ein Erweitern der Lösungsräume für architektonisches Entwerfen gedacht, erfordert offenes Planen, die Beziehungen zwischen Raum und sozialem Gebrauch neu zu überdenken. Ein Leitgedanke ist hier jener des Gebrauchs als Ereignis. Er versucht der Veränderung, dem Sich-Entwickeln sowie dem Temporären Rechnung zu tragen und nutzt die Boundary-Qualität von Raum. Er erfordert schwebende Kategorisierungen sozialer Praktiken in der Nutzung von Raum. Eine Annäherung an solche schwebenden Kategorisierungen stellt das Konzept des Zwischen-Raums dar. Ein Zwischen-Raum vermag die ihn umgebenden Räume zu reflektieren, sich gegen diese abzuschotten oder sie in einer Weise zu paraphrasieren, die keine klaren Kategorisierungen zulässt. Er will als transitorischer Raum, als Nische für periphere oder temporäre Aktivitäten genutzt werden, will räumliche Begrenzungen, Schwellen, Öffnungen oder Übergangsbereiche schaffen. Häufig sind Zwischen-Räume Bewegungs-Räume – Korridore, Rampen oder Passagen. Ihr spezifischer Charakter liegt in der Bewegung des Durchschreitens und Durcheilens, einschließlich der zufälligen Begegnungen, die dabei stattfinden.

Zwischen-Räumen kommt im Entwurf des Kino-Centers Eurocity eine zentrale Bedeutung zu. Sie umhüllen die gestapelten Volumina der Kinosäle und machen Platz für spontane Nutzungen und temporäre Installationen.

Der Raum zwischen Pleasure Dome[2] und den Gasometern ist als ein Zwischen-Raum konzipiert. Er schafft Übergänge von der licht- und farbendurchtränkten Wand des Pleasure Dome[2] mit ihrer visuellen Durchlässigkeit zur Herbheit der begrünten Gasometersockel sowie zur tristen Abfolge von Einfahrten. Die Strukturierung dieser Übergangszone wird in Metaphern, Skizzen und Assoziationsbildern beschrieben.

Einen anderen Weg des Schaffens offener Formen der Raumorganisation zeigt das Wettbewerbsprojekt ZMF (Zentrum für medizinische Grundlagenforschung). Hier erweist sich die Raumqualität aus der Überlagerung zweier Prozesse. Ausgangspunkt ist die neutrale Struktur eines mäandernden Bands aneinandergereihter Funktionsräume. Über die Verformung dieses Volumens und das gleichzeitige Herausschälen von Teilen entsteht eine spezifische Raumkonstellation. Sie ist durch die Verbindung von neutraler Serialität mit einer Fülle von unterschiedlichen Binnen- und Außenräumen, Höfen und Innenhöfen, Einschnitten und Schluchten charakterisiert. Die Grundform eines Flügels verstärkt den körperbetonten Modellierungsprozess. Hier wird deutlich, wie über innere Verformungen in einem neutralen Volumen spezifische Raumqualitäten geschaffen werden können. Offenheit für variable Nutzung lässt sich nicht allein aus der Neutralität des Raums, sondern aus der Kombination von Neutralität und Spezifikation erzielen.

OPEN PLANNING

The design work on the gasometer site employs place markers systematically. Instead of specific objects the design defines different spatial qualities. One of these spatial qualities is the showcase. Its layers of meaning are described by means of a specific combination of metaphors and images. As an osmotic wall the showcase mediates between inside and outside, between public space, consumer and entertainment worlds. The showcase can be entered, passed through or used as an exhibition space (as in the Austria Email project). Working with place markers means viewing the showcase or the provisional specification of the facade principle as a hypothesis.

Open Spatial Organisation – Evolving Uses

Open planning, conceived of as an approach to expanding those spaces which offer solutions for architectural design, demands a rethinking of the relationship between space and social use. Use as an event here provides a guiding idea that attempts to take account of change, development and the temporary and exploits the boundary quality of space. It demands flexible categorisations of social practices in the use of space.

The concept of the space in-between represents an approach to such pending categorisations. The space in-between can reflect the spaces surrounding it, it can cut itself off from them or paraphrase them in a way that allows no clear categorisations. It offers itself for use as transitory space, as a niche for peripheral or temporary activities. it attempts to create spatial definitions, thresholds, openings or transitional areas. Frequently the spaces in-between are spaces for movement such as corridors, ramps or passageways. Their specific character lies in the motion of passing or hurrying through them and includes the incidental encounters which take place in them.

Spaces in-between are ascribed a central importance in the design of the Eurocity cinema center. They surround the stacked volumes of the cinemas themselves creating space for spontaneous uses and temporary installations.

The space between the Pleasure Dome[2] and the gasometers is conceived of as an intervening space. It establishes transitions from the visual transparency of the light and colour impregnated wall of the Pleasure Dome[2] to the severity of the grassy gasometer plinth and the bleak succession of entranceways. The structuring of this transitional zone is described in metaphors, sketches and images of association.

The ZMF (Zentrum für medizinische Grundlagenforschung) competition project illustrates other ways of creating open forms of spatial organisation. Here spatial quality is a result of overlaying two processes. The starting point is a neutral structure of a meandering band of aligned functional spaces. Through the distortion of this volume and by peeling out parts a specific spatial constellation is produced that is characterised by the connection of neutral serialism with a rich variety of internal and external spaces, squares, internal courtyards, incisions and canyons. The basic form of a wing strengthens the emphasised physicality of the modelling process. Here it becomes clear how specific spatial qualities can be created by internal distortions in a neutral volume. Openness for flexible use is achieved not only through the neutrality of space but also as a result of the combination of neutrality and specification.

OFFENES PLANEN

Ein anderes zentrales Merkmal dieses Entwurfs ist die Einbeziehung von Technik. Das Gesamtvolumen wird von einer abgelösten Haut umhüllt. Seine Funktion ist die Unterstützung aerodynamischer Prozesse. Der im Raum zwischen Schleier und Außenwand vorbeistreichende Wind soll dieserart eingefangen und die Druckdifferenzen zur Durchlüftung des Gebäudes genutzt werden. Diese auf den ersten Blick nicht erkennbare Funktion wird durch die Gestaltung des Schleiers vermittelt. An manchen Stellen geöffnet, wirkt die Umhüllung wie eine atmende, von Kiemen durchsetzte Fischhaut. Anderseits hat sie den Anschein eines zarten Filters, der den Austausch zwischen Innen und Außen moduliert. An manchen Stellen dicht, an anderen wiederum geöffnet, filtert er das eindringende Licht und modifiziert die Sichtbarkeit nach außen. Der atmende Schleier symbolisiert mit einfachen Mitteln Bewegung (den Wind) und Variabilität (Flächen unterschiedlicher Dichte, Öffnungen).

Eine weitere Möglichkeit des Offenhaltens von Raumorganisation nutzt das Ausstellungsprojekt „YOUgend". Die Ausstellung, als Implantat in einem revitalisierten alten Gebäude geplant, besteht aus einer Landschaft von geschlossenen Stimmungsräumen, ihnen folgenden Vertiefungszonen, offenen Rampen und Stegen. Diese stille Architektur bildet eine Bühne für Erzählungen. Mittels Ton, Licht, Filmausschnitten, Farben und Projektionen werden Stimmungen erzeugt und Ereignisse dargestellt. Hier zeigen sich einige der Möglichkeiten des Instrumentierens gebauter Räume für variable, evolvierende Nutzungen. Die darzustellenden Inhalte müssen nicht vorweg gedanklich in der Architektur selbst festgelegt werden. Weder muss der Raum um das Objekt gebaut noch das Objekt an gegebene Raumkonstellationen angepasst werden. Es wird möglich, mit unterschiedlichen Raumfüllungen zu experimentieren. Implantate unterstützen die variable Nutzung neutraler Strukturen und funktionell unbestimmter Räume. Diese Verwendung von Technik als raumbildendem und darstellendem Element zugleich verweist auf eine andere Art der Flexibilität als jene mit traditionellen gestalterischen Mitteln. Sie reflektiert die Idee von Gebrauch als Ereignis.

Vielfältige Konfigurationen

Die Umsetzung eines Konzepts für offenes Planen bedarf einer Methode. Darunter verstehen wir ein Set von Möglichkeiten, Entwerfen und Planen als einen informellen und fließenden kooperativen Arbeitsprozess zu organisieren. Beginnend beim konzeptuellen Ansatz, dem Arbeiten mit Metaphern, Vorstellungsbildern und Assoziationen, erfordert dies Instrumente und Strategien der Konfrontation des Entwurfskonzepts mit den Gegebenheiten sowie des Umgangs mit Gegensätzlichkeiten.

Die skizzierten Formen der Entwicklung und Kommunikation eines Entwurfskonzepts – das Thema als metaphorisch verdichtete Beschreibung von Grundgestaltungsprinzipien, das Bild in seiner zum Dialog einladenden interpretativen Flexibilität – sind nicht nur wichtige Elemente des Planungsprozesses selbst. Sie prägen auch das zu entwerfende Objekt, helfen dessen Bedeutungsschichten zu vervielfältigen und damit kulturell verfestigte Formen des Wahrnehmens und Interpretierens von Räumen aufzubrechen.

OPEN PLANNING

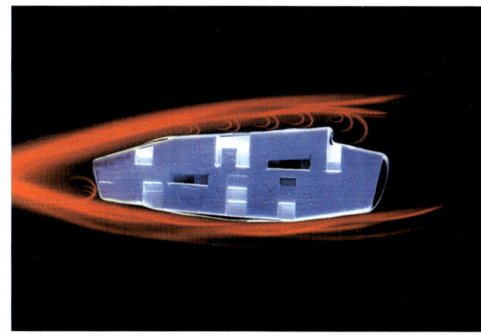

A further central characteristic of this design is the way in which technology is integrated. The entire volume is enclosed by a detached skin, its function is to support aerodynamic processes. The wind passing between the veil and the external wall is to be captured and the differences in pressure exploited to ventilate the building. This function, not identifiable at first glance, is communicated by the design of the veil. Open at several places the shell is like the breathing skin of a fish, complete with gills. Yet on the other hand, it has the appearance of a delicate filter that modulates the exchange between inside and outside. Sealed at several points and open at others, it filters the light entering and modifies the visibility towards the outside. Employing simple means this breathing veil symbolises movement (the wind) and variability (surfaces of different density, openings).

The exhibition project "YOUgend" exploits a further possibility inherent in the process of keeping spatial organisation open. The exhibition, planned as an implantation in a revitalised old building, consists of a landscape of closed atmospheric spaces followed by zones for deeper investigation, open ramps and staircases. This still architecture offers a stage for narratives. By means of sound, light, film excerpts, colours and projections moods are created and events represented. Some of the possibilities which the instrumentation of built space offers for variable, evolving functions are illustrated here. The architecture itself must not initially anticipate the contents to be represented. The space must not be built around the object nor the object adapted to the existing spatial constellation. It becomes possible to experiment with different ways of filling the space. Implantations support the variable use of neutral structures and functionally undetermined space.

The use of technology as an element that is, at one and the same time, spatially formative and representative indicates another kind of flexibility very different to that achieved with traditional design methods. It reflects the idea of use as an event.

Varied Configurations

To apply a concept for open planning we require a method. Under this term we understand the organisation of a set of possibilities, designs and planning as an informal, flowing, co-operative work process. Starting with the conceptual idea, the work with metaphors, impressions and associations, this requires instruments and strategies to handle the confrontation between the design concept and the existing situation and also a way of dealing with contradictions.

The sketched forms of the development and communication of a design concept – the theme as a metaphorically intensified description of basic design principles, the image with an interpretative flexibility that invites dialogue – are not merely important elements of the planning process itself. They also influence the object to be designed, helping to multiply its layers of meaning and thus to break up culturally petrified forms of perceiving and interpreting spaces.

OFFENES PLANEN

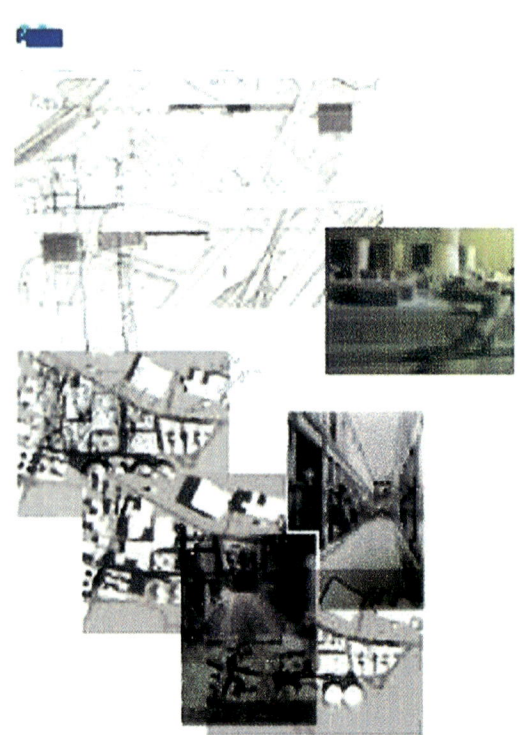
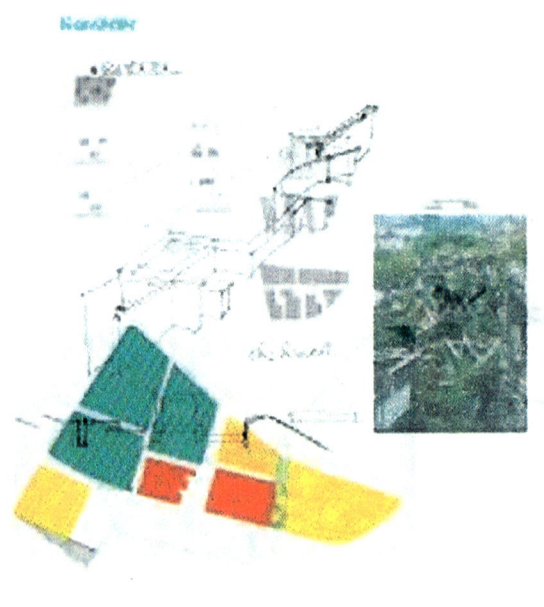

OPEN PLANNING

Wohnbebauung Engerthstraße
Wien–Leopoldstadt, Wettbewerb 1984

An diesem frühen, manifestartigen Entwurf kommt die von Formideen und soziokulturellen Querbezügen sprühende städtebauliche Grundhaltung Rüdiger Lainers bereits klar zum Ausdruck – unabhängig von der konkreten, zeitbezogenen Formensprache. Gemeinsam mit der Kulturwissenschaftlerin Gertraud Auer wurde ein System sich überlagernder Ordnungen entwickelt, die sich aufbauen, verformen und wieder verlieren. Das Prinzip zur Erzeugung lebendiger Varianz basiert auf verzogenen geometrischen Rastern, die von dazwischengewürfelten Zufälligkeiten verformt, parasitär agglomeriert und räumlich konterkariert werden. Damit soll der offene Prozess der Stadtbildung beispielartig interpretiert werden – im Bewusstsein, dass im Falle einer faktischen Ausführung vieles noch einmal anders werden kann und auch anders wird.

Das ausgedehnte rechteckige Bebauungsfeld ist eingespannt zwischen der zwei Baublöcke tiefen Donauuferbebauung und der Industriebrache des aufgelassenen Nordbahnhofs, die bis heute als vielversprechendes städtebauliches Erwartungsgebiet unverändert blieb. Nach Norden, zur Engerthstraße und zum vielbefahrenen Handelskai, schützt ein langer, von kurzen Quertrakten rhythmisierter Riegel vor den Emissionen des Verkehrs. Ironisch wird er von den Autoren als Vollwertwohnen apostrophiert; die Swimmingpools am Dach persiflieren den in Wien unter diesem Namen und mit diesem „Markenzeichen" verbreiteten Massenwohnbau. Davor scharen sich in leicht versetzten Reihen zwei Dutzend siebengeschoßiger Türme. Mit durchschnittlich einer Wohnung pro Geschoß und zahlreichen individuellen Veränderungen und Applikationen bilden sie den nonkonformistischen Gegensatz zu dem als „Wall" bezeichneten Nordtrakt, dessen südorientierte Wohnungen aber – ungeachtet des postulierten Gegensatzes – hinter breiten Balkonen über attraktive Grundrisse verfügen. Nach Süden grenzt ein vielfach überbrückter „Wassergraben" vom Nordbahnhofgelände ab, bietet aber zugleich betonte Verbindungen. Mit vielfältigen kultur- und zeitgeschichtlichen Hinweisen substituiert das Projekt den urbanen Kontext der Stadt Wien, der sich in einem so großen Quartier selber erst wieder entwickeln muss. Zugleich übt es mit dem inszenierten Rückzug hinter Wall und Wassergraben Kritik an einer zunehmenden Unwirtlichkeit des öffentlichen Raumes. Die ungebrochene Lebensfreude, die sich im architektonischen Ausdruck manifestiert, macht es aber auch zu einem realistischen Projekt, das nie in Gefahr steht, in Zynismus abzugleiten. W.Z.

Engerthstrasse Housing Development
Vienna–Leopoldstadt, Competition Entry, 1984

Rüdiger Lainer's basic urban stance, exploding with formal ideas and socio-cultural cross-references, is already clearly expressed in this early, manifesto-like design – quite independent of the concrete formal language that is a reflection of its date of origin. Together with the cultural scientist, Gertraud Auer, a system was developed of superimposed orders which build up and deform, to vanish again. The principle was to produce a lively variety based on distorted geometric grids which are deformed, agglomerated in a parasitical manner and spatially counterbalanced by accidental interventions. The intention was to offer an exemplary interpretation of the open process of urban formation while remaining fully aware of the fact that, should the project actually be carried out, much could, and probably would, turn out very differently.

The extensive rectangular development area stretches between the buildings along the Danube, which are two blocks deep, and the disused former industrial area around the Nordbahnhof, which still remains a highly promising area of urban expectations. To the north, towards Engerthstrasse and the busy Handelskai a long slab, rhythmically articulated by short transverse blocks offers protection from traffic fumes. It is ironically entitled "Vollwertwohnen" (Whole Nutrition Living) by the designers, the swimming pools on the roof make fun of mass housing projects in Vienna bearing this name and "trade mark." In front two dozen seven-storey towers are set in slightly staggered rows. With, on average, one apartment per storey and numerous individual adaptations and applications they form a non-conformist counterpoint to the north tract defined as a "wall." However its south-facing apartments have, despite the postulated antithesis, attractive floor plans behind wide balconies. Towards the south a "moat" with a number of bridges separates the site from the Nordbahnhof complex while, at the same time, offering emphasised connections. With a variety of cultural and historical references the project offers a substitute for that urban context of the city of Vienna which, in such a large district, must first develop again in the course of the years. At the same time the dramatic withdrawal behind the wall and moat is an implicit criticism of the increasing unattractiveness of public space. The untroubled joie-de-vivre manifest in the architectural expression makes this a realistic project which never runs the risk of slipping into cynicism. W.Z.

ENGERTHSTRASSE

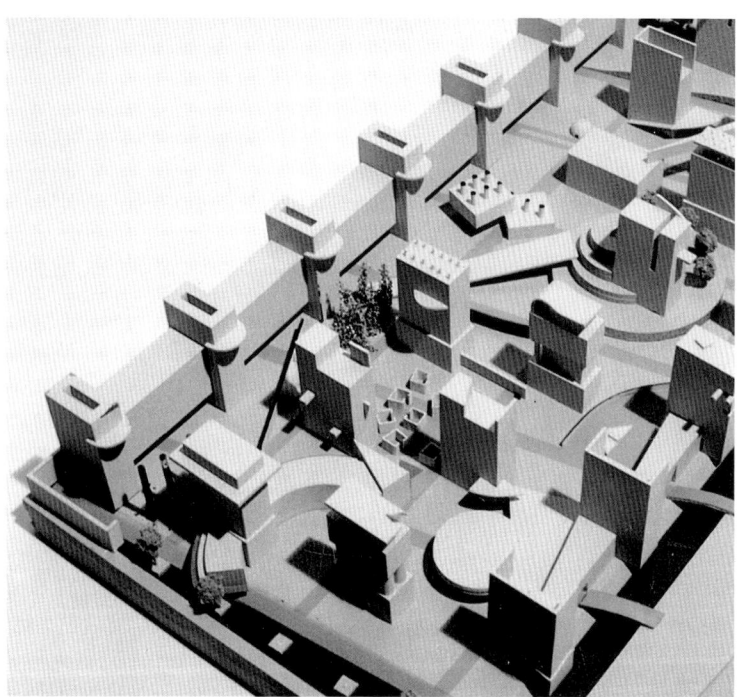
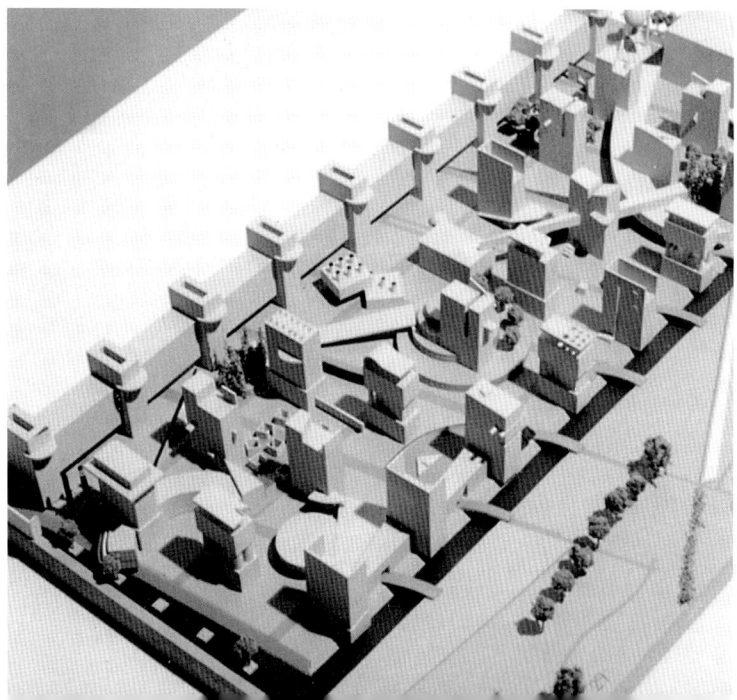

Dieses Projekt ist ein realistisches. Es ist real im entwicklungsgeschichtlichen Sinn. Die Entwicklung der Stadt läßt sich nicht loslösen von der ökonomischen und ökologischen Verelendung, angekündigt im „Terrorist Chic" der Film- und Unterhaltungsindustrie, täglich gelebt in den Metropolen jenseits der Meere, blicklos betrieben von den Sachwaltern eines Wachstums. Der Städter zieht sich in die Burg zurück, dem Riot gehört die Stadt. Zwischen den Wällen das vom Übertechnisierten zum Archaischen pendelnde Unterhaltungsangebot, die Künstlichkeit der Beziehungen, gelehrt wie im Managementseminar. R.L.

This project is realistic. It is real in the sense of the history of development. The development of the city can not be separated from the increasing economic and ecological misery announced in the "terrorist chic" of the film- and entertainment industry and experienced daily in cities overseas, blindly operated by the administrators of growth. The city dwellers retreat to the fortress, the city belongs to the riot. Between the ramparts lie the entertainment offered, alternating between the archaic and an exaggeration of technology, and the artificiality of relationships, taught as in a management seminar. R.L.

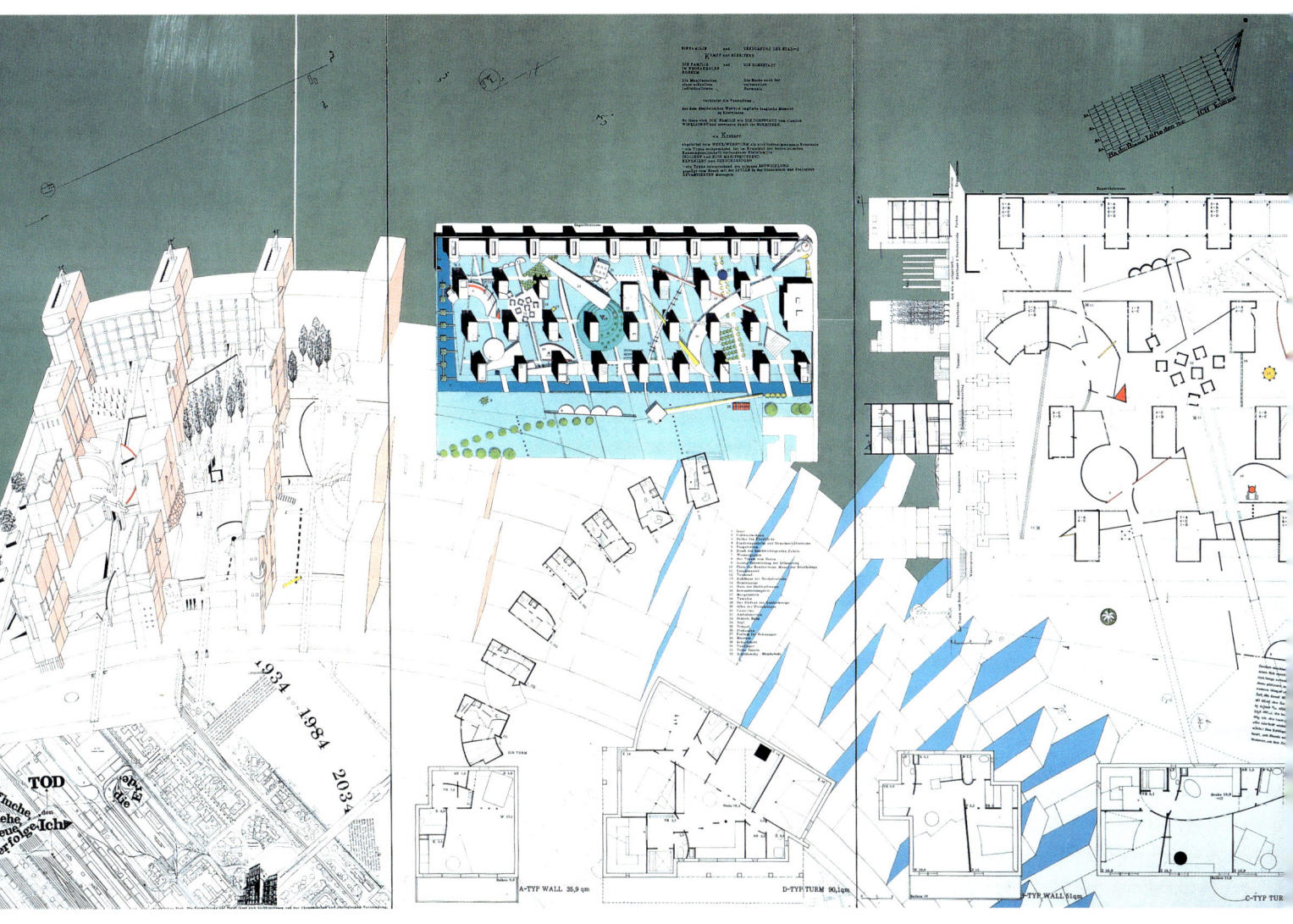

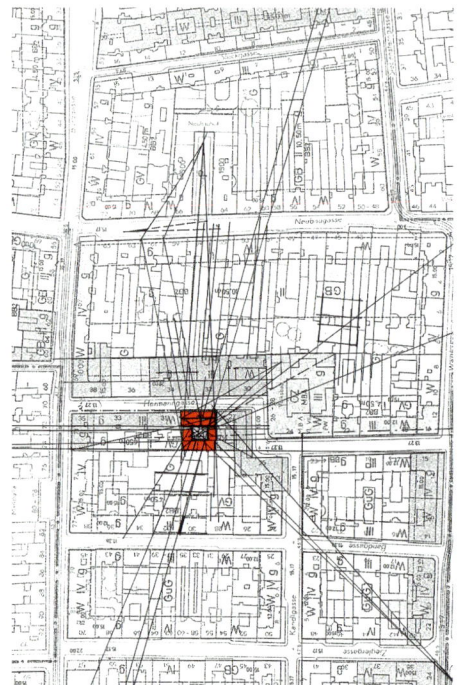

THE "LANDING PADS" FOR THE
IMPLANTATIONS, DEVELOPED
FROM THE CONTEXT
DIE AUS DEM KONTEXT
ENTWICKELTEN „LANDEBAHNEN
DER IMPLANTATE

Umbau Hermanngasse 29
Wien–Neubau, 1990

Der dicht bebaute siebte Wiener Gemeindebezirk weist noch eine erstaunlich große Zahl Häuser aus der ersten Hälfte des 19. Jahrhunderts auf. So auch in der Hermanngasse, einem schmalen Seitenast der Burggasse, die zudem doppelt abgewinkelt ist. Die zwei- bis dreigeschoßigen, breitgelagerten Biedermeierhäuser unterscheiden sich durch geringere Gebäudetiefen und niedrigere Raumhöhen von ihren meist gründerzeitlichen Nachbarn und wirken bereits aus Proportionsgründen anheimelnd, oft sogar putzig. In der Regel stehen sie unter Denkmalschutz. In den Höfen hinter den geraden Straßentrakten wurden anstelle der Schuppen und Stallungen bald Betriebsgebäude für allerlei Manufakturen und Werkstätten errichtet, denn „Neubau", so der Name des Bezirks, war ein Handwerkerviertel.

Hinter dem dreigeschoßigen Biedermeierhaus mit der Nummer 29, mit schmaler Durchfahrt zum Hof in der Mittelachse, erhebt sich auf U-förmigem Grundriss ein viergeschoßiges Betriebsgebäude, dessen Räume – höher und größer als jene im Vorderhaus – von Kappendecken überspannt sind. Beide Gebäudeteile wurden in der Struktur saniert, Mauern trockengelegt, Dächer gedichtet und gedämmt, Heizung und Sanitäranlagen eingebaut. In die ungleiche Struktur waren dreizehn Wohnungen einzuplanen, wobei die möglichen Ein- und Umbauten mit den künftigen Bewohnern besprochen und entwickelt wurden. Während vorne eine Mittelmauer den Grundriss teilt, sind die Räume hinten einhüftig und zumeist nur vom Hof her belichtet. Vor allem fehlten sowohl vorne als auch hinten die Bäder sowie die Toiletten in entsprechender

Conversion Hermanngasse 29
Vienna–Neubau, 1990

Vienna's densely built seventh district still has an amazingly large number of buildings dating from the first half of the 19th century. This is the case too in Hermanngasse, a small side street off Burggasse which twice makes a further turn. The wide-fronted, two to three-storey Biedermeier houses differ from their mostly Gründerzeit neighbours in that the blocks are less deep and the rooms lower, their proportions alone making them homely, indeed often quaint. Generally speaking these buildings are under a preservation order. In the courtyards behind the street fronts buildings for all kinds of manufacturing industries and workshops soon replaced the original sheds and stables, for "Neubau", which is the name of this neighbourhood, was once a district of craftsmen.

Behind number 29, a three-storey Biedermeier house with a narrow, centrally positioned driveway through to the courtyard, stands a four-storey industrial premises based on a U-shaped plan. Its rooms, higher and larger than those in the front building, are spanned by a series of shallow vaults. The basic structure of both buildings was renovated and the walls treated for damp, the roofs repaired and insulated, heating and sanitary facilities installed. In this disparate structure thirteen apartments were to be planned whereby the rebuilding and insertions were discussed and developed with the future residents. Whereas in the front building a central spine wall divides the floor plan the rooms behind face in one direction, mostly receiving light from the courtyard only. Above all, both in the front building and at

HERMANNGASSE

THE IMPLANTATIONS AND THEIR GEOMETRIC INCORPORATION
DIE IMPLANTATE UND IHRE GEOMETRISCHE EINORDNUNG

INTERNAL STANDARD GARAGE DOOR AS A TEMPORARY SPACE DIVIDER
INNERES SERIENGARAGENTOR ALS TEMPORÄRER RAUMTRENNER

Zahl und an der richtigen Stelle, was nicht nur räumliche, sondern vor allem installationstechnische Probleme zu lösen aufgab. Die Komplexität der Bedingungen erforderte, die verschiedenen Wohneinheiten wie in einem dreidimensionalen Puzzle in den Bestand hineinzukomponieren.

Während vorne die Haupträume mehrheitlich vorgegeben waren und da und dort durch Entfernen einer nichttragenden Zwischenwand vergrößert wurden, befanden sich hinten große Produktionsräume, die jedoch für eine Aufteilung zu wenig sinnvolle Zugänge aufwiesen, weshalb mehrere Stiegen zu errichten oder zu ergänzen waren. Zugleich wurde das gesamte Bauwerk sanft erneuert, etwa die blättrigen Farbschichten im Stiegenhaus als geschichtsträchtige Oberflächen belassen, die Kastenfenster repariert und neu gestrichen, einfache Schiffböden verlegt und die Wände geweißt. Die neuen Einbauten sind meist leicht konstruiert, aus Metall, Holz, Wellkunststoff, Profilglas und oftmals sogar aus Bambus. Die Böden der Bäder sind, nach Bewohnerwünschen, in Asphalt oder Fliesen gehalten. Allen Einbauten gemeinsam ist das episodische, scheinbar vorübergehende, versatzstück- und möbelmäßige, das sich vom Bestand in der Anmutung unterscheidet, da sie nicht Festigkeit und Kontinuität suggerieren wie die verputzten Ziegelmauern, die Kappen- und Betondecken, sondern Spontaneität und Veränderung. Und doch ist jede dieser kleinen Geschichten sorgfältig zu Ende erzählt, jede Inszenierung im Detail genau durchkonstruiert und technisch dauerhaft ausgeführt. Nach acht Jahren Benutzung ist eigentlich alles noch wie beim Einzug: die flachen Kiesel am Boden eines Bades, die Stufen und der Steg aus Bambus, die hölzernen Plissée-Stiegen und die Garagentore als temporäre Raumtrenner.

the rear, the lack of an adequate number of bathrooms and toilets in the right location was a major problem which demanded the solution of spatial, and above all technical, problems relating to the installation of services. The complexity of the requirements demanded that the various dwelling units be inserted in the existing building as in a three-dimensional puzzle.

Whereas in the street front building the main rooms were already defined and were merely enlarged here and there by removing a partition wall, at the rear the large production rooms had too few access corridors to allow sensible planning which meant that several staircases had to be built or extended. At the same time the entire building was gently renovated: the flaking layers of paint in the staircase were left as an historic surface, the double windows repaired and painted, simple wooden floorboards laid and the walls painted white. The new insertions are mainly light in terms of construction, made of metal, wood, corrugated plastic, profiled glass and often even bamboo. The floors of the bathrooms are, according to the residents' wishes, of asphalt or tiles. All new elements have in common the fact that they are episodic, apparently temporary set pieces much like furniture differing from the old substance in that, unlike the rendered brick walls, the concrete and vaulted roofs, they do not suggest solidity and continuity but spontaneity and change. And yet each of these little stories is recounted to the very end, every narrative worked out in detail and carried out in a technically durable manner. After eight years of use everything remains as on the day people moved in: the flat pebbles on the floor of a bathroom, the steps and footbridge made of bamboo, the folded

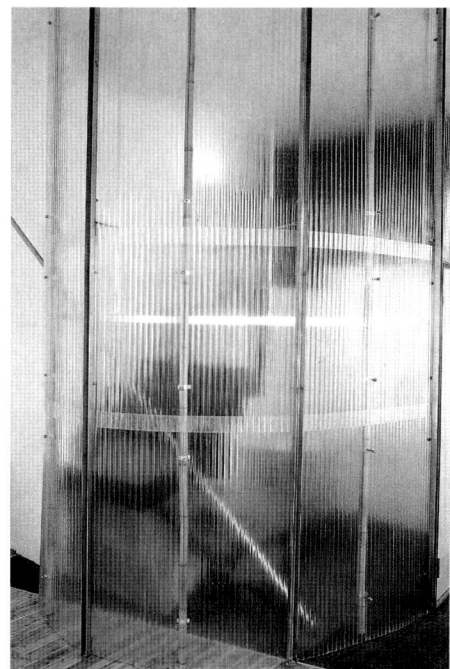

**TRANSLUCENT WALL IN THE BATHROOMS
BAMBOO- AND STAINLESS STEEL UPRIGHTS,
CORRUGATED POLYESTER
TRANSLUZENTE WAND DER BADEZIMMER
BAMBUS- UND NIROSTEHER, WELLPOLYESTER**

**SECTION
SCHNITT**

Beide Hausteile wurden im Verlauf des Entwurfs zu einem Mikrokosmos von Raumkonzepten, zu einem Ideenlaboratorium fürs städtische Wohnen, das dank der Neugier der künftigen Bewohner und dem Forscherdrang des Architekten zahlreiche Entwicklungen für die Sanitärräume und die inneren Erschließungen hervorbrachte. Die Wohnräume blieben neutral, die Küchen einfach. Da finden sich keine Prestigeobjekte mit teuren Materialien und schweren, Ewigkeit beanspruchenden Bauteilen, vielmehr sind die Interventionen beseelt von aufmunternder Heiterkeit, vom Ansatz, das Wohnen und die von der Altsubstanz gestellten Probleme leicht zu nehmen, im Bewusstsein, dass das Leben der toten, wenn auch geschichtsträchtigen Materie überlegen ist.

In der nordwestlichen Ecke des Hoftrakts war das Tageslicht knapp, weshalb hier die Decken zwei Geschoße tief aufgerissen und darüber mit einem verglasten Oberlicht versehen wurden. Der auf diese Weise gebildete Vertikalraum hält die beiden offenen Geschoße energisch zusammen. Das flache Dach des Hoftrakts wurde auf tiefer Humusschicht begrünt; ein in den Jahren üppig herangewachsener, lauschiger Garten kann auf zwei Arten erreicht werden: über das eine Haupttreppenhaus oder über eine schmale Stiege, die sich zuletzt im Luftraum eines Lichtschachts nach oben wendelt. Dies erlaubt einen Rundgang durch die innere Erschließungsstruktur beider Hausteile, die mit ihren knappen Gängen, zahlreichen Stufen und Verwinkelungen ansprechend geheimnisvoll, somit privat und zugleich kleinstädtisch – das heißt zugleich öffentlich – wirkt. Vieles wurde an dieser Neubelebung alter Bausubstanz angedacht, ausgelotet und getestet, was an späteren Bauwerken als Teil des Konzepts in gereifter oder abgeklärter Form wieder auftaucht. Das Chancenpotential, das eine derartige Bauaufgabe einem jungen Architekten bietet, hat Rüdiger Lainer an diesem Objekt optimal entfaltet und die daraus gewonnenen Erfahrungen danach bei seinen neu errichteten Wohnbauten angewendet.

timber stairs and the garage door as a temporary room divider. In the course of the design both parts of the house became a microcosm of spatial concepts, a laboratory of ideas for urban living which, thanks to the curiosity of the future residents and the architect's urge to research, produced numerous ideas for the sanitary facilities and the internal circulation. The living rooms remain neutral, the kitchens simple. There are no prestigious objects made of expensive materials and heavy elements laying claim to eternity, on the contrary, the interventions are animated by an encouraging cheerfulness, by the idea of taking living and the problems posed by the old substance easily, fully conscious that life is superior to the dead, but historic, material.

In the north-west corner of the courtyard tract daylight was in short supply which is why the floors in two storeys were opened up and a glazed roof light placed on top. The vertical space thus created keeps both open storeys together. The flat roof of the courtyard wing was given a thick layer of humus for planting, a leafy garden which has developed over the years can be reached in two ways: via the main staircase or by means of a narrow stairs which revolves upwards in the void of a light shaft. This move allows one to make a tour of the internal circulation of both parts of the house which, with their narrow corridors, numerous steps and angles, seems secretive and thus private and yet also like a small town and therefore public. In this rejuvenation of the old building substance much that was considered, tested and probed was to re-emerge in later projects as part of the concept in a matured or developed form. Rüdiger Lainer optimally exploited the possibilities which the opportunity of a building project such as this offers a young architect, the experience which he gained was then applied to his later housing projects.

SHARED ROOF TERRACE
GEMEINSAME DACHTERRASSE

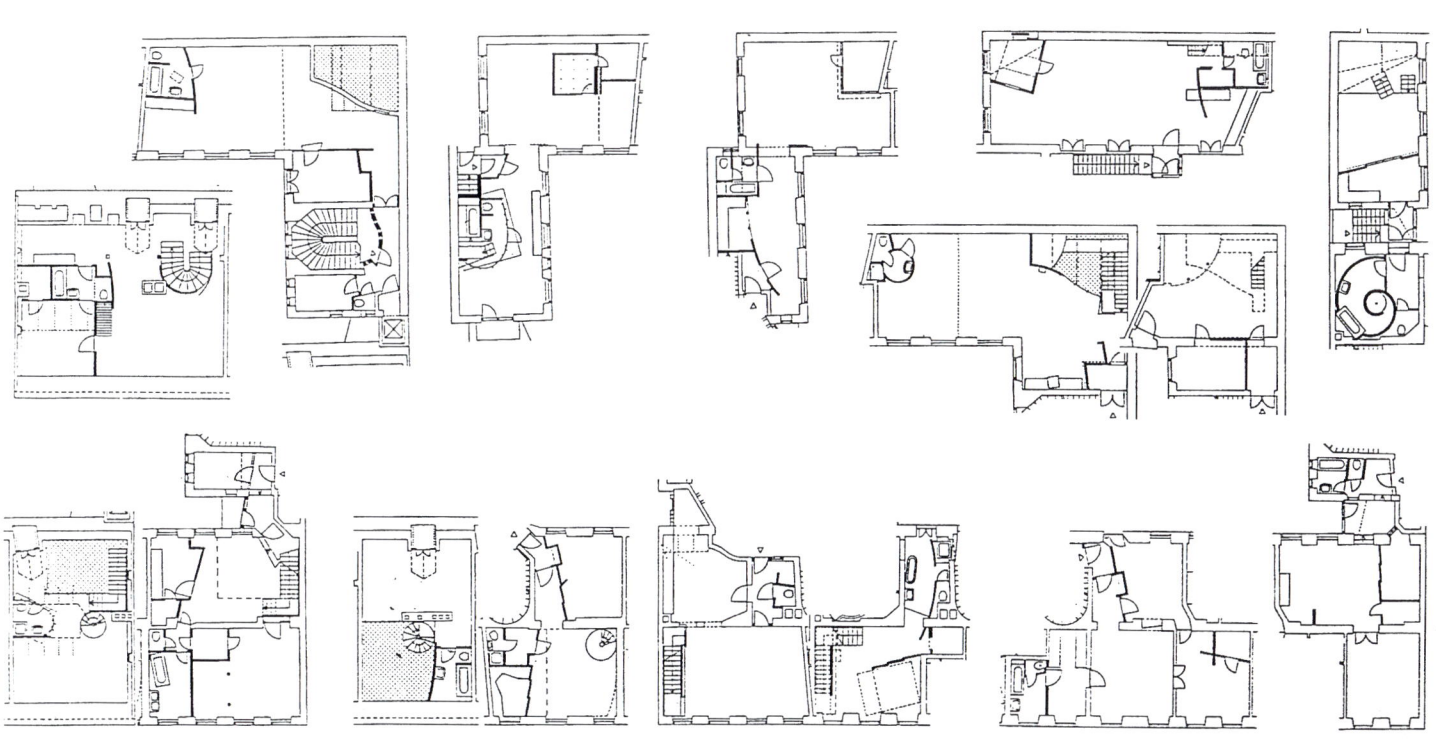

TWELVE UNITS
ZWÖLF EINHEITEN

FORM IS POLITICAL

WOHNBAU I

Die drei Wiener Wohnbauten Waidhausenstraße/Penzing (1991), Benjowskigasse/Aspern (1991) und Rothenburgstraße/Altmannsdorf (1992) sind mit ähnlichen architektonisch-städtebaulichen Ansätzen entworfen, obwohl ersterer als Baulückenverbauung, der andere als verdichtender Siedlungsbau und letzterer als Vorstadtsolitär zu planen war. Drei Aspekte waren bei allen Anlagen wichtig und zeugen von der konzeptionellen Verwandtschaft: Das plastisch-expressive Erscheinungsbild, gleichsam das „Gesicht" der Bauwerke, das dem öffentlichen Raum der Straße zugewendet ist; die individuelle, identitätstiftende Durchgestaltung der Wohnungen; sowie die räumlich attraktive, das Bauwerk insgesamt aufwertende innere Erschließung, deren teilöffentlicher Charakter durch ein Hereinziehen des Außenraumes bewusst gepflegt wird.

HOUSING I

The three Viennese housing developments Waidhausenstrasse, Penzing (1991), Benjowskigasse, Aspern (1991) and Rothenburgstrasse, Altmannsdorf (1992) were designed from a similar architectural and urban starting point, although the first of the three involved filling a vacant site, the second planning a dense estate development, and the third a suburban solitaire. In each of these developments three aspects were important and reveal a conceptual relationship: the sculpturally expressive appearance which is the "face" of the building turned towards the public space of the street, the individual design of the apartments which establishes an identity and the spatially attractive internal circulation which enhances the building, its partly public character cultivated by the incorporation of external space.

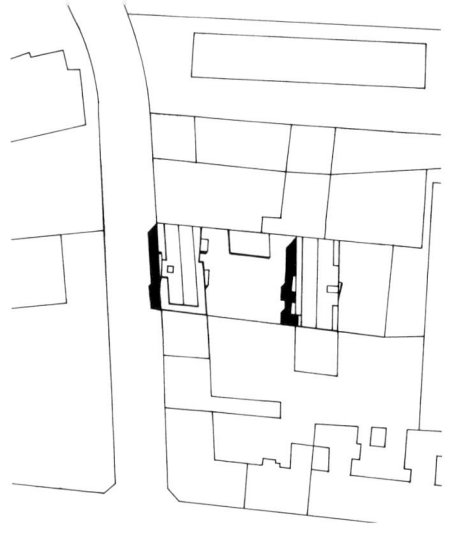
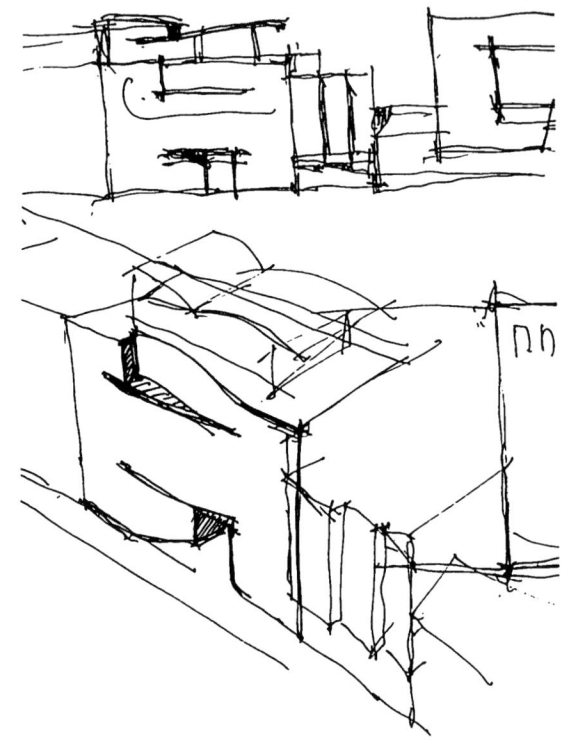

Wohnbau Waidhausenstraße 24
Wien–Penzing, 1991

Die über Jahrzehnte und Jahrhunderte oft in Schüben sich ausbreitende und entwickelnde Großstadt lässt da und dort in ihrem räumlichen Gefüge städtebauliche Kanten entstehen, die, nicht ausformuliert, Fragment bleiben, weil der wirtschaftliche Atem nicht ausreichte. Der obere Ast der Waidhausenstraße bildet zum Grünraum der friedhofsnahen Gärtnereien und Gewerbebetriebe eine nach Westen orientierte Kante, deren gründerzeitlicher Ansatz lückenhaft blieb. In den sechziger Jahren kamen auf dem vorgegebenen Parzellenmuster der Straßen- und Hoftrakt einer Wohnanlage dazu, die an den niedrigen Bestand anschlossen. Zweieinhalb Jahrzehnte später folgten zwei weitere Abschnitte nach denselben städtebaulichen Vorgaben im Sinne einer Baulückenverbauung, obwohl dazwischen noch eine Parzelle leer blieb. Den südlichen Teil bearbeitete Rüdiger Lainer mit seinem Team.

Prinzipiell weisen der Straßen- und der Hoftrakt dieselbe, nur gespiegelte typologische Konfiguration auf: an einem Stiegenhaus mit Lift liegen pro Geschoß zwei Dreizimmerwohnungen und eine Einzimmerwohnung. Die schräg angeschnittene Form des Grundstücks bietet zu einer üblichen orthogonalen Ordnung eine weitere Richtung an, die dem Grundriss an entscheidenden Stellen überlagert wurde, so dass sich aus den Interferenzen architektonisch Gewinn schlagen ließ.

Housing Development Waidhausenstrasse 24
Vienna–Penzing, 1991

The city, which developed and expanded over the decades and centuries in phases, allowed here and there urban edges to develop within its spatial network that, due to lack of economic vitality, remain unformulated fragments. The upper branch of Waidhausenstrasse forms a west-oriented edge to a green space composed of nursery gardens related to the local cemetery and industrial premises, its Gründerzeit starting point remaining somewhat incomplete. In the sixties the street and courtyard tract of a housing development were erected upon the predetermined site pattern adjoining lower existing buildings. Two and a half decades later two further developments based on the same urban premise followed with the intention of filling a gap although one site was left empty. Rüdiger Lainer and his team developed the southern section.

In principle the street and courtyard tract have the same typological configuration, merely mirrored. Two three-room apartments and a single-room apartment lie on each floor, served by a staircase with lift. In addition to the usual orthogonal order the angular incision in the site offered a further direction which is applied to the plan at significant points deriving an architectural profit from the interferences.

WAIDHAUSENSTRASSE

Weiters wurden in derselben Trag- und Erschließungsstruktur drei Grundrisstypen entwickelt, unter denen die Mieter wählen konnten. Der erste Typ weist einen mittigen Gang auf, von dem aus Küche, Wohnzimmer, Sanitärgruppe und Schlafteil zugänglich sind; der zweite verfügt über einen durch die gesamte Trakttiefe reichenden offenen Wohnteil aus Wohnzimmer und Küche, über den der Schlafteil zugänglich ist; den dritten zeichnet ein großes Wohnzimmer aus, das unmittelbar durch die Wohnungstür betreten wird, die Küche ist abgetrennt und die Sanitärgruppe konzentriert. Damit wurde latenten Wünschen nach unterschiedlichen Wohnformen ein Angebot gestellt. In der Folge hielt sich das Bedürfnis nach offenen und nach unterteilten Wohnbereichen die Waage.

Die Räume der Erschließung, Hausgänge und Stiegenhaus sind individuell behandelt: An der Straße liegt der Zugang zum Vorder- und Hinterhaus. Der Gehsteig ist räumlich und belagsmäßig hineingezogen; ansteigend führt der Weg auf einigen flachen Stufen durchs Haus in den Hof und zum Hinterhaus. Eine Reihe Rundstützen aus Schleuderbeton begleitet diesen Weg: Die ersten zwei verstärken mit ihrer Präsenz die Eingangszone. Die beiden nächsten flankieren den kastenartigen Zugang zum Vorderhaus, der seitlich zur Linken etwas vorspringt. Damit gelingt eine Umdeutung der Zugangsrichtung um 90 Winkelgrade, während der nach hinten führende Weg nur leicht in die Normalrichtung zur Hinterfassade gebeugt wird. Dieses subtile Spiel von Richtungen und ineinanderfließenden Raumzonen führt zu einer differenziert erlebbaren Folge räumlicher Aussagen und Stimmungen, die insofern gewachsen wirkt, als sie aus verschiedenen inhaltlichen Wurzeln heraus entwickelt wurde. Das dichte Gewebe gestalterischer Vektoren evoziert nicht zuletzt jene Urbanität, die selbst an der Peripherie großstädtisch, genauer: wienerisch ist. Die Fassaden bilden diesen Diskurs aus Richtungen plastisch ab, wobei hier das Element der verglasten Loggien dazukommt. Die Straßenfront gehorcht anderen Regeln: das klare Bild zweier ineinander verschränkter Wandflächen wird im flachen Relief von der Farbgebung nach dem Konzept von Oskar Putz verstärkt. Damit gewinnt sie unspektakulär ein eigenständiges „Gesicht". Diese Art der Gliederung reiht sich sensibel in die Zeile der Nachbarhäuser, thematisiert den Hauptzugang als Durchgang, nicht als „Eingang", weil die Außenwände hineingezogen wurden. Die immer wieder spürbare gestalterische Freude hält sich dabei an tektonisch-räumliche Aspekte und vermeidet die Hereinnahme außerarchitektonischer „Erzählungen".

Additionally three floor plan types were developed, between which the tenants could make their choice, within the common load-bearing and circulation system. The first type has a central corridor from which kitchen, living room, sanitary facilities and the bedrooms are reached, the second has an open living area composed of kitchen and living room extending through the depth of the building from which there is access to the sleeping area, the third type has a large living room entered directly from the entrance door, the kitchen is separated and the sanitary facilities form a concentrated block. In this way a response was made to the latent desire for different living forms. As a consequence the need for open or separated living areas was kept in balance.

The circulation spaces, common corridors and staircase are treated individually. The approach to the front and back building lies on the street. The footpath is incorporated in the design both spatially and as regards the surfacing. The route leads upwards via a few low steps through the building into the courtyard to the rear building. A series of circular columns made of spun concrete accompany this route. The presence of the first two strengthens the entrance zone, the next two flank the box-like access to the front building which at the side projects somewhat to the left. This move achieves a realignment of the direction of approach by 90 degrees whereas the route leading to the rear is merely slightly swivelled to make a right angle to the rear facade. This subtle play with directions and spatial zones flowing one into the other leads to a sequence of spatial statements and moods that can be individually experienced and that seems to have grown up gradually as, in terms of content, it was developed from different roots. This dense weave of design vectors evokes an urbanity which, even on the periphery, seems metropolitan or, to put it better, Viennese. The facades offer a depiction of this discourse on directions with the added element of the glazed loggias. The street front obeys different rules: the clear image of two interlocking wall surfaces is strenghtened by a colour scheme based on a concept by Oskar Putz. In an unspectacular fashion it thus acquires an independent "face." This method of articulation fits in sensitively in the row of neighbouring buildings and deals thematically with the main approach as a passageway rather than as an "entrance" by incorporating the external walls. The delight in design which can be felt at many points is confined to architectural and spatial elements avoiding the introduction of non-architectural "narratives."

FRONT BUILDING, WEST | VORDERHAUS WEST

REAR BUILDING, EAST | HINTERHAUS OST

FRONT BUILDING, WEST
VORDERHAUS WEST

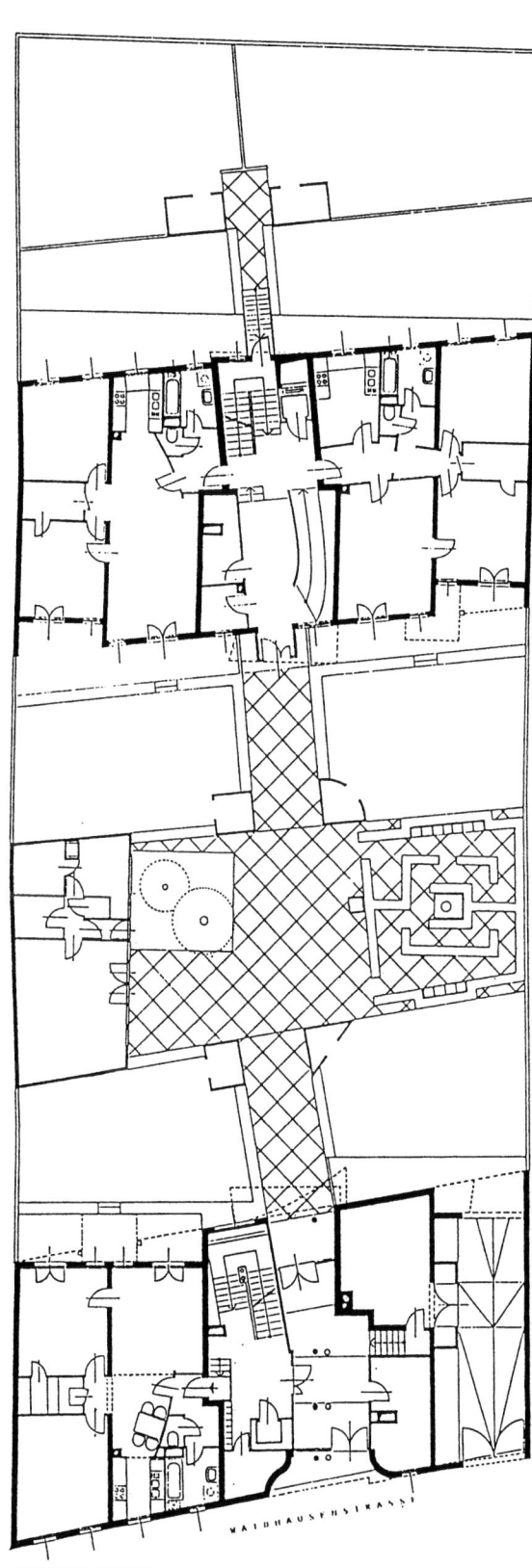

**GROUND FLOOR
FRONT AND REAR BUILDING
VORDER- UND HINTERHAUS
ERDGESCHOSS** 1:333

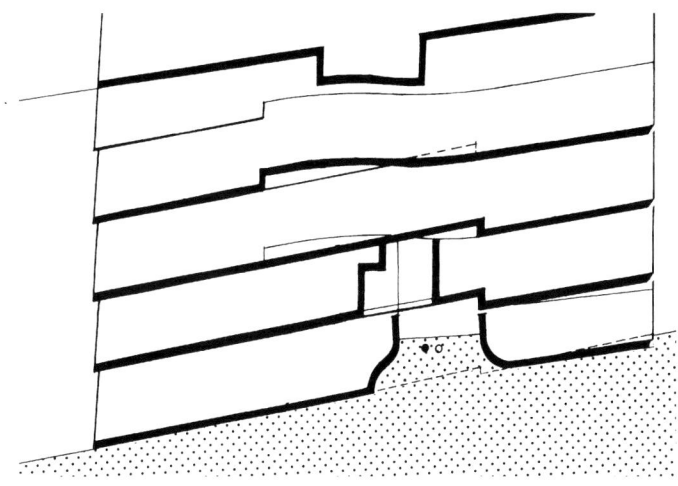

**LAYERING OF THE FACADE
SCHICHTUNG DER FASSADE**

**2ND FLOOR REAR BUILDING
2. OBERGESCHOSS HINTERHAUS** 1:333

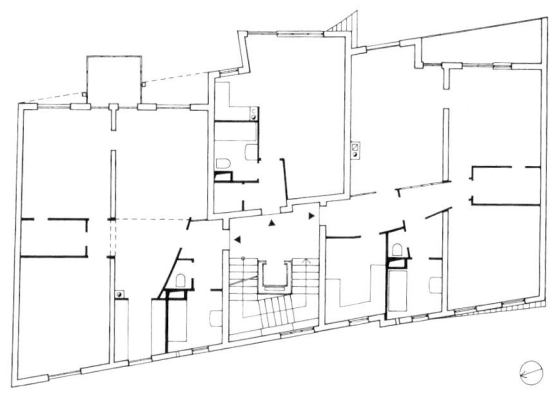

**2ND FLOOR FRONT BUILDING
2. OBERGESCHOSS VORDERHAUS** 1:333

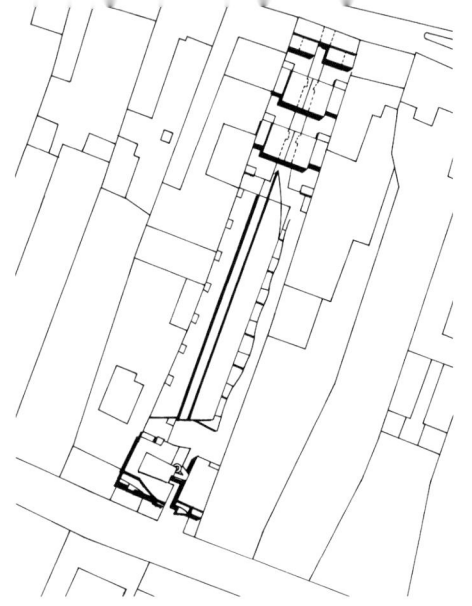
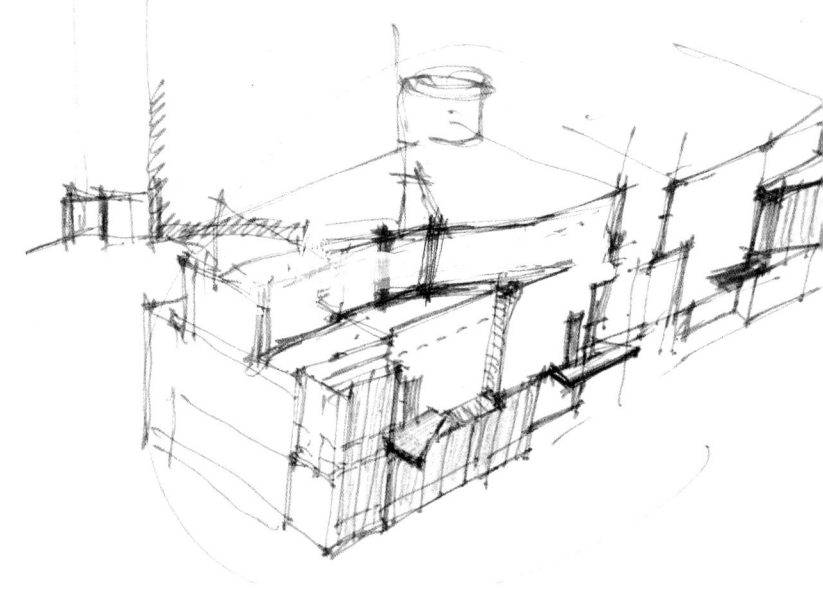

**Wohnhausanlage Siegesplatz 21/Benjowskigasse
Wien–Aspern, 1991**

Vom südwestorientierten Anger des alten Dorfkerns von Aspern, aus historischem Anlass Siegesplatz geheißen, zieht sich das schmale Grundstück über 100 Meter nach Süden bis zum ehemaligen Hintausweg, der heutigen Benjowskigasse. Die klassische, von der landwirtschaftlichen Nutzung bestimmte, von einem kleinen Hakenhof ausgehende Handtuchparzelle wurde aus siedlungsbaulichen Überlegungen in drei Abschnitte geteilt: Am Siegesplatz reiht sich das erste Gebäude in die niedrige Zeile der geschlossenen Angerbebauung. Es wird mittig von einem Torweg durchstoßen; zwei südorientierte, zum Doppelhaus addierte Maisonnettewohnungen verfügen jeweils über einen kleinen vorgelagerten Gartenhof. Dieser Typ wird, gleichsam bekräftigend, noch zweimal wiederholt, wobei das Erdgeschoß bis an die seitlichen Grenzen reicht, das Obergeschoß jedoch zurückgestaffelt ist.

Die Mittelzone des Grundstücks wird mit einer Zeile aus sieben Reihenhäusern belegt, die als Ost-Westtypen die mögliche Besonnung optimal nutzen: Eingang, Essplatz und obergeschoßige Schlafräume im Osten, Wohnraum, Gartenhof und Terrasse für das Abendwohnen im Westen. Der durch das gesamte Grundstück führende Weg lenkt östlich an der Zeile vorbei. Im Süden, an der Benjowskigasse war vom Bebauungsplan wieder geschlossene Bauweise angesagt, diesmal mit zwei Vollgeschoßen. Hier bearbeitet Rüdiger Lainer das Thema des von einer schmalen Gasse geteilten Doppelbaukörpers, das bei späteren Bauten wieder aufscheint. Die Stiege wird teilweise im Luftraum über der Gasse geführt. Wir werden an den Film „mon oncle" von Jacques Tati erinnert, in dem der Onkel, zum Erstaunen und Gaudi des Publikums, mehrmals wieder zum Vorschein kommt, während er über Treppen und Loggien zu seiner Dachwohnung hinaufsteigt.

**Housing Development Siegesplatz 21/Benjowskigasse
Vienna–Aspern, 1991**

From the south-west oriented village green in the old center of Aspern, that is called for historic reasons Siegesplatz (Victory Square), the narrow site extends for more than a hundred metres southwards to the old rear alley-way today named Benjowskigasse. This handkerchief-sized plot is a classic example of a site determined by agricultural use and is derived from an angled farm house type. It was divided into three sections for reasons relating to the problems of housing development: the first building on Siegesplatz is placed in the low continuous row formed by the neighbouring buildings along the green. It is penetrated at the center by a gateway; two south-facing maisonette apartments are combined to form a double house, each has a small garden courtyard at the front. In an intensifying gesture this type is twice repeated, the ground floor extending to the side boundaries whereas the upper floor is set back.

The central zone of the site is occupied by a row of seven terrace houses, their east-west orientation guaranteeing an opimal exploitation of sunshine. Entrance, dining area and the bedrooms on the upper floor are on the east side, living room, garden courtyard and terrace for evening use face west. To the south, along Benjowskigasse, the development plan required once again a continuous building pattern, in this case with two full storeys. Here Rüdiger Lainer developed the theme of a double building element divided by a narrow lane which reappears in later buildings. We are reminded of Jacques Tati's film "mon oncle" in which the uncle, to the astonishment and delight of the public, appears several times while climbing, via staircase and loggias to his attic apartment.

SIEGESPLATZ

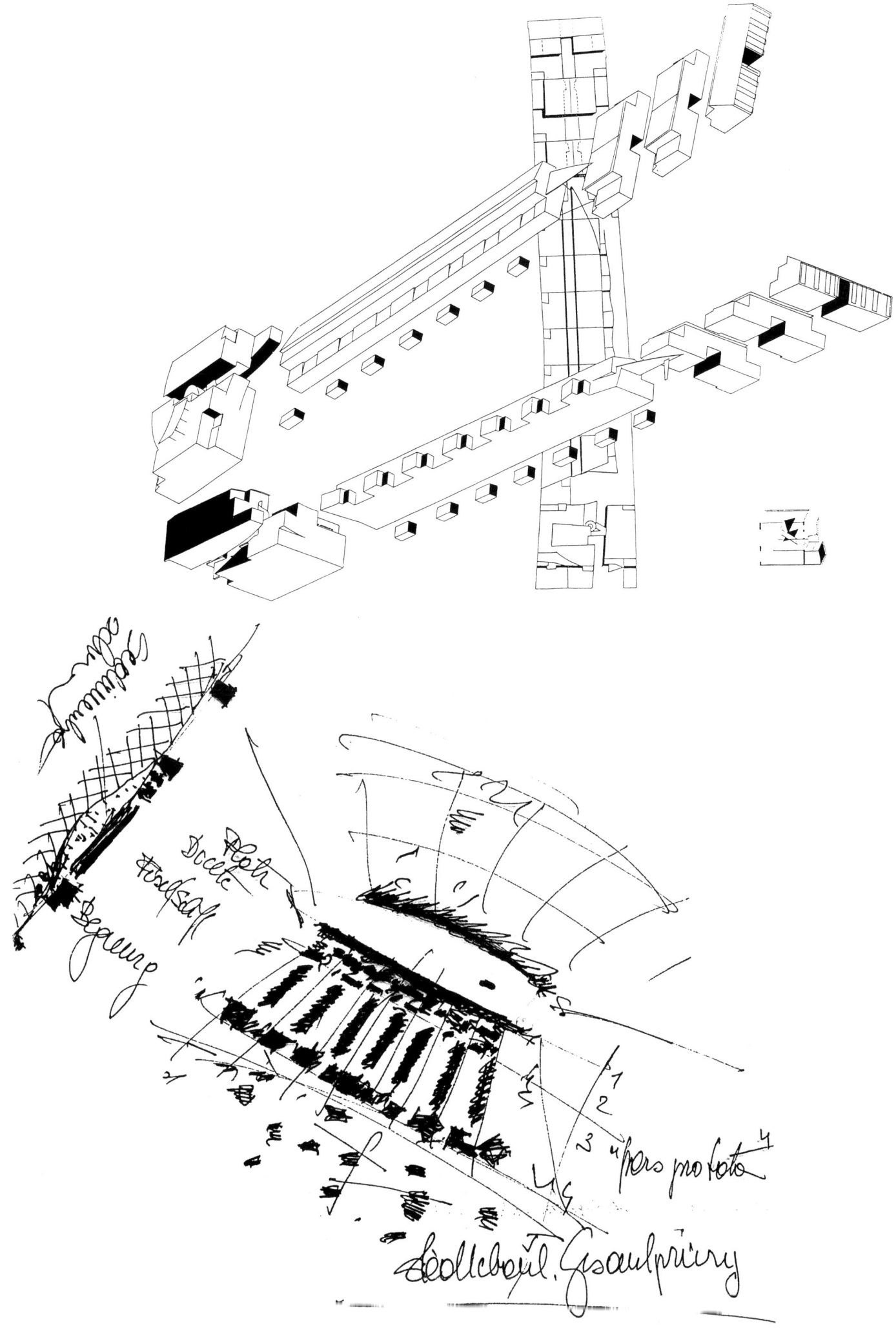

TERRACE HOUSES WEST | REIHENHÄUSER WEST

Der größere Abschnitt enthält in den unteren beiden Geschoßen zwei Maisonnetten und darüber eine große Geschoßwohnung; der kleinere liegt über der Abfahrt zur Tiefgarage sowie über deren Aufgang. Darüber befinden sich zwei kleinere Wohnungen. Die Hauptfassade zur Benjowskigasse, die in Umkehr der ursprünglichen Ordnung im Dorf nun den Hauptzugang akzentuiert, ist in teils geschwungene, teils trapezförmig aus der Ordnung springende Wandscheiben aufgelöst. Zu beiden Seiten könnten Gebäude ähnlicher Größe anschließen, doch steht der geteilte Baukörper noch solitär da. Das Schwergewicht der Fassadengestaltung wird in die Mittelzone gelegt, wo Mauerflächen dominieren.

Zu den künftigen Nachbarbauten wird die Fassade weicher mit verglasten Loggien und Balkonen. Sowohl auf siedlungsbaulicher als auch auf architektonischer Ebene bildet die Anlage insgesamt den nachvollziehbaren, prototypischen Ansatz einer maßvollen Verdichtung im Kontext der ursprünglichen Dorfstruktur, die längst nicht mehr landwirtschaftlich, sondern vorstädtisch geprägt ist. Die an der Straße gelegenen Wohnungen sind individueller, die gleichgearteten Reihenhäuser in der Mittelzone sind dafür vom Straßenlärm besser abgeschirmt. So wird einerseits die Lagegunst ausgleichend gehandhabt, andererseits die spezifische Stellung im Siedlungsgefüge als Anlass für eine lebendige Formbildung genommen. Die Anlage ist daher nicht als isolierte Figur zu betrachten, sondern als differenzierte Einfügung, die mit den heutigen Nachbarn ebenso interagiert wie sie für künftige Entwicklungen offen ist.

The larger section contains on both lower floors two maisonettes and above a large, single-storey apartment, the smaller section lies above the approach to and exit from the underground garage. Above there are two smaller apartments. The main facade on to Benjowskigasse, which reverses the original order in the village and accentuates the main approach, is broken up into wall slabs partly curved, partly trapezoid shaped which jump out of the ordering system. On either side buildings of similar height could be attached but at present the divided block stands alone. The main emphasis of the facade design is placed in the central zone where wall surfaces are dominant.

Towards the future neighbouring buildings the facade becomes softer with glazed loggias and balconies. On both the level of housing and architecture the complex forms a comprehensible, prototypical starting point demonstrating a measured increase in density within the existing village structure which for some time now is no longer rural but suburban in character. The apartments on the street side are more individual, the terrace houses in the central zone are better screened from traffic noise. The advantages of both locations are thus fairly treated and the specific position within the development mesh is exploited as a motivation for a lively development of form. This complex should not be viewed as an isolated figure but as a differentiated insertion which interacts with the present-day neighbours while remaining open for future developments.

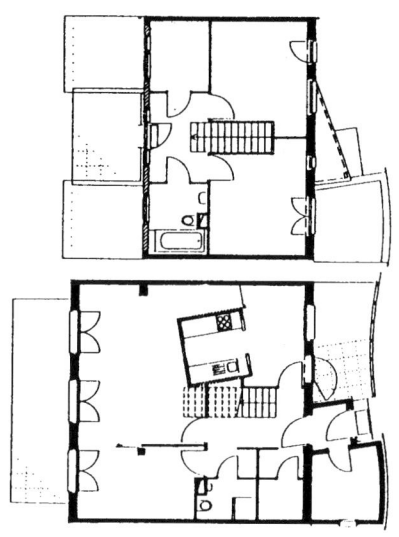

TERRACE HOUSES, FLOOR PLAN
REIHENHÄUSER GRUNDRISS 1:333

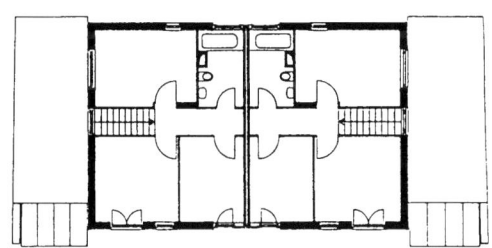

GATEHOUSE UPPER FLOOR
TORHAUS OBERGESCHOSS 1:333

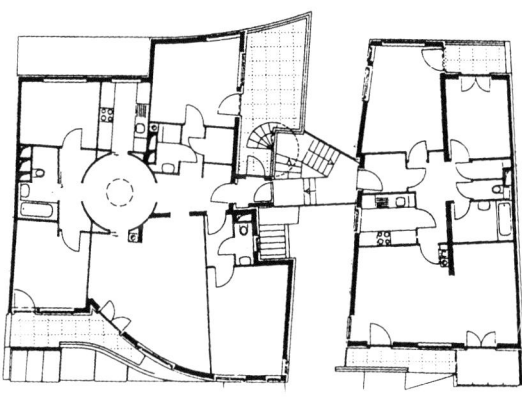

2ST FLOOR DIVIDED HOUSE
2. OBERGESCHOSS GETEILTES HAUS 1:333

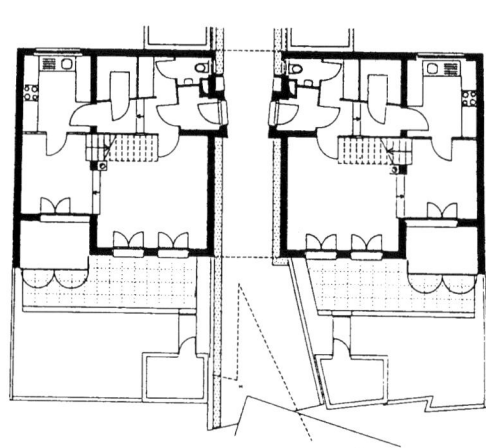

GATEHOUSE GROUND FLOOR
TORHAUS ERDGESCHOSS 1:333

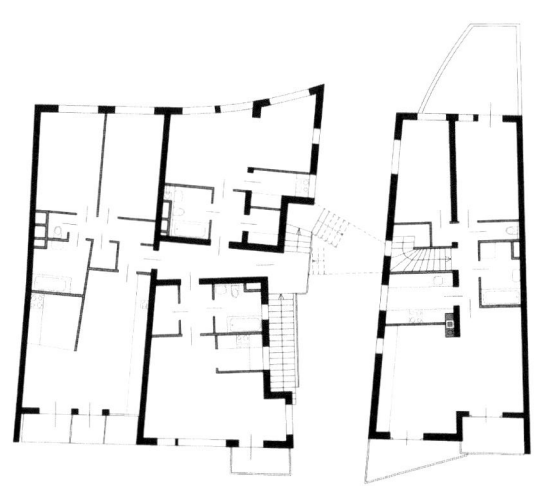

1ST FLOOR DIVIDED HOUSE
1. OBERGESCHOSS GETEILTES HAUS 1:333

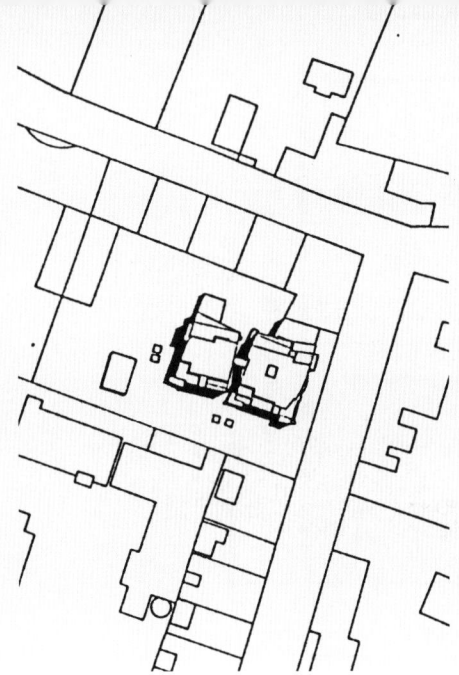
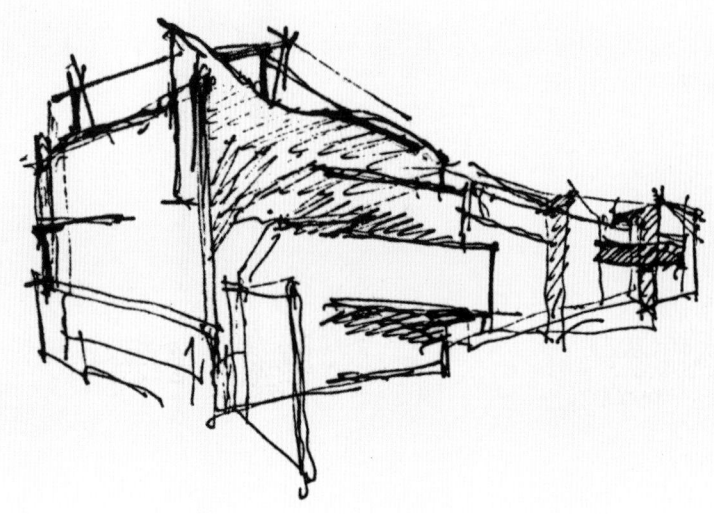

Wohnhausanlage Rothenburgstraße 2
Wien–Altmannsdorf, 1992

Im Übergang von einer neuen Blockrandbebauung zu niedrigen Vorstadtstrukturen mit eingemischten Gewerbebauten wurde der neue Doppelbaukörper mit der signifikanten Physiognomie seiner bewegten Stirnseite zur Rothenburgstraße platziert. Die gebäudenahen Flächen des Umraumes sind den Erdgeschoßwohnungen zugeordnet; der rückwärtige Teil dient als Gemeinschaftsgarten, wo auch ein zeltartig zartes Kinderhaus aus Stahl, Glas und Wellkunststoff steht. Dieser Gartenteil ist mit dem engen Gassenraum, der zwischen Vorder- und Hinterhaus eingeschnitten ist, durch Hartbelagwege verbunden.

Das Bauwerk ist in zwei etwa gleichgroße Teilkörper gegliedert, die durch eine transparente Korridorbrücke eng und zugleich filigran gekoppelt sind. Die Erschließung führt zielstrebig entlang der Mittelachse durch die Häuser nach hinten, spaltet sich in den weiterführenden Gang und in eine einläufige nach oben führende Stiege. Der Lift ist leicht aus den Hauptachsen gedreht, so dass sein Prisma vor der Lifttür eine kleine Raumzone akzentuiert. Um den Erschließungskern fügen sich in meist rechtwinkliger Ordnung die Sanitärräume und Abstellkammern; dann folgen die Küchen, die wegen Licht und Luft meist an die Fassade grenzen. Die Wohnräume und Zimmer der mehrheitlich relativ großen Wohnungen erzeugen eine äußerste Raumschicht, die von einer oft weich bewegten Hülle gefaßt wird. Als räumliche Außenposten setzen die Balkone nahe bei oder an den Gebäudeecken an und stoßen in den Umraum vor.

Housing Development Rothenburgstrasse 2
Vienna–Altmannsdorf, 1992

This new double block was placed so that the significant physiognomy of its animated end elevation faces on to Rothenburgstrasse at the point of transition from a new block perimeter development to lower suburban structures with incorporated small industrial premises. Areas of the surroundings lying close to the building are allotted to the ground floor apartments. The rear section serves as a communal garden with a delicate, tent-like play-house made of steel, glass and corrugated plastic. This garden area is linked by hard-surfaced paths to the narrow lane incised between front and rear buildings.

The building is divided into two elements of approximately equal size. They are linked both closely and in a filigree manner by a transparent corridor bridge. The access route leads purposefully along the center axis through the buildings to the rear splitting into a corridor leading further and a single-flight staircase rising upwards. The lift is moved slightly off the main axis, its prism thus accentuating a small spatial zone in front of the lift door. The sanitary facilities and storage spaces are arranged around the circulation core, mostly in a rectilinear order, the kitchens follow and, for reasons of light and ventilation, generally border the facades. The living rooms and other rooms of the mostly relatively large apartments produce an outermost spatial layer contained by a shell that is often gently animated. The balconies are spatial outposts, close to or at the corners, that thrust into the surrounding space.

ROTHENBURGSTRASSE

NORTH VIEW
ANSICHT NORD

Die Straßenfassade entwickelt sich von rechts nach links – in die Richtung, in der man von der Hetzendorfer Straße in die Rothenburgstraße hineinfährt. Vom festen Vertikalelement der teilverglasten Balkone ziehen sich, sowohl fahnen- als auch schirmartig überlagert, weich ausschwingende Wandscheiben über die Stirnfront, welche die beiden zurückhaltender gestalteten Teilbaukörper zum öffentlichen Raum hin vertritt. Die Farbgebung von Oskar Putz stützt einerseits die Trennung, andererseits relativiert sie das Relief durch monochrome Gleichheit.

Das äußere Relief korrespondiert mit der inneren Raumaufteilung, so dass die Wohnungen über die spezifische Ausnutzung ihrer Lage im Baukörper hinaus individuelle Identität gewinnen. Mehrere nichttragende Wände würden einen offeneren Grundriss erlauben, der mit einer Folge von Schiebetüren entlang der Fassade räumlich attraktiv wirken würde. Für Familien mit heranwachsenden Kindern können sich allerdings Abgrenzungsprobleme ergeben, weshalb diese Grundrissdisposition selten gewählt wird. Die Grunddisposition legt die Küchen in die Nähe des Vorraums, von dem aus sie auch erschlossen sind. In fast allen Fällen wird aber auch ein Zugang vom Wohnbereich angeboten, der als Erschließungsalternative die Wohnung aufwertet. Die Kleinwohnungen sind naturgemäß knapper arrangiert. Die für Wiener Verhältnisse vergleichsweise kleine Wohnbauaufgabe ist auf mehreren Ebenen engagiert bearbeitet. So wurde den städtebaulichen Aspekten angemessen Rechnung getragen, die innere Erschließung räumlich attraktiv gestaltet und sorgsam belichtet sowie dem individuellen Wohnen eine sinnvolle räumlich-funktionelle Basis angeboten. Die räumliche Lockerung zum Gebäudemantel hin verdeutlicht das Bemühen, den Grad an vorgegebener Ordnung zugunsten von freieren Entfaltungsmöglichkeiten niedrig zu halten.

The street facade develops from right to left – the direction in which one drives into Rothenburgstrasse from Hetzendorferstrasse. From the fixed vertical elements of the partly glazed balconies wall panels, swinging gently outwards and overlapping like flags or screens, extend along the end elevation which represents in the public space the two parts that are designed in a more restrained manner. Oskar Putz' colour scheme underlines the separation while at the same time modifying the relief as a result of its monochrome equality.

The external relief corresponds with the internal planning of the spaces so that the apartments gain an individual identity beyond the exploitation of their position in the building. The number of non load-bearing walls would permit a more open floor plan which, with a series of sliding doors along the facade, would be spatially attractive. However, for families with growing children, this could create problems of privacy which is why this particular floor plan arrangement is seldom chosen. The basic plan places the kitchen close to the hall from which it is reached. In almost all cases there is also access from the living area establishing a circulation alternative that enhances the apartment. The small apartments are naturally more tightly planned.

This housing development, relatively small by Viennese standards, is handled in a committed way on several levels. The urban aspects were given appropriate consideration, the internal circulation attractively designed and carefully lighted and individual life styles offered a sensible, spatially functional basis. The spatial loosening as one moves towards the building's exterior illustrates the effort to restrict the degree of prescribed order in favour of more free possibilities of development.

4ᵀᴴ FLOOR
4. OBERGESCHOSS 1:333

3ᴿᴰ FLOOR
3. OBERGESCHOSS 1:333

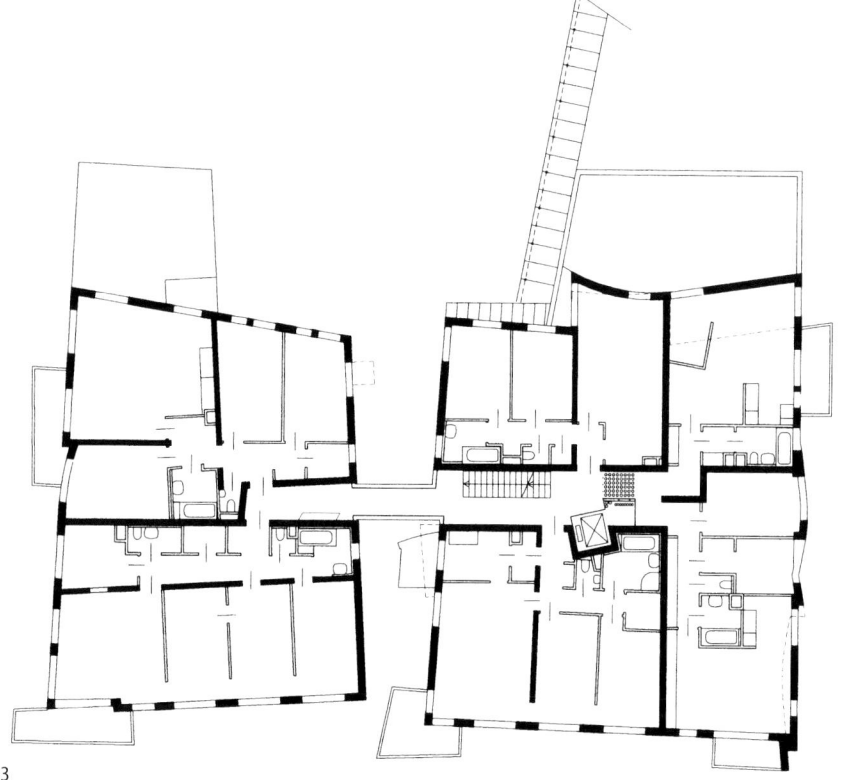

1ˢᵀ FLOOR
1. OBERGESCHOSS 1:333

**CHILDREN'S HOUSE
KINDERHAUS**

NEUTRAL AND SPECIFIC

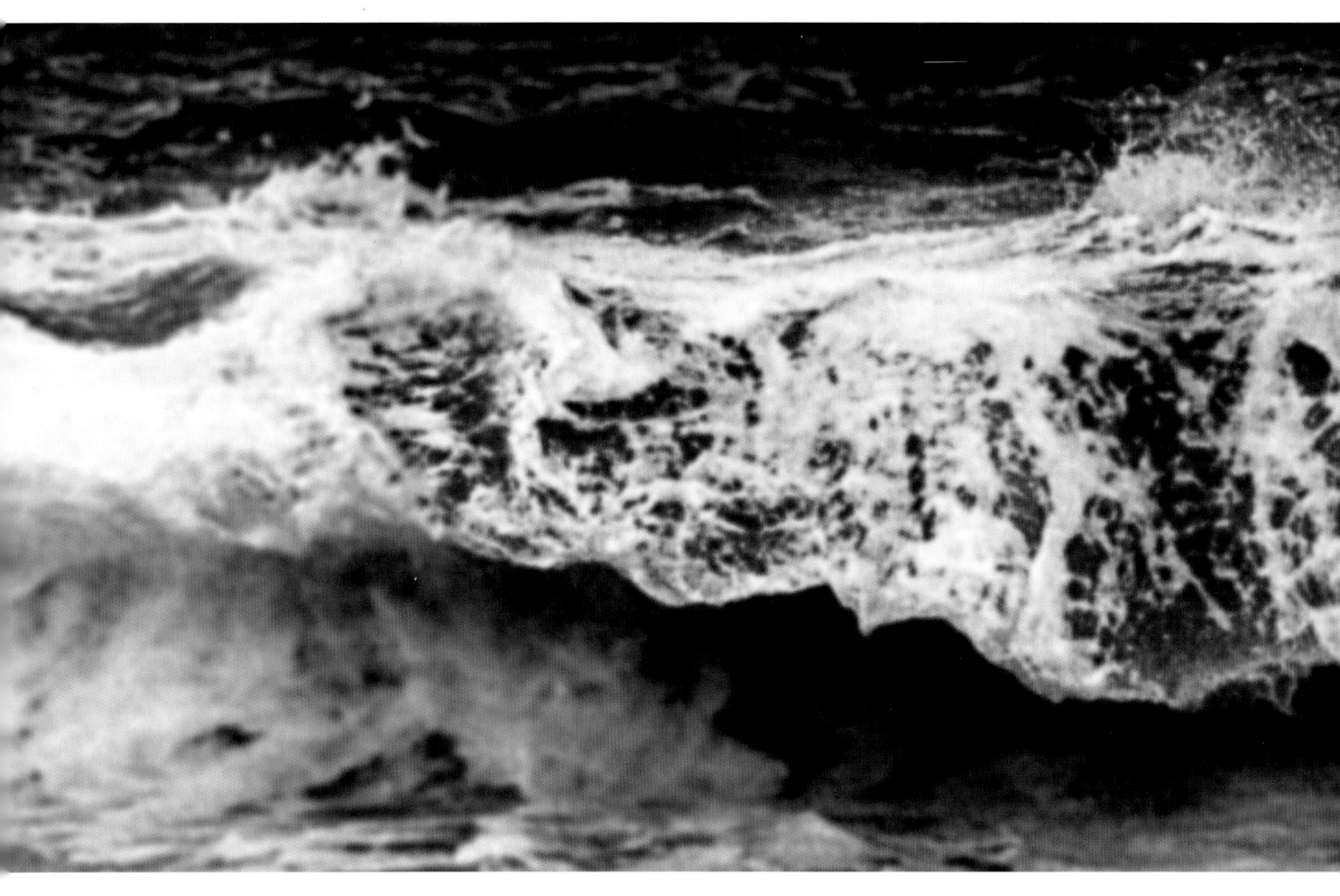

WOHNBAU II

Basierend auf den Erfahrungen mit kostengünstigen Tragstrukturen für die Schule Absberggasse und das Penthouse Seilergasse versucht Rüdiger Lainer mit seinen jüngsten Wohnbauprojekten die Hauptanliegen der früheren Arbeiten – individueller Charakter und innere Veränderbarkeit der Wohnungen, ansprechende innere und äußere Erschließung sowie ein vielfältiges Angebot für das Außenwohnen – zu verbinden mit ökonomischen Tragsystemen, verstärkter Vorfertigung und der gezielten Anwendung von Bepflanzung in Form „vertikaler Grünräume". Mit dem Angebot von teilweise offenen, das heißt unspezifisch gehaltenen Strukturen, die erst durch die Belegung und die Benützung ihren individuell differenzierten Charakter gewinnen, wird vom Prinzip der bildhaften, durch bauplastische Gliederung erzeugten Individualität abgegangen. Mit den strukturalen und bauvolumetrischen Vorgaben wird die städtebauliche Integration bewältigt, ohne aber dem individuell konkreten Ausdruck vorgreifen zu wollen, der im Hinblick auf die Anonymität und den Wechsel künftiger Bewohner durch den Architekten nicht voraussehbar ist. Im Sinne seines Verständnisses einer offenen Planung zeigt seine Entwurfsmethodik „Wege auf, die Stärken und konzeptuelle Integrität eines Entwurfskonzepts zu bewahren und es gleichzeitig gegenüber sich verändernden und im Planungsverlauf erst konkretisierenden Anforderungen offen zu halten".

HOUSING II

Drawing from the experience with economical structural systems which he acquired in designing the Absberggasse school and the Seilergasse penthouse, Rüdiger Lainer attempts in his most recent housing projects to combine the primary concerns of his earlier work – the individual character and internal flexibility of the dwellings, sophisticated internal and external circulation and a variety of possibilities for outdoor living – with economical structures, an increased use of pre-fabrication and the considered application of planting in the form of "vertical green space." The supply of partly open, that is unspecified structures, which first acquire their individually differentiated character when occupied and used, represents a departure from the design principle of figurative individuality that results from sculptural articulation. Within the structural and volumetric constraints he deals with the problem of urban integration without ever anticipating an individual concrete expression, which, in view of the fact that he does not know who the future residents will be nor how often a change of tenancy will occur, cannot be predicted by the architect. Within the framework of his understanding of open planning Lainer's design approach illustrates "ways of preserving the strengths and conceptual integrity of a design approach while keeping it open to those changing demands which first acquire concrete form in the course of the planning process."

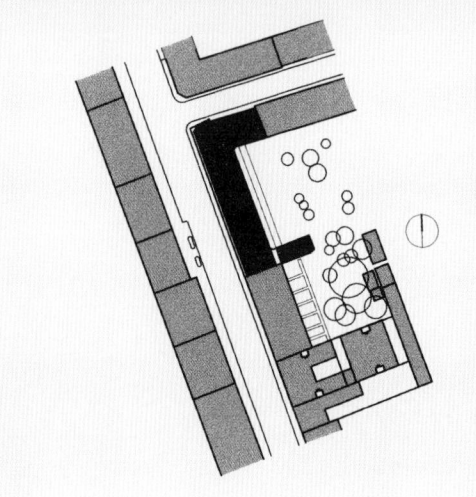

Dachaufbau Favoritenstraße 27
Wien–Wieden, 1998–

Ein alltägliches, viergeschoßiges Mietshaus von 1835 an der Ecke Favoritenstraße/Karolinengasse, des Gevierts Viktor- und Weyringergasse, sollte um zwei beziehungsweise ein Geschoß aufgestockt werden. Während auf den meisten Nachbarzellen mehrere Trakte die in die Tiefe gestaffelten, schmalen Lichthöfe einzwängen, beschränkt sich der biedermeierliche Winkelbau auf den Blockrand und schließt mit einem schmalen Seitenflügel einen weiträumigen begrünten Hof ein.

Auf die einfache Gebäudestruktur mit kräftigen Außenmauern und einer Kaminwand in der Mitte sowie festgelegten Treppenhäusern antwortet das Projekt mit einer Leichtbaukonstruktion mit Querschotten, zwischen denen jeweils eine Kleinwohnung Platz findet. Zusammenschlüsse zu größeren Wohneinheiten sind möglich. Als wesentliches, neu hinzugefügtes Element tritt die Erschließung hervor. Sie ist hofseitig auf schlanken Stützen aufgeständert und in zwei Raumschichten geteilt. Außen liegt ein zweigeschoßiger Laubengang, der beide Stiegenhäuser verbindet und auch den abgewinkelten Trakt an der Karolinengasse erreicht.

Zwischen Steg und Hauswand ist eine 2,40 Meter breite Zone eingeschoben, die den neu errichteten Lift für alle Geschoße, aber vor allem balkonartige Wohnungsvorplätze enthält, über die man in die eigentlichen Vorräume gelangt. Dazwischen liegen breite Lufträume. Auf diese Weise verfügen die meisten Wohnungen über eine kleine Fläche, auf der die Bewohner sich im Freien aufhalten können. Im Stützgerüst besteht diese Möglichkeit auch für die darunter liegenden Wohnungen des Altbaus.

Rooftop Extension Favoritenstrasse 27
Vienna–Wieden, 1998–

The intention was to extend an ordinary, four-storey tenement house, dating from 1835, standing on the corner of Favoritenstrasse and Karolinengasse in the Viktorgasse-Weyringergasse quarter, by adding one/two storeys. Whereas on most of the neighbouring plots a succession of tracts frames narrow light wells that are staggered along the depth of the site, this angled Biedermeier building consists merely of the street-front building and a narrow side wing which together enclose an extensive, leafy courtyard.

This project responds to the building's simple structure with a light-weight structural system employing cross walls between which there is space for a small apartment, it is also possible to combine these units to form larger dwellings. The circulation system emerges as a significant new element. On the courtyard side it is carried on slender supports and separated into two spatial layers. In the outer layer a two-storey gallery connects both staircases and also extends to the tract that runs at an angle along Karolinengasse.

Between this gallery and the wall of the building a zone, 2.40 metres deep, is inserted containing the newly-built lift serving all floor levels but, above all, balcony-like "forecourts" to the apartments which one must cross to enter the actual hall of the dwellings. Wide voids extend between these elements. This concept means that most of the apartments offer the residents a small outdoor space. The structural frame provides this possibility for the apartments in the old building lying below.

FAVORITENSTRASSE

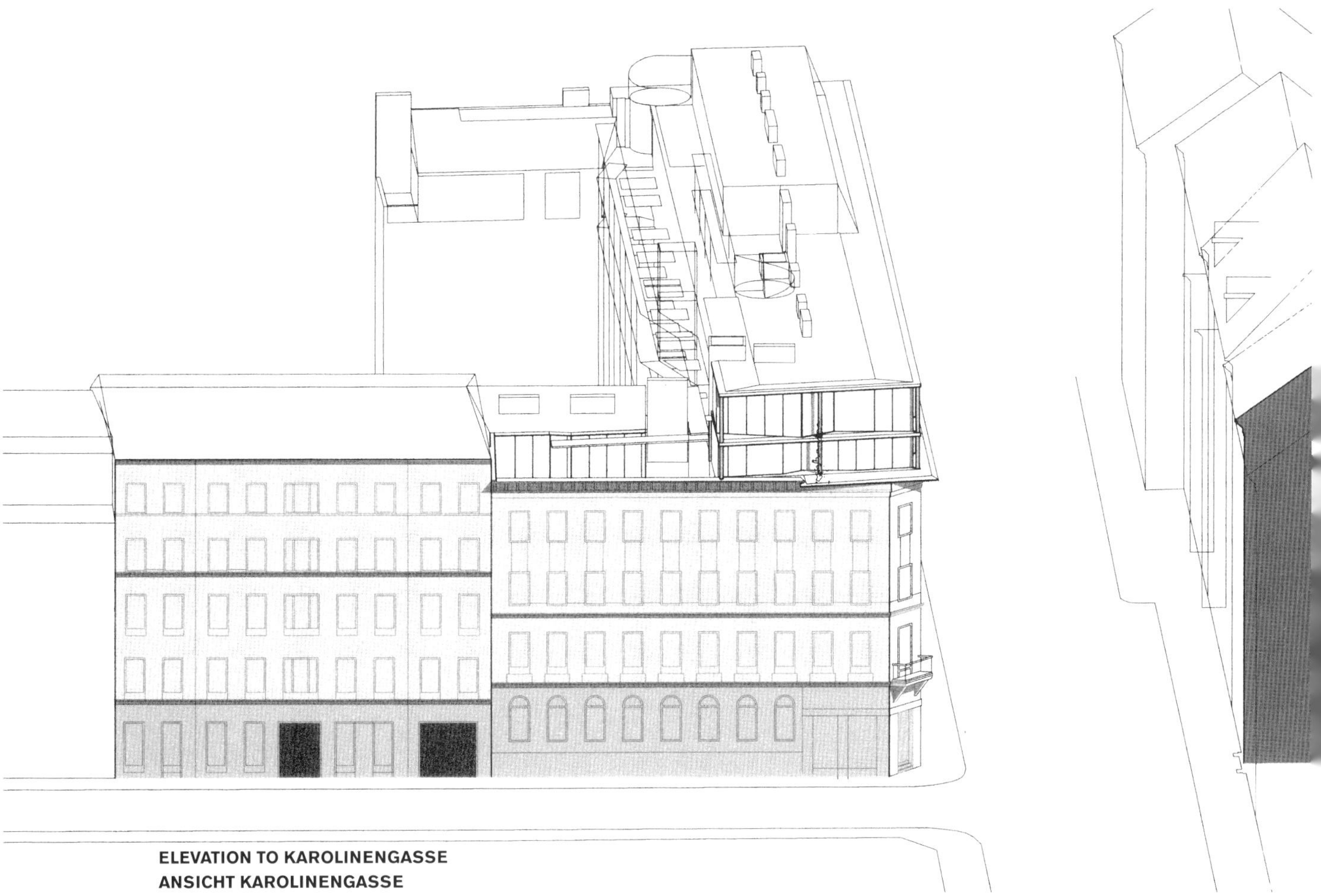

ELEVATION TO KAROLINENGASSE
ANSICHT KAROLINENGASSE

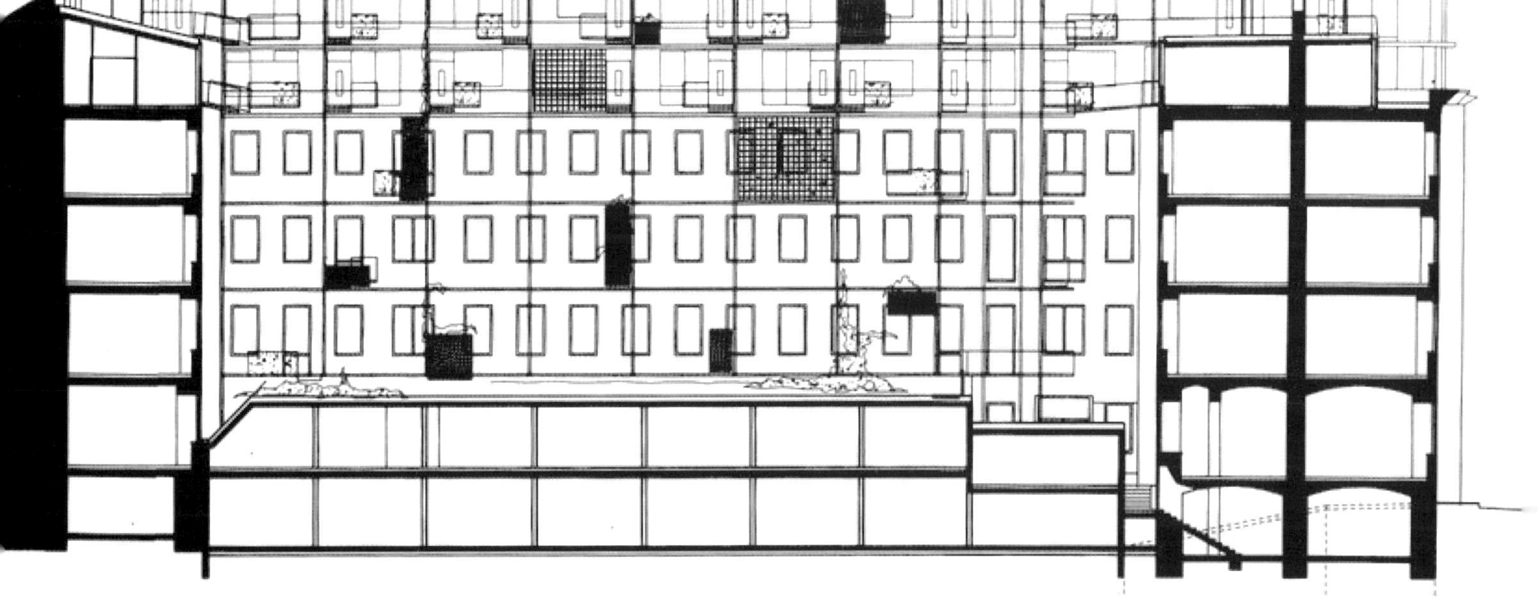

VIEW FROM THE GARDEN
GARTENANSICHT 1:333

Die Erschließung gewinnt dadurch über ihre erste Funktion hinaus weitere Optionen, ob diese nun Küchenkräuter, Sommerfrühstück oder Nachmittagstee heißen. Zuoberst sind eine mit Lift oder Treppe erreichbare, allgemeine Dachterrasse sowie zwei großzügige Penthouse-Wohnungen vorgesehen. Die gestalterische Unabhängigkeit der neuen, in Leichtbauweise zu erstellenden Gebäudeschicht gegenüber dem massiv errichteten Bestand wird vom alten Gesims betont, das von den darüber liegenden, vorstehenden Geschoßdecken aufgenommen wird. Zur Karolinengasse wandelt sich die plane Fensterwand zu einem flach gestaffelten Relief, das als „weiche" Stirnseite den eigenständigen Charakter des aufgesetzten Bauteils vermittelnd ausdrückt. Ein vorgesehener Bewuchs mit Pflanzen ist in die Gesamtwirkung einbezogen, so dass sich über der massiven Fassade eine Doppelreihe schlanker Stützen, umrankt mit grünem Flor, vor den Glaswänden hinzieht. Diese Polarität ist nicht schroff, sondern sanft angelegt. Hofseitig entsteht eine gänzlich neue Ansicht: dem orthogonalen Tragraster sind in aleatorischer Weise beziehungsweise nach Wunsch, Balkonplattformen und Rankgerüste überlagert. Dahinter verlaufen die emotionslosen Reihen der bestehenden Fenster. Die Belebung ist aber nicht bloß optischer Natur, sondern wird vom Außenwohnen der Mieter wesentlich mitbestimmt.

The circulation thus acquires further options in addition to its primary function, whether it be for growing kitchen herbs, taking breakfast in summer or afternoon tea. At the very top a shared roof terrace reached by the lift or a staircase and two large penthouse apartments are planned. The independence, in design terms, of the new building layer constructed in a light-weight system from the massively built existing building is emphasised, above all, by the old cornice which is taken up by the projecting floor slabs above. On Karolinengasse the flush window wall transforms into a shallow, folded relief which, as a "soft" end elevation, conveys the independent character of the new element placed on top of the old building. The planned planting is incorporated in the total effect so that above the massive facade a double row of slender supports, entwined with greenery, extends in front of the glass walls. This polarity is not crudely but gently applied. On the courtyard side an entirely new elevation is created, the orthogonal structural grid is overlaid, in an aleatory fashion or according to the tenants' wishes with balcony platforms and trellises. Behind these extend the emotionless rows of the existing windows. This animation is not merely a visual effect but also, to a considerable degree, results from the residents' outdoor life.

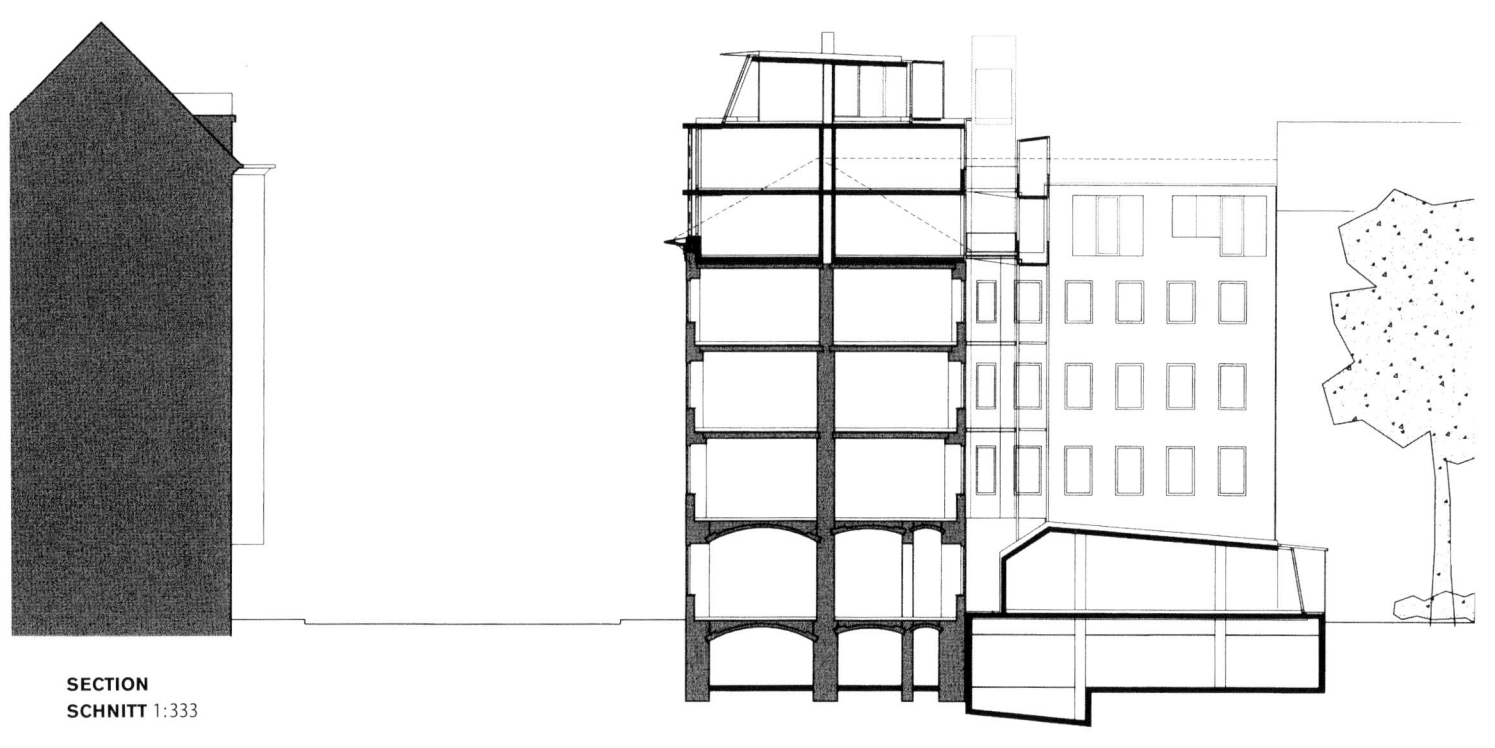

SECTION
SCHNITT 1:333

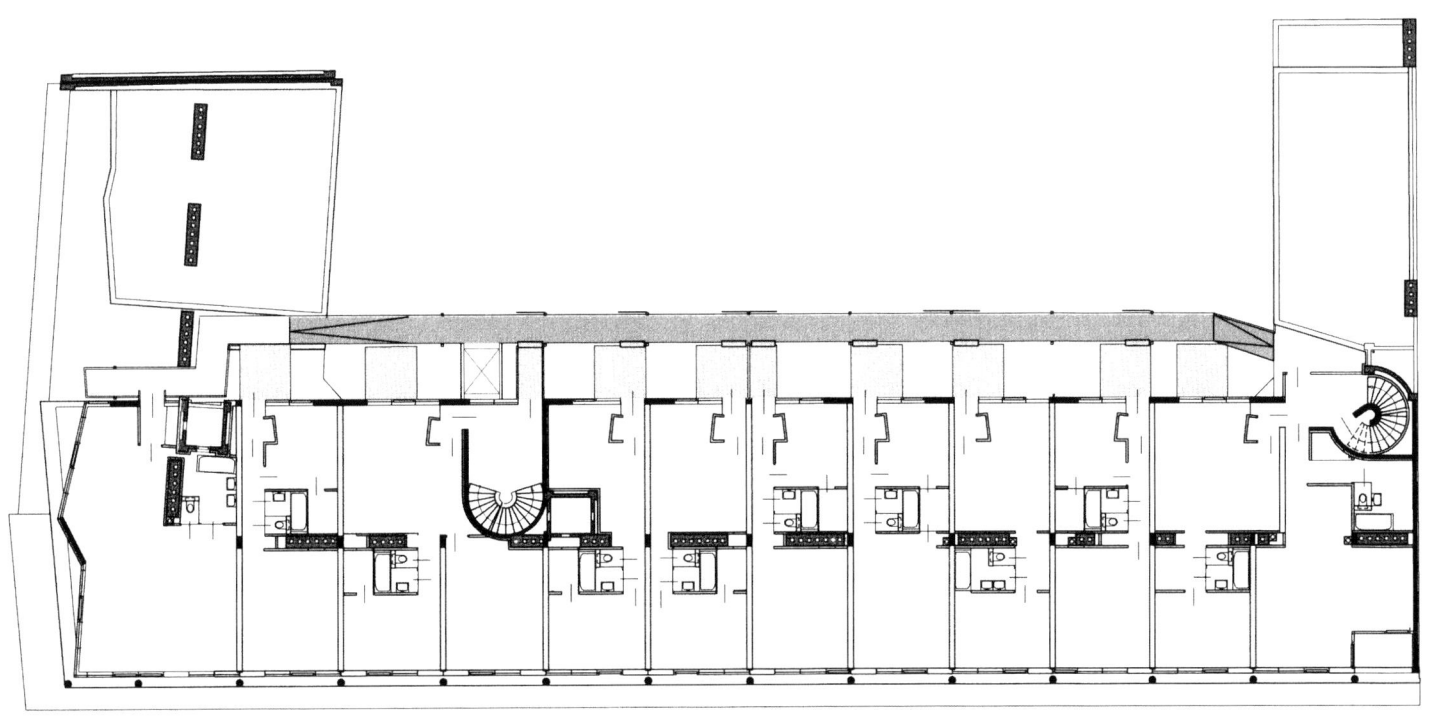

ADDITIVE, REVERSABLE BASIC SYSTEM WITH INSERTED SANITARY AND KITCHEN CELLS
ADDITIVES SCHALTBARES GRUNDSYSTEM MIT EINGESETZTEN SANITÄR- UND KÜCHENZELLEN 1:333

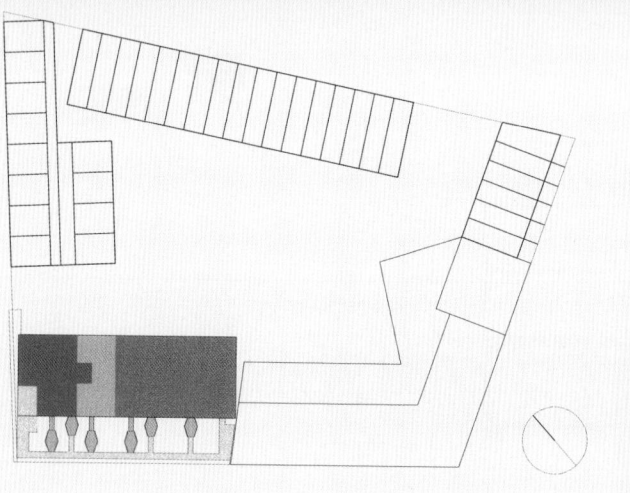

Wohnbau Wiedner Hauptstraße/Schußwallgasse
Wien–Wieden, 1998–

Für einen Baublock zwischen Gürtel und Wiedner Hauptstraße wurde gemeinsam mit Szedenik/Schindler und ARTEC ein städtebauliches Gesamtkonzept entwickelt. Für den Bauteil an der Schußwallgasse hat Rüdiger Lainer seine aktuellen Überlegungen für einen kostengünstigen und zugleich urbanen, lebensoffenen Wohnbau zu einem Konzentrat verdichtet, bei dem die vielgestaltigbildhafte Individualität seiner früheren Wohnbauten einer strukturellen Anlage zur Wahrnehmung individueller Entwicklungschancen gewichen ist. Der Strukturaufbau erfolgt in Raumschichten, die parallel zur Straßenfront verlaufen. Zur Straße nach Westen zieht sich laubenartig die Erschließung auf allen Geschoßen hin. Stiege und Lift am einen Ende sorgen für die Vertikalbeziehungen. Vom Laubengang gelangt man zuerst in kanzelartige Ausweitungen, die jeweils einer Wohnung vorgeordnet sind. Diese von zwei gewölbten Wandschirmen definierten Bereiche dienen unter anderem als Balkone. Zusammen mit dem Laubengang sollen sie intensiv mit Pflanzen bewachsen sein. Das heißt, vor der Fassade des Hauses erhebt sich mit einigem Abstand ein hoher, vertikaler Grünraum, der „hängende Garten", in den zahlreiche „Gondeln" eingenistet sind, die verschiedenen Formen des Außenwohnens dienen. Von diesen Balkonen führen längere Stege durch eine offene Licht- und Luftschicht zum eigentlichen Haus, dem eine weitere Schicht vorgelagert ist, die verandenartige Vorräume enthält, welche außerdem als Puffer oder Diele fungieren. Dahinter liegen die Grundeinheiten von ca. 50 m² Fläche, zwei Zimmer, Küche, Bad, WC und Schrankfläche. Im Sinne einer nachfrageorientierten Flexibilität

Apartment Building Wiedner Hauptstrasse/
Schusswallgasse, Wien–Wieden, 1998–

Together with Szedenik/Schindler and ARTEC an urban outline concept was developed for a block between the Gürtel and Wiedner Hauptstrasse. For the building element along Schusswallgasse Rüdiger Lainer intensified his current considerations on reasonably priced and urban open housing to create a concentrate in which the variegated pictorial quality of his earlier housing projects is replaced by a structural system that takes account of individual possibilities of development. The structural build-up takes the form of a series of spatial layers running parallel to the street-front. Westwards, towards the street, the gallery-like circulation system extends in front of all floors of the building. The staircase and lift at one end provide the vertical connection. On coming from the access gallery one first reaches pulpit-like extensions placed in front of each apartment. These areas, defined by two curved wall screens serve, in part, as balconies. Together with the access deck they are to be densely planted. This means that, in front of the facade of the building a high, vertical green space, the "hanging garden," with numerous inserted "gondolas" will develop that will serve various forms of outdoor life. Longer footbridges lead from these balconies to the building itself passing through an open layer of light and air. A further layer placed in front of the house itself contains veranda-like halls which also serve as a buffer zone. Behind these are the dwelling units with a floor area of around 50 m², made up of two rooms, kitchen, bathroom, WC and storage space. In the interest of market-oriented flexibility one and a half or two of these units

WIEDNER HAUPTSTRASSE

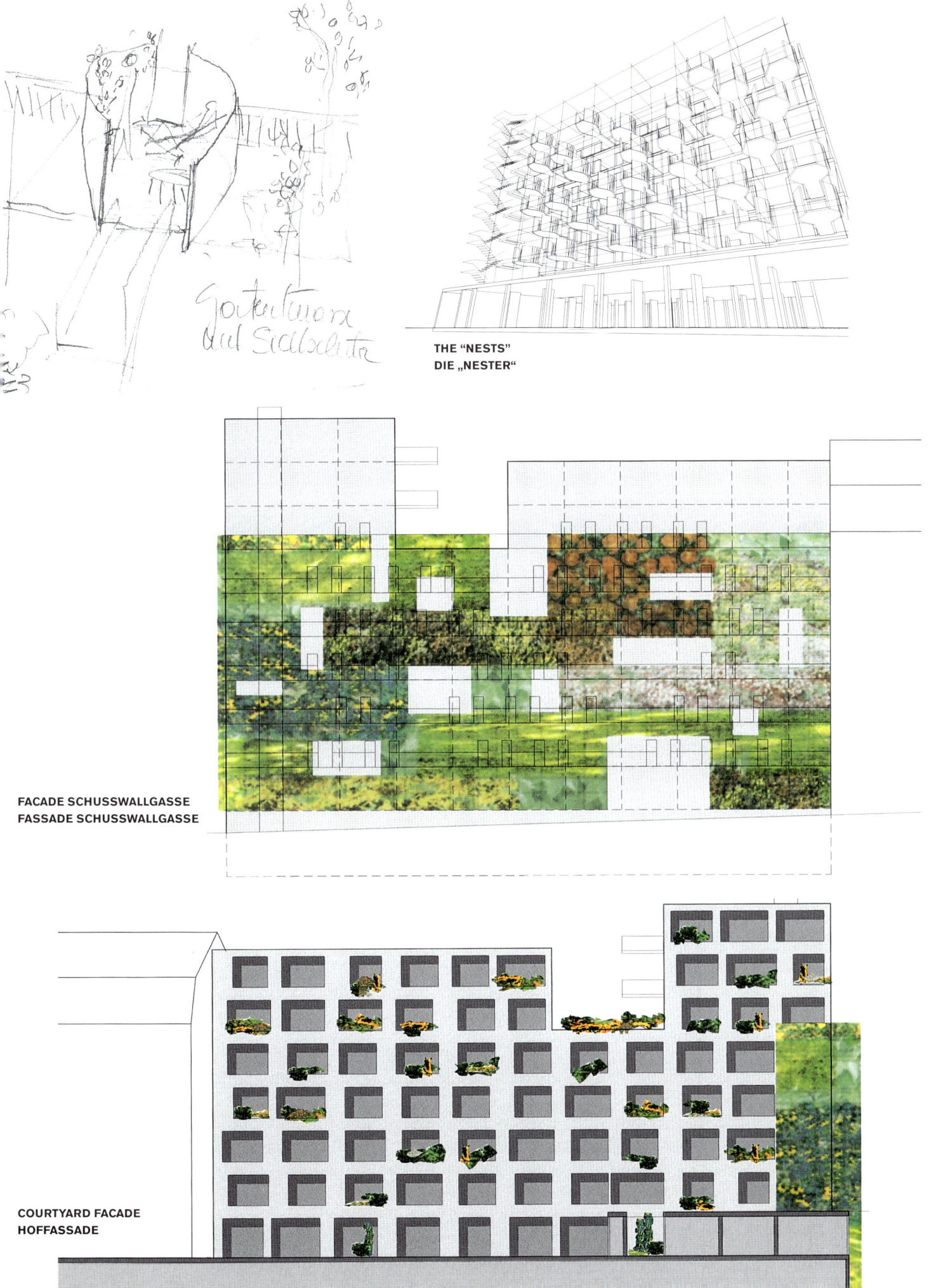

THE "NESTS"
DIE „NESTER"

FACADE SCHUSSWALLGASSE
FASSADE SCHUSSWALLGASSE

COURTYARD FACADE
HOFFASSADE

lassen sich eineinhalb oder zwei derartige Einheiten zu einer größeren Wohnung zusammenschließen. Nur die Lage gewisser Tragelemente und die der Installationsschächte ist fixiert, das Übrige lässt sich in gewissen Grenzen frei festlegen, wobei die Sanitärzellen in einer Zone oder Raumschicht nahe den Schächten liegen sollten.

Nach Osten ist eine weitere Raumschicht mit Bepflanzung vorgelagert, die schallabsorbierend wirkt. Mit der seriell durchkonstruierten Anlage werden niedrige Erstellungskosten angestrebt und mit der außenliegenden Erschließung wird im Baukörper Platz gespart. Der Aufbau in Raumschichten, die je einige potentielle Eigenschaften aufweisen, von denen künftige Bewohner jene wahrnehmen können, die ihnen zusagen, ist als offenes Konzept zu verstehen. Mit dem unspezifischen Angebot bleibt dem Bewohner mehr Freiheit, seinen Bereich selber zu kultivieren. Das Bild dieser Vielfalt entsteht erst im Lauf der Benutzung, wobei veränderte Bewohnerverhältnisse auch später noch zu einem neuen Ausdruck führen können.

Der städtischen Lage wird mit einer bis in den Hof reichenden Geschäftsfläche entsprochen, deren Dach ebenfalls begrünt ist. Das Mezzaningeschoß ist für Bürozwecke vorgesehen. Die Fassade nach Osten wird mit Modulelementen in Grenzen leicht variiert, sodass ein auf den ersten Blick gleichmäßiger Eindruck im Detail differenziert wird und gesamthaft ein changierender Eindruck entsteht.

can be combined to create a larger apartment. It is merely the position of certain structural elements and the service ducts which are fixed, everything else can, within certain limits, be freely planned whereby the sanitary cells should, naturally, be placed in a zone or spatial layer close to the vertical ducts.

To the east a further spatial zone with planting is placed in front of the building and is intended to absorb noise from the street. This development, constructed on the principle of serially repeated elements, aims firstly at achieving low building costs; the externally placed circulation saves space inside the building. The establishment of spatial layers offers a range of potential qualities from which the future residents can select those that most appeal to them and can therefore be understood as an open concept. This non-specific supply allows the residents more freedom to define their areas themselves. The image that reflects this variety will develop in the course of use, whereby changes in the structure of the resident population can later lead to a new expression.

The urban nature of the location is reflected in a retail area extending into the courtyard, its roof is also covered in greenery. The mezzanine level is intended for office use. The east facade will be slightly varied, within limits, by the use of modular elements so that the impression of uniformity conveyed by a first look will be modified and a varying and varied impression will develop.

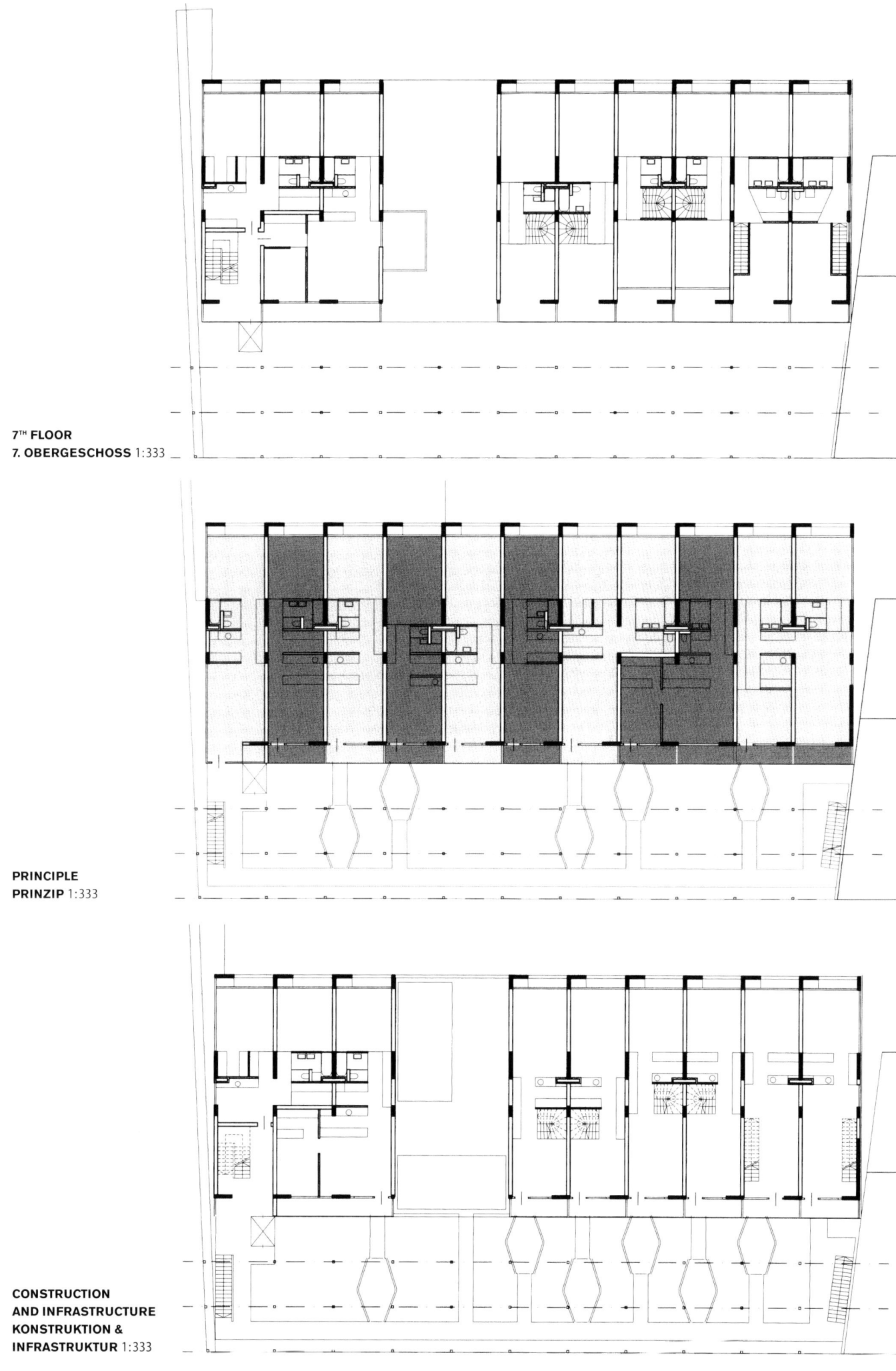

7TH FLOOR
7. OBERGESCHOSS 1:333

PRINCIPLE
PRINZIP 1:333

CONSTRUCTION AND INFRASTRUCTURE
KONSTRUKTION & INFRASTRUKTUR 1:333

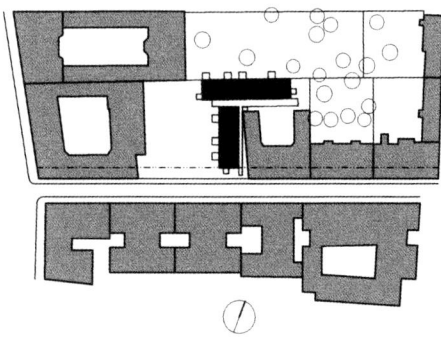 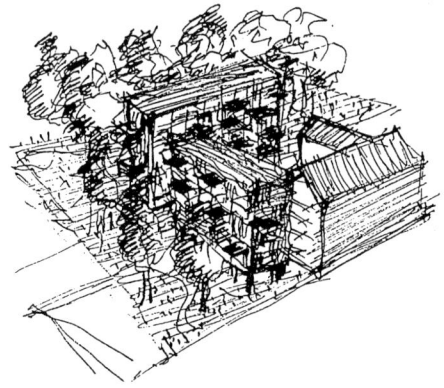

Wohnbau Taubstummengasse 12
Wien–Wieden, 1998–

Die Vorgaben des Bebauungsplanes ergaben für die unregelmäßig mit Schuppen und Werkstätten belegte Baulücke keine städtebaulich überzeugende Lösung. Sie liegt an einer Schnittstelle zwischen mittelgroßer Parzellenstruktur mit mehrheitlich öffentlichen Bauten an der Favoriten- und der Gußhausstraße sowie der kleinteiligeren Zinshausstruktur an der Taubstummengasse aus der Zeit vor Zurückverlegung der vorderen Baufluchtlinie. Eine Befensterung des Bestands ließ ein Schließen der Lücke nicht zu. Zudem verfügt der Binnenbereich des Gevierts, zu dem die Baulücke räumlich vermittelt, über einen schönen alten Baubestand. Die Aufgabe lautete daher, für diese Übergangsstelle die geeignete städtebauliche Ausnahmelösung zu entwickeln. Das als Alternative vorgeschlagene Konzept platziert zwei rechtwinklig zueinander stehende Trakte in enger Beziehung zu dem östlich angrenzenden alten Straßentrakter und den von dessen Seitenflügeln gefassten Hof. Damit bleibt die Lücke offen und der parkartige Binnenbereich des Gevierts tritt an dieser Stelle mit dem Straßenraum wirksam in Beziehung. Der eine geplante Neubautrakt steht, leicht zurückgesetzt und im Erdgeschoß aufgestelzt, rechtwinklig zur Taubstummengasse, und ist recht nahe an die Feuermauer des zur Erneuerung vorgesehenen Biedermeierhauses gerückt. In den schluchtartigen Raum zwischen neu und alt wird die Laubengangerschließung gelegt, die T-förmig auch den hinten querstehenden zweiten Wohntrakt bedient. Im Anschlusspunkt steht der Lift und führt eine Fluchttreppe nach unten. Die aufgelöste Tragstruktur der beiden Neubautrakte erlaubt eine Aufteilung in einen differenzierten Wohnungsmix. An der Hauptwohnseite beider Trakte kragen kistenartig angedockt, mit halbtransparenten Seitenwänden gut abgeschirmte Loggien aus, die dem Außenwohnen dienen. Gesamthaft betrachtet, werden an diesem Entwurf kostengünstiges Bauen, kontextueller Städtebau, die mehrdeutige Rolle der gut dimensionierten Erschließungsflächen und ein qualifiziertes Außenwohnen thematisiert. Dabei steht der erneuerte Bestand zu den beiden Neubautrakten in einem dualen Verhältnis. Diese lösen jenen nicht ab, sondern die drei Elemente bewältigen zusammen den Abschluss der Straßenzelle und die stadträumliche Überleitung in den baumbestandenen Binnenbereich.

Apartment Blocks Taubstummengasse 12
Vienna–Wieden, 1998–

The constraints of the development plan did not permit a solution convincing in urban terms for the vacant site occupied by sheds and workshops, which lies on the interface between a medium-sized plot structure with largely open buildings on Favoritenstrasse and Gusshausstrasse and the more dense tenement block structure on Taubstummengasse that dates from a time before the front building line was set back. The fenestration of the existing buildings did not allow the gap to be closed. In addition at the center of the block to which this vacant site provides a spatial introduction there are a number of fine old trees. Therefore the task was to develop a suitable exceptional urban solution for this transitional urban area. The concept, presented as an alternative, places two buildings at right angles to each other in a close relationship to the old neighbouring street tract to the east and to the courtyard formed by its side wings. Thus the gap remains open and the internal, park-like space of the block engages at this point in a direct relationship with the street space. One of the newly planned wings stands, set back slightly and carried on supports, at right angles to Taubstummengasse close to the party wall of the old Biedermeier building which is to be restored. The gallery access placed in the canyon-like space between new and old is T-shaped in plan and also serves the second transverse residential block behind. The lift stands at the junction and an escape staircase leads downwards. The broken-up structure of the two new wings facilitates a differentiated housing mix. On the main residential side of both wings loggias, attached like boxes and screened by semi-transparent side walls, project providing space for outdoor living. Seen as a whole this project deals thematically with reasonably priced building, contextual urban planning, the ambiguous role of well-proportioned circulation areas and quality outdoor living. The renovated existing building stands in a dualistic relationship to both new buildings. These do not replace the old building but together the three elements terminate the row of the street forming an urban spatial transition to the internal space with the trees.

TAUBSTUMMENGASSE

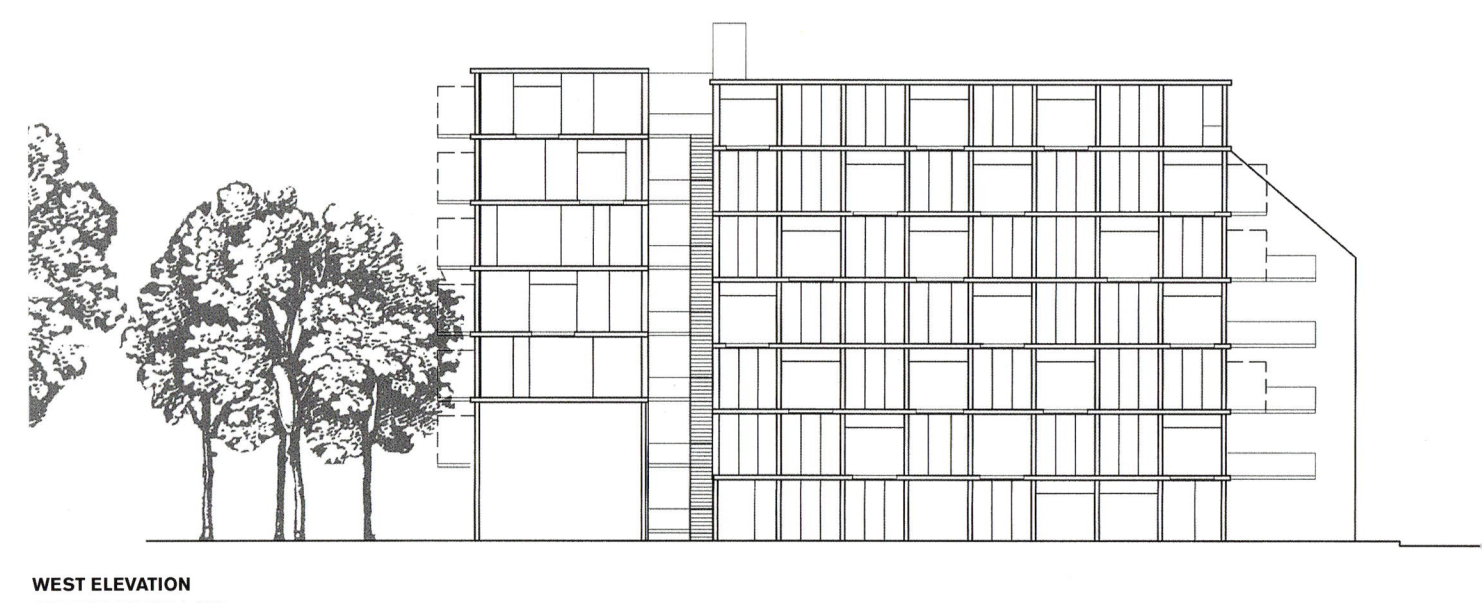

WEST ELEVATION
ANSICHT WEST 1:333

SECTION EAST – WEST
SCHNITT OST – WEST

SECTION NORTH – SOUTH
SCHNITT NORD – SÜD

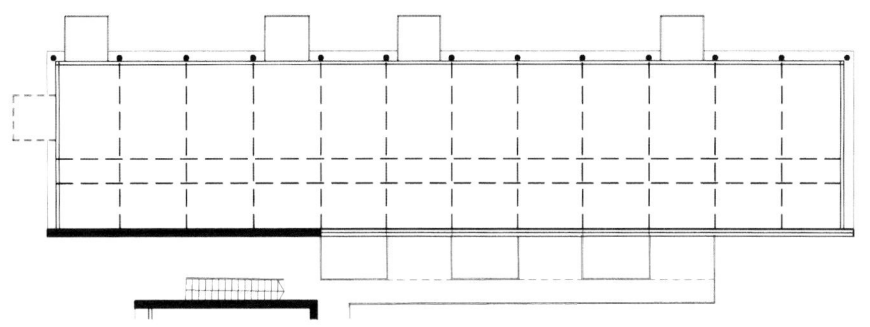

SCHEMATIC PLAN
SCHEMA GRUNDRISS 1:333

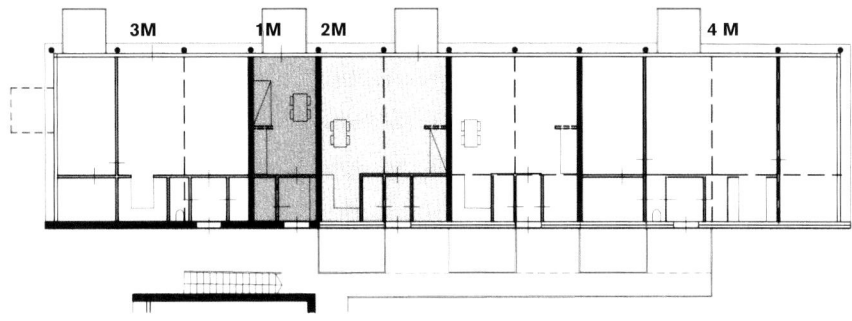

COMBINATIONS OF THE MODULI
KOMBINATORIK DER MODULI

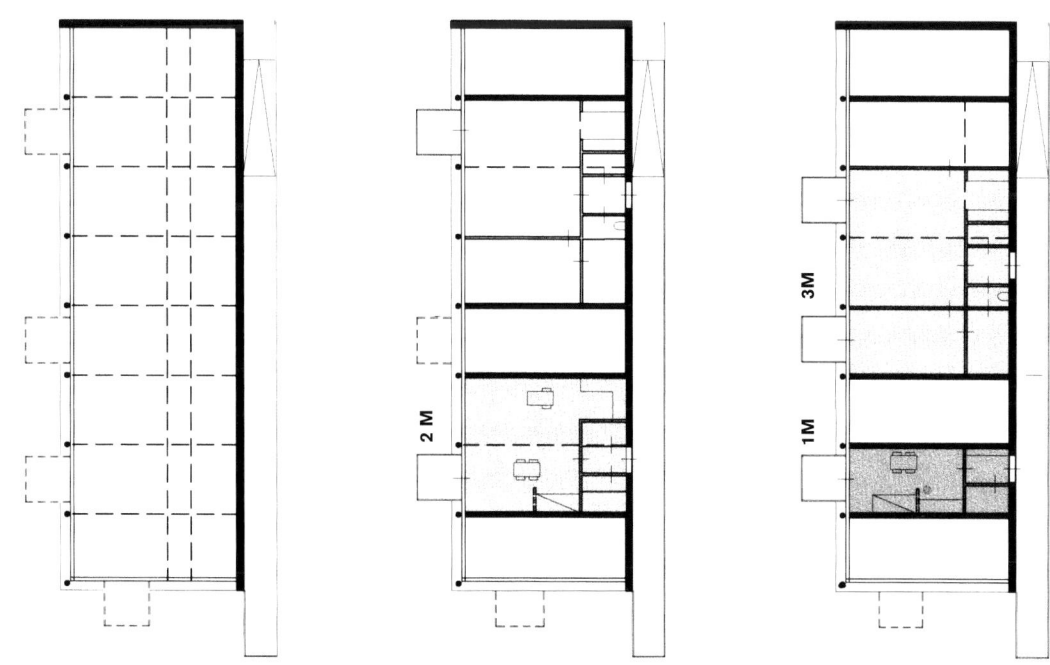

FLEXIBLE PLAN COMBINATIONS
FLEXIBLE GRUNDRISS KOMBINATION

Wohnanlage Altmannsdorfer Anger
Wien–Meidling, 1998

Das Planungsgebiet weist eine heterogene Umgebung mit oft ganzjährig bewohnten Kleingartenhäusern auf. Das Konzept sieht ein Raumgitter als Tragstruktur vor, in dem die modulartigen, geschlossenen Elemente der Wohnungen und verschiedene Typen von Außenwohnräumen, wie Atrien, Loggien, Balkone und Terrassen, in einer locker gepackten, ausgeprägt freiraumbezogenen Mischung eingelagert sind. Das Erschließungssystem kommt mit direkten Eingängen, eigenen Stiegen und angedockten Außenstiegen dem Bedürfnis nach Individualität entgegen, womit der oft hermetische Charakter von Geschoßwohnungen an dieser peripheren Lage im Sinne „gestapelter Einfamilienhäuser" relativiert wird.

Die Verwendung von Holz als Konstruktionsmaterial nützt einerseits dessen geringe Wärmeleitfähigkeit zur kraftschlüssigen Durchdringung von Klimatrennschichten, andererseits die Palette an Werkstoffen und Halbfabrikaten zur weitgehenden Standardisierung und Vorfertigung sowie die ökologisch unbedenkliche Herkunft des Holzes aus nachhaltiger Produktion. Der Gefährdung wegen seiner Brennbarkeit wird im Inneren mit schützenden Fertigteilelementen begegnet. In den Außenbereichen rechnen die Entwerfer mit einer geringeren Brandlast, der auch die kräftig dimensionierten Holzquerschnitte mit ihrem verzögerten Abbrand entgegenstehen. Mehrere Module des Raumgitters ergeben, nach Bedarf und Sinnfälligkeit addiert, kleinere oder größere Wohnungen. Während Erdgeschoß und erstes Obergeschoß mit direkten Bezügen zum Garten ausgerüstet sind, werden für das Außenwohnen im zweiten und dritten Obergeschoß und im Dachgeschoß eher Loggien, Terrassen und Atrien vorgesehen. Vor diese stark plastische, unregelmäßige volumetrische Struktur ist ein Tragraster als Teil des Raumgitters gestellt, der das Ganze rahmt und zusammenfasst. Er lässt sich zudem für Balkone und Stege nützen. Als Zeichen für den lebendig-spielerischen Charakter des Projekts sind die Stützen der vorangestellten Gitterstruktur in Form von Baumstämmen mit Aststümpfen gezeichnet. Damit wird das rationale Gitter mit Elementen bildhafter Natürlichkeit relativiert.

Altmannsdorfer Anger Housing Development
Vienna–Meidling, 1998

The planning area has a heterogeneous structure with allotment garden houses many of which are occupied throughout the year. The concept envisages a spatial mesh as load-bearing structure in which the modular, closed elements of the dwellings and various types of spaces for outdoor living such as atria, loggias, balconies and terraces are inserted in a loosely packed mixture that has a marked orientation to external space. The circulation system responds to the need for individuality with direct entrances, individual staircases and attached external staircases which modify the often hermetic character of multi-storey housing in such a peripheral location by employing the concept of "stacked single-family houses."

The use of wood as a structural material exploits, on the one hand, this material's low thermal transmission to achieve a flexible interpenetration of climatically distinct layers, while, on the other hand, employing a palette of materials and semi-finished products that allows a high degree of standardisation and pre-fabrication while also utilising the ecologically impeccable origins of wood from sustainable production. The inflammabilty of timber is countered in the interior by the use of protective, pre-fabricated elements, externally the designers envisaged a reduced danger of fire which the generously dimensioned timber sections should be able to handle as they burn down more slowly. Several modules of the spatial grid produce, when combined as reason and necessity require, smaller or larger dwellings. Whereas the ground and first floor have a direct relationship to the garden, on the second and third storeys and on the top floor loggias, terraces and atria are envisaged for outdoor life. Part of the spatial mesh, a load-bearing grid placed in front of this strongly sculptural, irregular volumetric structure, frames and holds together the entire building. It can also be used for balconies and footbridges. The supports of this structure, which is placed in front of the actual building, take the form of tree trunks with sawn-off branches and are symbols of the lively, playful nature of the project. The rational, axial nature of the work is thus modified by the use of pictorial, natural elements.

ALTMANNSDORF

SPATIAL MESH
RAUMGITTER

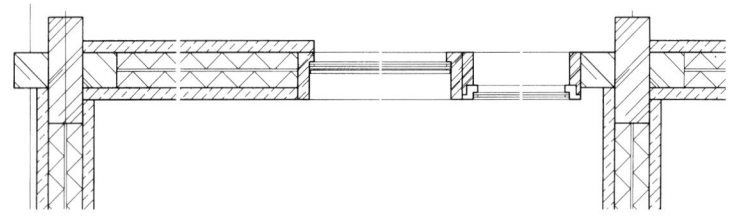

HORIZONTAL SECTION
HORIZONTALSCHNITT 1:30

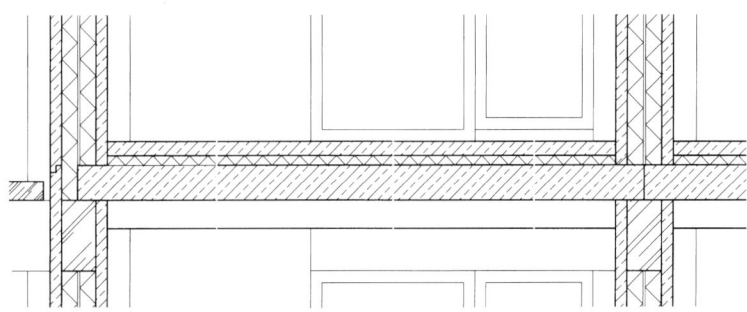

VERTICAL SECTION
VERTIKALSCHNITT 1:30

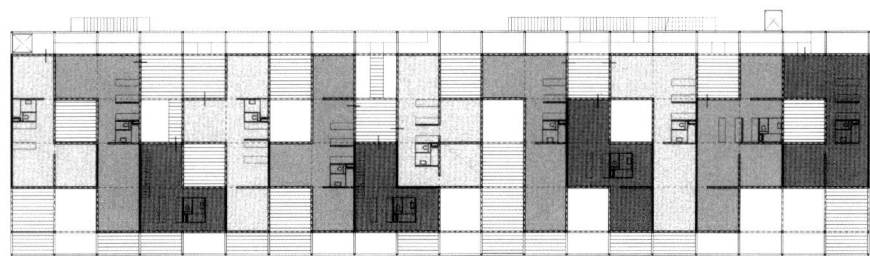

3RD FLOOR
3. OBERGESCHOSS 1:666

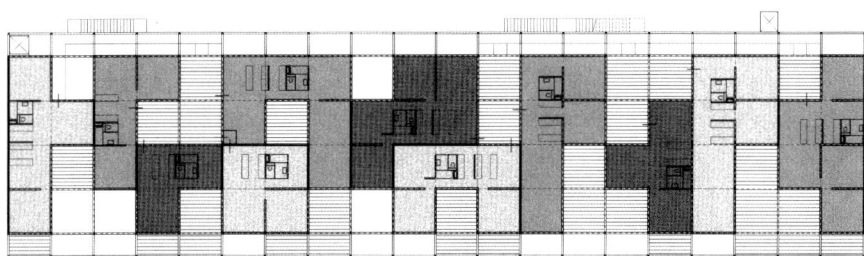

2ND FLOOR
2. OBERGESCHOSS 1:666

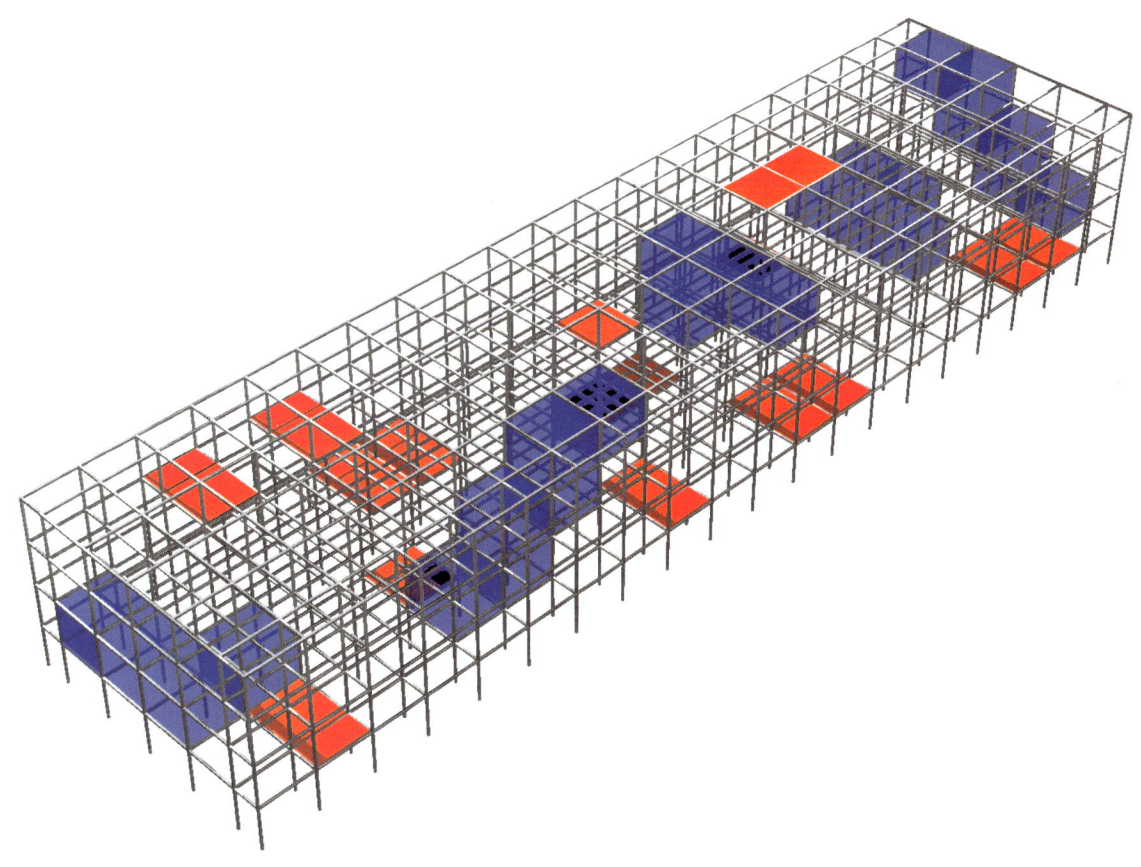

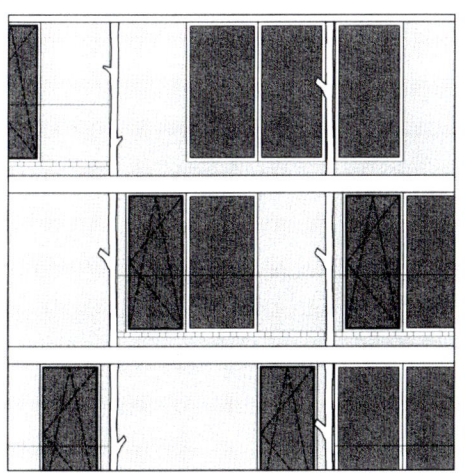

ELEVATION DETAIL
DETAIL ANSICHT

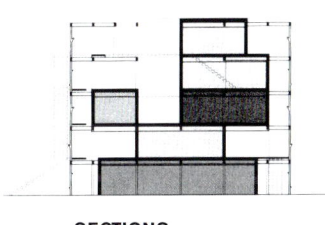

SECTIONS
SCHNITTE 1:666

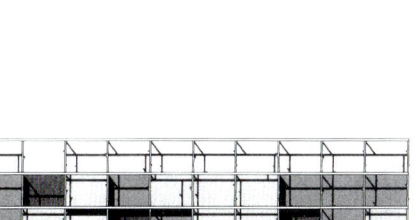

ELEVATION
ANSICHT 1:666

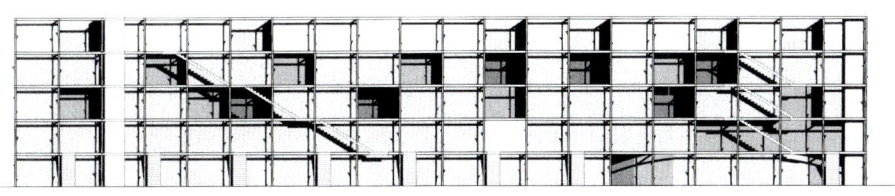

ELEVATION
ANSICHT 1:666

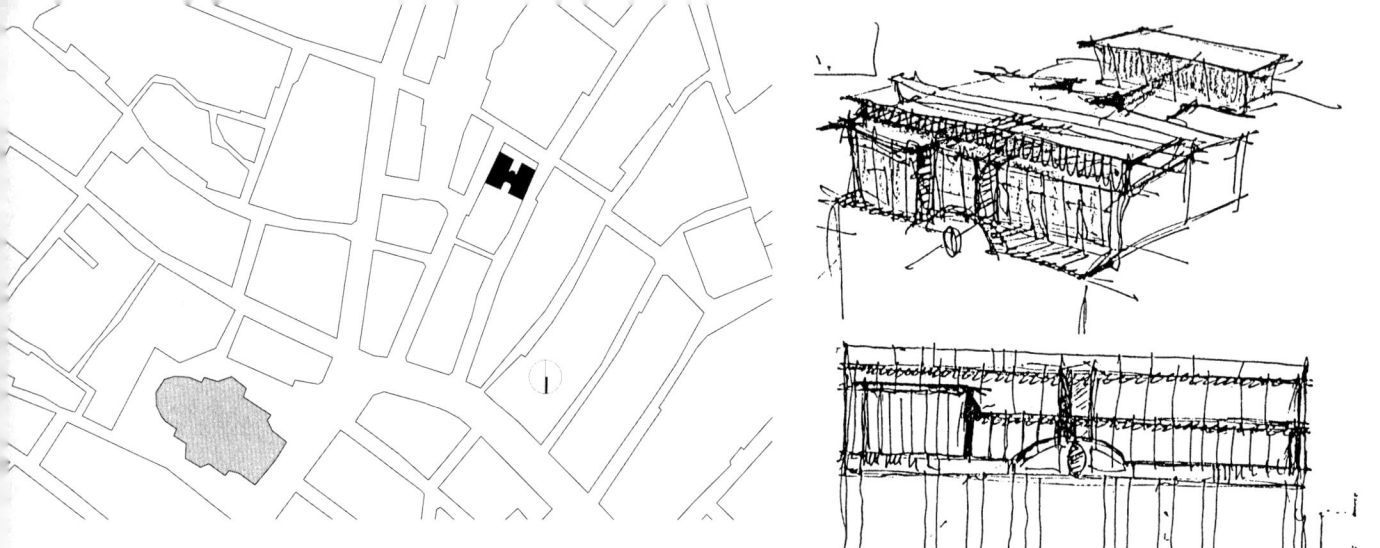

Penthouse Seilergasse 16
Wien–Innere Stadt, 1995

Hinter der Attikamauer des hohen Stadthauses, dessen Fassade von Jugendstil zu Neubarock changiert, erhebt sich über die gesamte Breite der Ansicht ein zweigeschoßiger Glaspavillon, der von der engen Seilergasse aus nicht zu sehen ist. Die quergelagerte Ordnung verleiht ihm Ruhe, und in der Ausdehnung stimmt er mit den blech- oder ziegelgedeckten und meist gaupenbesetzten Dächern der Nachbarschaft überein. Damit passt er strukturell in die Dachlandschaft der Wiener Innenstadt, deren Ansichten in der Regel nur straßenseitig kontrolliert werden, aber hofseitig oft recht wild sind, was in einer Sicht von oben durchaus feststellbar wird. In einer Art Umkehrprinzip sind die öffenbaren Elemente in der zweigeschoßigen Glaswand als hölzerne Türen mit breiten Rahmen und transparenter Füllung ausgeführt. Ihr Rhythmus entspricht dem von Gaupen. Und wenn abends die Beleuchtung die Innenräume preiszugeben scheint, wird das Penthouse zum besonderen Objekt, vergleichbar der Atelierwohnung in dem nicht weit entfernten ehemaligen Café auf dem Herrengassenhochhaus von Theiss und Jaksch.

Durch den nur gedämpft beleuchteten Hausgang erreicht der Besucher von der Straße her das alte Stiegenhaus mit Lift, das zwei Rücken an Rücken stehenden Straßentrakten als Erschließung dient. Auf dem letzten Stiegenabsatz überlagert eine Blechplatte den alten Fliesenbelag um Stufenhöhe und führt zu zwei verzinkten Metalltüren, hinter denen die fünf als Büro oder Wohnung nutzbaren Einheiten zu erreichen sind. Die rechte der beiden Eingangstüren öffnet sich auf einen knappen, von einem schmalen

Penthouse Seilergasse 16
Vienna–Inner City, 1995

Behind the roof parapet of this high city building with a facade which alternates between Jugendstil and neo-baroque a two-storey glass pavilion rises across the entire width of the elevation which is not visible from Seilergasse, the narrow street below. The transverse order lends it calm, its dimensions correspond with the neighbouring metal or tile covered roofs, most with dormer windows. Thus it fits in structurally with the roofscape of the Viennese inner city where, as a rule, only the street front elevations are controlled and the inner courtyard sides are often quite wild, as can be seen in a view from above. In a kind of reversal of normal principles the openable elements in the two-storey glass wall are wooden doors with broad frames and transparent panels. Their rhythm relates to that of the dormer windows. When, in the evening, the lighting seems to reveal the interior the penthouse becomes a special object comparable with the atelier apartment in the former café on top of the high-rise building in Herrengasse by Theiss and Jaksch, which is not far away.

Along a dimly lit entrance corridor the visitor coming from the street reaches the old staircase and lift that serves two street tracts standing back to back. On the top landing a metal sheet was laid the height of a step above the old tiling and leads to two galvanised metal doors behind which the five units, which can be used as apartments or offices, are reached, the right-hand entrance door opens onto a tight vestibule lit by a narrow window from which two further doors lead to independent units. Through the left-hand main entrance you arrive in a bright, airy

SEILERGASSE

Fenster belichteten Vorraum, von dem zwei weitere Türen zu entsprechend unabhängigen Einheiten führen. Durch den linken Hauptzugang gelangt man in eine oben verglaste, helle und luftige Eingangshalle, eher wie ein Geschäftsfoyer wirkend, von dem aus das auf derselben Ebene liegende Büro zugänglich ist und eine plissierte Stahlbetontreppe zum oberen Geschoß führt, die als Skulptur den trapezförmig zugeschnittenen Raum beherrscht. Auf Stegen bewegt man sich zur oberen Büroeinheit sowie nach hinten durch den Luftraum des Foyers zu der im rückwärtigen Teil gelegenen fünften Nutzungseinheit.

Die Kaminmauer in der Mittellinie des Vordertrakts, reduziert auf die erforderlichen Züge, und die ein Geschoß hohe hofseitige Außenmauer legen den hinteren Grundrissbereich fest. Vorne tragen schlanke Stahlstützen die Unterzüge, über denen sich Profilblechdecken hinziehen. Die gesamte, betont leicht ausgeführte Tragkonstruktion ist mit weißer Farbe dematerialisiert und fügt sich so zum Loftcharakter der durchgehend offenen Grundrisse, die nur durch Schrankwände zoniert sind. Küchen und Bäder liegen hinter Glaswänden – für letztere mattiert –, doch lassen sie sich auch wegfalten, sodass ein Bad im großen Raum und mit Ausblick genossen werden kann.

Vor beiden Geschoßen des Dachaufbaus spannen sich die Glaswände, die oben, um die Kante gezogen, ein Stück in die Decke übergehen, das räumliche Gefühl nährend, sich nicht ganz darin und auch nicht ganz draußen zu befinden. Indem die Steher der Metallkonstruktion an die eingangs genannten Holztüren anschließen, steht für den Ausblick immer eine ungeteilte, wandhohe Glasscheibe zur Verfügung; damit wurde die Raumtrennung für

entrance hall lit from above which seems like a foyer in a business premises. From this hall you can reach the office lying on the same level. A reinforced concrete staircase in the form of a folded plate that leads to the upper floor is a sculpture dominating the trapezoid-shaped space. You move towards the upper office unit across footbridges and towards the rear through the void of the foyer to the fifth functional unit lying at the back.

The wall along the center line of the front tract containing the chimney flues was reduced to the necessary number of flues, together with the storey-height external wall to the courtyard it defines the floor plan of the rear section. At the front slender steel columns carry beams above which profiled metal floor slabs extend. The entire emphatically light construction is dematerialised by the use of white paint and thus matches the loft-like character of the completely open floor plans which are zoned only by storage units. Kitchens and bathrooms are behind glass walls – in the case of the bathrooms matt – but these too can be folded away so that you can take a bath in a large space and enjoy the view.

The glass walls stretch in front of both storeys of the roof top addition. At the top, continued around the edge, they extend partly into the ceiling strengthening the feeling of being neither completely inside nor outside. As the uprights of the metal construction are placed beside the wooden doors mentioned earlier there is always an undivided, full-height glass pane through which the view can be enjoyed. Thus, in terms of everyday perception, the separation of space is sublimated. In addition to the broad panorama consisting of a sea of roofs, gables, ridges and

FRONTVIEW
ANSICHT 1:333

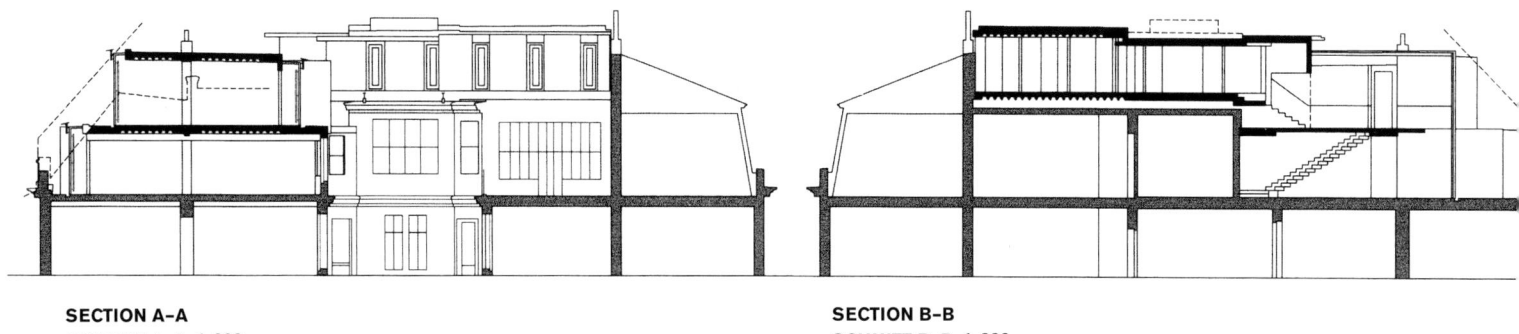

SECTION A-A
SCHNITT A-A 1:333

SECTION B-B
SCHNITT B-B 1:333

das alltägliche Empfinden sublimiert. Neben dem breiten Panorama auf das Meer aus Dächern, Giebeln, Firsten und Lukarnen sind einzelne Ausblicksfenster in die Seitenwände geschnitten, die je nach Standort den Blick auf Teile des Stephansdomes rahmen.

Substratflächen mit Magerflora ziehen sich vor den Glaswänden hin und bedecken auch das oberste Dach, das eine für alle Wohnungen zugängliche Plattform trägt. Damit wird der Eindruck eines seit längerer Zeit bestehenden Kiesklebedaches hervorgerufen und an gewöhnliche, aus dem 19. Jahrhundert überkommene Elemente im Bereich von Dachateliers und -kammern erinnert. Diese bereits klassisch gewordene „zweite Peripherie" finden wir in jeder Großstadt. Obwohl der Wohn- und Arbeitsort im innersten Zentrum liegt, gelang es, mit den gestalterischen Maßnahmen eine Stimmung angenehmer Entrücktheit hervorzurufen: Da ist die Kraft umgenutzter Fabrikshallen, die kreative Muße alter Hofeinbauten und verwilderter, biotopartiger Flachdächer. Und wenn man an lauen Sommerabenden auf der Dachterrasse zu den Mauerseglern hochblickt, die schrill schreiend die Luft durchschneiden, en passant auch einen Turmfalken klickern hört neben dem Gurren der unvermeidlichen Stadttauben, vereinigen sich scheinbar widersprüchliche Elemente von Peripherie und Zentrum zu einer Stimmung zufriedener Gewissheit, dass es sich inmitten der Großstadt gut wohnen und arbeiten lässt.

skylights there are individual viewing windows cut into the side walls which, according to position, frame a view of part of St. Stephen's cathedral.

Areas of substrate with scrub vegetation extend in front of the glass walls and also cover the uppermost roof which carries an additional platform accessible to all apartments. The impression of a gravel clad roof in existence for some time thus conveyed evokes memories of commonplace elements from the 19th century world of attic rooms and ateliers. We find this "second periphery," which has already achieved the status of a classic, in every major city. Although this dwelling and workplace lies in the very center of the city the design measures have succeeded in creating a pleasant trance. The power of refunctioned factory halls, the creative calm of old courtyard buildings and flat roofs which, through the growth of wild vegetation have become biotopes, are present here. On balmy summer evenings when you look up from the roof terrace to the swifts screaming shrilly as they slice through the air or hear, en passant, a kestrel calling or the cooing of the unavoidable city pigeons, apparently contradictory elements of periphery and center combine to create a mood of contented certainty that it is possible to live and work pleasantly in the center of the city.

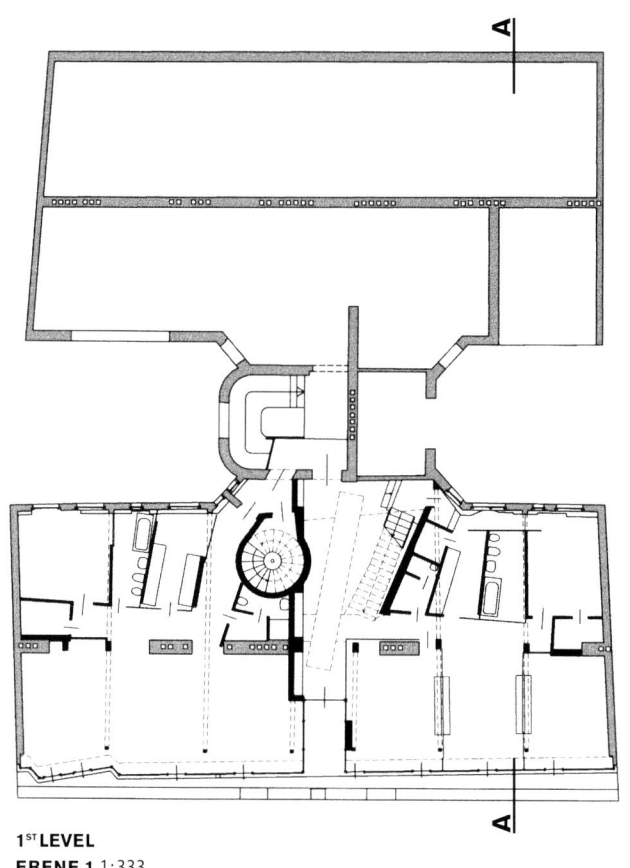

1ST LEVEL
EBENE 1 1:333

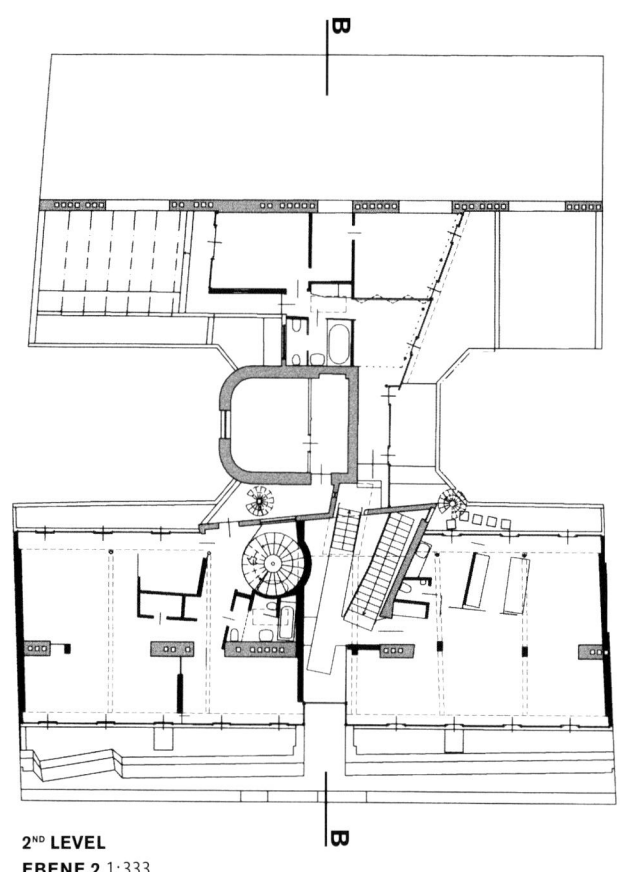

2ND LEVEL
EBENE 2 1:333

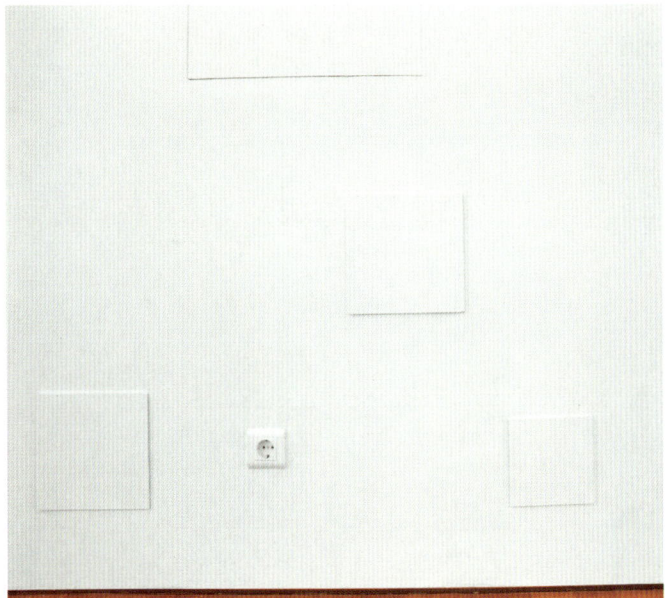

TECHNICAL LID AS A CONCEALED PICTURE
TECHNISCHE DECKEL ALS VERBORGENES BILD

THE BIG BOX "MONDRIAN MEETS RYMAN"
DER GROSSE KASTEN „MONDRIAN MEETS RYMAN"

Umbau Palais Equitable, Mezzanin
Wien–Innere Stadt, 1997

Das Palais Equitable ist ein eindrückliches Bauwerk, das die wichtigste Front am Stock im Eisen-Platz mit Blick zum Stephansdom nachhaltig behauptet. Und der majolika-verflieste Innenhof zeugt von industriell-gründerzeitlicher Prachtentfaltung. Sein Entwerfer, Baurat Andreas Streit, schaffte es 1888, den Sockel vom Erdgeschoß über ein Zwischengeschoß bis zum Mezzanin über drei Ebenen zu ziehen und darüber erst mit dem Piano Nobile anzusetzen. Von der Höhe über den Fußgängerströmen ist aber bereits das Mezzanin ein sehr nobles Geschoß. Die großen quadratischen Fenster weisen es noch dem Geschäftsteil zu, vermitteln aber der Raumstimmung im Inneren internationales Chicago-Flair.

Diese Großzügigkeit nimmt der Umbauentwurf insofern auf, als er die primäre massive Struktur der Außen-, Hof- und vor allem der Mittelmauern abgeklärt wirken lässt und alle weiteren Einbauten oder Trennelemente als tertiär Hinzugefügtes behandelt.

Sie stehen wie Versatzstücke auf dem sämtliche Räume durchfließenden, warmfarbigen Parkett aus Doussieholzriemen mittlerer Länge. Vertikal verglaste Streifen setzen Trennwände von den Mauern ab, Sanitär- und weitere Serviceräume sind containerartig an die befensterte Mauer zum Prachtstiegenhaus gelegt, die Gangfläche zieht sich in variabler Breite U-förmig herum. Die Loslösung von den schweren Mauern wird so weit getrieben, dass die Türen in scheibenartige Wandschirme davor oder dahinter verlegt werden. Die relativ große Mauerstärke wird daher im Bereich der Öffnungen entweder gangseitig oder büroseitig nutzbar. Im Sitzungssaal am

Conversion of the Mezzanine Level of the
Palais Equitable, Vienna–Inner City, 1997

The Palais Equitable is an impressive building, a fact persistently asserted by its main front on Stock im Eisen Platz with a view of St. Stephen's cathedral. The internal courtyard with majolica tiling is an example of industrial Gründerzeit magnificence. The designer, Baurat Andreas Streit, who created the building in 1888, extended the plinth from the ground floor through an intermediate level to the mezzanine, that is through three levels, and only then placed the piano nobile on top. Its height above the streaming masses of pedestrians means that even the mezzanine is a very noble storey. The large quadratic windows indicate that it is still part of the business section of the building but lend the rooms in the interior an international Chicago flair.

The design of the conversion adopts this generosity in that it allows the primary massive structure of the external-, courtyard- and above all the central walls to preserve and reveal its function treating all further insertions or separating elements as tertiary additions. They stand like set pieces on the warm coloured parquet floor that flows through all the rooms which is made of Doussie wood strips of medium length. Vertical strips of glazing separate the partition walls from the load-bearing main walls. Sanitary and other service spaces are placed like containers against the wall that has windows facing onto the ceremonial staircase, the corridor extends as a U of varying width. This concept of separation from the massive walls is carried so far that the doors are placed in panel-like screens in front or behind the

PALAIS EQUITABLE

DOOR AND SLIDING DOOR
SCHIEBETÜR UND DREHTÜR

RECEPTION CLUSTER
EMPFANGSCLUSTER

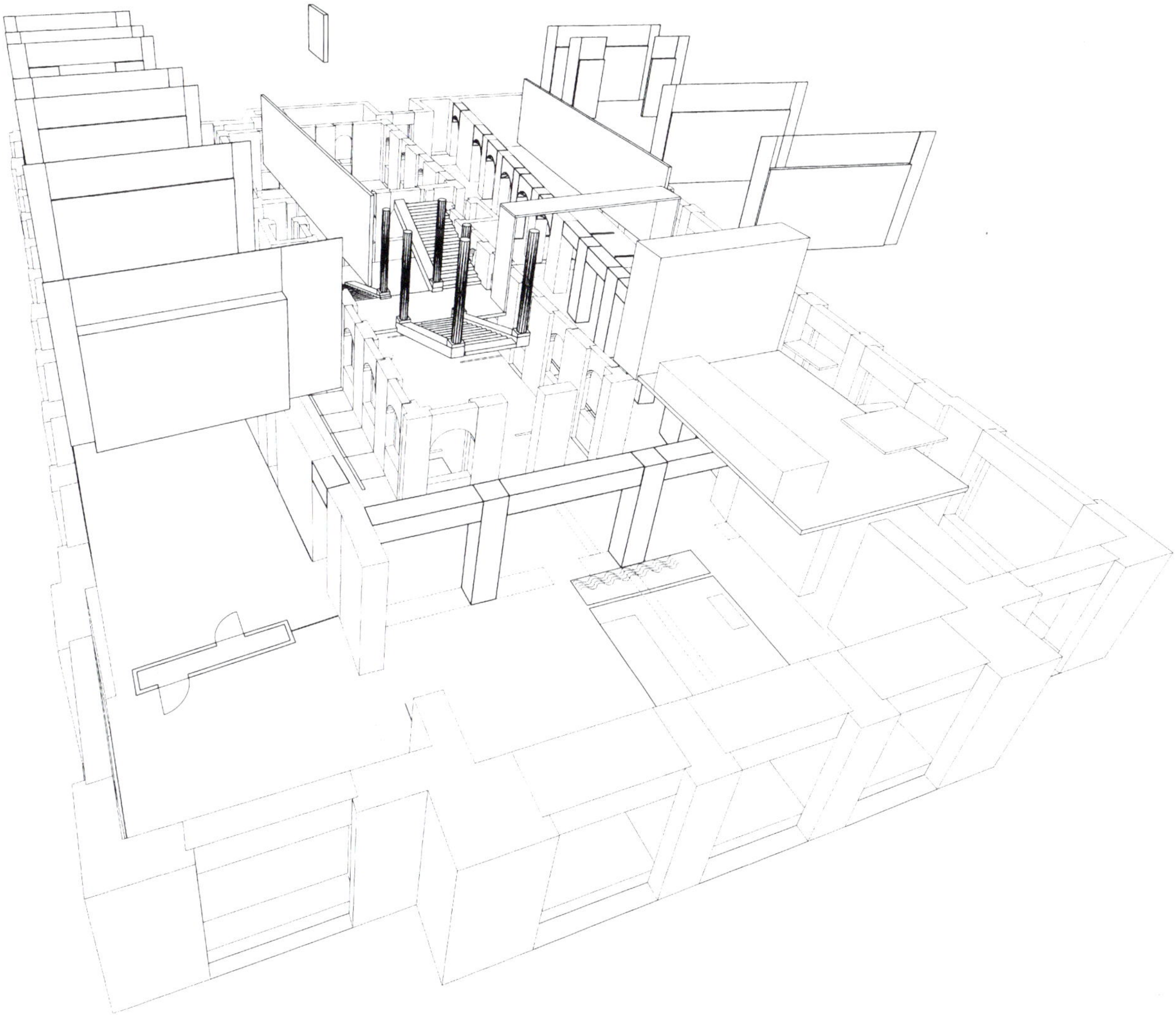

Ende des rechten Seitenflügels kommt dieses Prinzip ausgeklügelt zum Einsatz. Hier lassen sich große Türblätter beiseite drehen, um den davorliegenden Gang ins Geschehen einzubeziehen, etwa um im Rahmen einer umfangreichen Besprechung die Pausenerfrischung effizient und zeitgleich zur Wirkung zu bringen, oder aber, um bei Kunstanlässen, die sich auf eine reichhaltige Sammlung stützen können, genügend Wandelfläche anzubieten.

Als festeingebautes Kunstwerk deckt eine von Michael Kienzer in breiten Pinselschwüngen bemalte, durchleuchtete Glasscheibe dahinter befindliche Serviceräume. Das Bild seinerseits zoniert mit seiner Objektwirkung den Gang, weitet ihn virtuell aus und relativiert die beachtliche Längenausdehnung von über 30 Metern. Als eigenen Beitrag im Übergangsbereich von Architektur zu Kunst hat Rüdiger Lainer die Schrankwand am stirnseitigen Abschluss des Sitzungssaals gestaltet. Die grafisch-zweidimensionale Komposition aus weißen Rechteckflächen und den als dunkle Linien erscheinenden Fugen wandelt sich zu räumlicher Verspieltheit, wenn die Türen leicht geöffnet werden. Selbstverständlich läßt sich dahinter auch einiges an Büchern, Schriften und Akten einlagern, so dass diese Wand tiefgreifend belebt wird.

walls. The depth of the relatively thick walls can therefore be exploited at the openings, either on the corridor or office side. This principle is cleverly used in the conference room at the end of the right-hand wing. Here large door leafs can be opened up in order to incorporate the corridor area, for instance in the context of a larger conference, to allow the refreshments during the coffee break to be organised in a more efficient and contemporary manner or to provide sufficient hanging space for art events which have the support of an extensive collection.

A back-lit glass element painted by Michael Kienzer in broad brush strokes is a built-in art work that screens the service rooms behind it. Its effect as an object zones the corridor, widening it in a virtual sense and modifying its considerable length of over 30 metres. Rüdiger Lainer designed the storage wall at one end of the conference room, it is his personal contribution in the transitional area between architecture and art. The graphic, two-dimensional composition made of white rectangular surfaces and the joints between them, which appear as dark lines, is transformed into a spatial playfulness when the doors are partly opened. Naturally any amount of books, documents and files can be stored inside, giving this wall a life of its own.

E TABLE, COMBINED IN VARIOUS WAYS
SER TISCH IN UNTERSCHIEDLICHEN KOMBINATIONEN

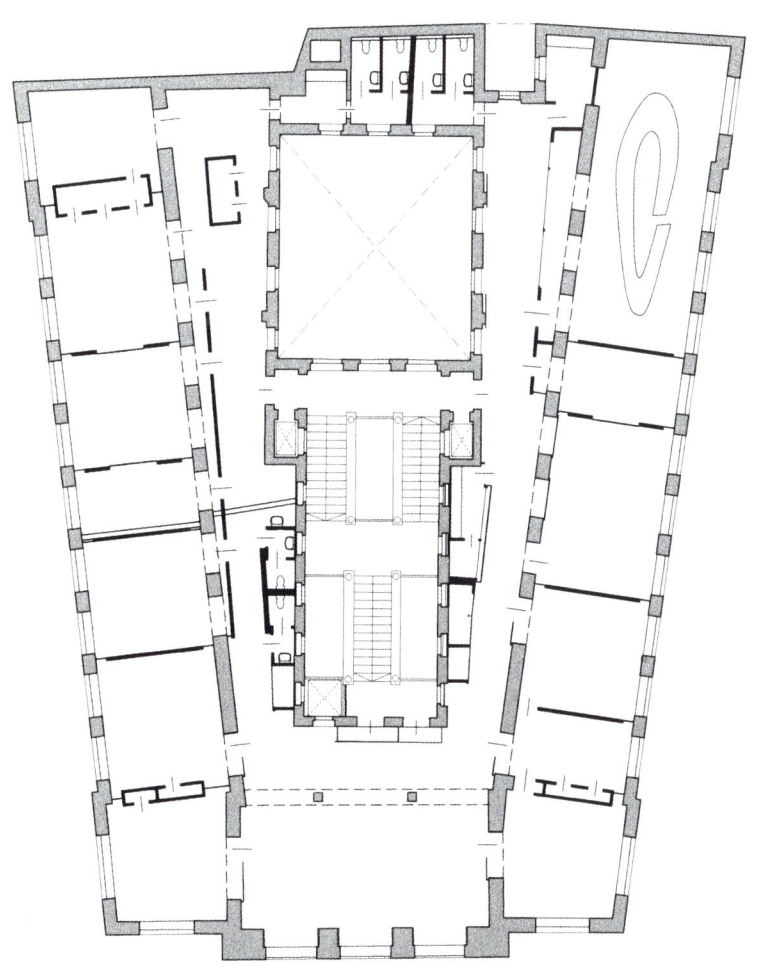

MEZZANINE
MEZZANIN 1:333

THE URBAN SCORE

DIE OFFENE STADT

Die Qualität der offenen Stadt liegt nicht primär in ihrer Erscheinungsform, in ihrer Ordnungsstruktur, sie liegt in den Kategorien, die man noch am ehesten der Peripherie zugesteht. In der Neutralität ihrer Struktur, die gerade das Zusammenhanglose, Vielfältige, Bruchstückhafte, Gegensätzliche des täglichen Gebrauchs ermöglicht. Wie ein Grundriss aus der Mitte des vorigen Jahrhunderts in simpler Nutzungsneutraliät eine Vielzahl von Gebrauchsmöglichkeiten bietet, bietet die traditionelle Stadt dieselbe Vielzahl von Gebrauchsmöglichkeiten im städtischen Anforderungsprofil. Dieser Befund trifft auch auf einen Irrtum des postmodernen Städtebaus und seiner Block- und Platzableger zu, nämlich die Form mit dem Gebrauch verwechselt zu haben. Wichtigste Anforderung an die neue Stadt ist es, sich mit der Aufgabenstellung der Undeterminiertheit auseinanderzusetzen. Die neuen Dinge in leerem wie vollem Volumen müssen vieles gleichzeitig sein können. Und doch, dies ist die große Herausforderung, muss es gelingen, sie mit einer Spezifität auszustatten und diese beiden Aspekte miteinander zu kombinieren. In der Dialektik von Planung und Skepsis, von Ordnung und Unordnung, von Geometrie und Landschaft, verbergen sich die Ansätze zur Aufhellung der gegenwärtigen städtebaulichen Problematik. R.L.

THE OPEN CITY

The quality of the traditional city is not expressed primarly in its outward appearance nor in its structure of order. Genuine quality lies predominantly in the categories one expects on the edges of the town. It is the neutrality of the structure of these areas which makes possible the disconnected, manifold, fragmentary and antagonistic aspects of everyday life. Just like a ground-plan dating from the mid-19th century, by its simple neutrality of utilisation, permits the multiple modes – the traditional town too, offers many options for utilisation. These findings also apply to an error of post-modern urban planning, namely the confusion of form with function. The most important task of the new town is to leave a great deal undetermined. The new things must be able to be this and that at the same time. Nevertheless, and this is the great challenge, there must be success in furnishing them with specific qualities and in combining these two aspects. In the dialectics of planning and scepticism, of order and disarray, of geometry and landscape, there are the rudiments which will permit the clarification of the present problems of urban planning. R.L.

Städtebauliches Leitprojekt
Altes Flugfeld Aspern, Wien, 1992–95

Mitte der siebziger Jahre wurde der Betrieb auf dem Flugfeld Aspern eingestellt und damit ein ca. 250 ha großes Gebiet für längerfristige Entwicklungen verfügbar. 1980 wurden ca. 120 ha dem Automobilkonzern General Motors zur Verfügung gestellt. Nach dem gewonnenen Wettbewerb 1992 wurde ein Leitprojekt als Grundlage für die künftige Entwicklung erarbeitet.
Anders als Erweiterungsprojekte, die an vorhandene Zentren und Stadträume anknüpfen, wird hier auf einem freien offenen Feld – das künftig einen intensiven Zusammenhang und Austausch mit dem weiteren urbanen Raum bildet – ein neuer Stadtteil errichtet. Die Gründung dieses Stadtteils bedurfte einer Reflexion und Neubestimmung dessen, was heute zeitgemäß Urbanität, Stadtkultur, modernes Wohnen und Leben sein kann.

Das Programm
Auf einer Fläche von ca. 130 ha sind vielfältige Nutzungsstrukturen zu planen. Wohnungen mit Folgeeinrichtungen, gemischte Nutzungen, Industrie und Gewerbegebiete sowie Kultur- und Freizeiteinrichtungen. Das Konzept soll flexibel entwickelbar sein und somit auch Veränderungen dieser Nutzungsstrukturen ermöglichen.

Die Stadt
Es ist eine Tatsache, dass die historischen Kerne der alten „Mittelpunktstädte" mit einem Bündel von Merkmalen – Vielgestaltigkeit, Abwechslungsreichtum, Kontrast von Dichte und Offenheit, sozialer und ästhetischer Ereignisse in Wahrnehmung und Benutzung – Qualitäten bieten, denen die herkömmlichen Stadtrandsiedlungen in keiner Weise entsprechen. Die Stadtvision der Leitidee für das Flugfeld Aspern orientiert sich nicht an einem formalen Bild (oder einer Erinnerung), sondern beruht auf der präzisen Neubestimmung von Funktionen, Raumqualitäten und deren Vernetzung. Grundlage ist die Realität des modernen Lebens, wie es sich in der Vielgestaltigkeit und dem beständigen Wandel städtischer Räume zeigt.

Urban Guideline Project
Former Aspern Airfield Vienna, 1992–95

In the mid-seventies operations on the Aspern airfield were closed down leaving a site of approx. 250 hectars available for long-term development. In 1980 approx. 120 hectares were placed at the disposal of General Motors. After winning the competition in 1992 Lainer's office worked on a guideline project as a basis for future development.
In contrast to expansion projects which link up with existing centers and urban spaces in this case a new urban district is to be set up on a free, open field which, in the future, will establish an intensive connection to and exchange with the wider urban space. The founding of this urban district required reflection upon and a new definition of what contemporary urbanity, urban culture, modern dwelling and life can mean today.

The Programme
On an area of around 130 hectares various structures of use are to be developed: apartments with the requisite facilities, mixed uses, industrial and commercial areas as well as cultural and leisure time facilities. The concept should be capable of flexible development and thus allow changes in these structures of use.

The City
It is a fact that the historic cores of the old "central point" cities with a package of characteristics – variety of form, rich diversity, contrast between density and openness, social and aesthetic occurrences relating to both perception and use – offer qualities which the standard estates on the urban periphery cannot match. The urban vision of the guideline for the Aspern airfield is not oriented on a formal image (or a memory) but is based on a precise, new definition of functions, spatial qualities and the way they are interlinked. The foundation is provided by the reality of modern life as illustrated in the varied form and constant change of urban spaces.

ALTES FLUGFELD ASPERI

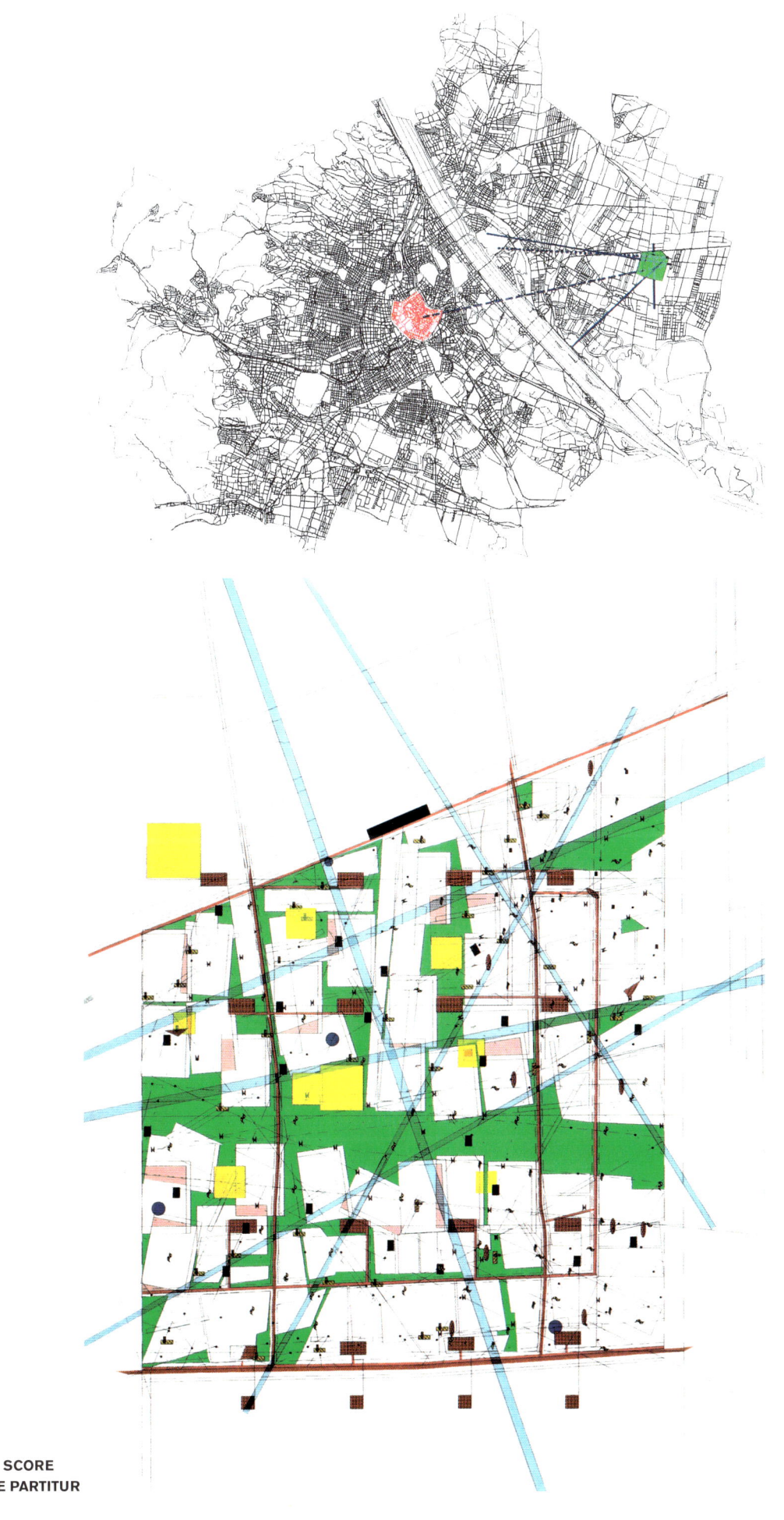

THE URBAN SCORE
DIE URBANE PARTITUR

Das Leitbild

In das Alte Flugfeld, seine Topographie und sein landschaftliches Umfeld schreibt sich ein Stadtteil ein, eine urbane Qualität von Lebensräumen mit besonderer Bezugnahme auf diese Naturbasis, deren landschaftlichen Reiz und die Lebens- und Freizeitqualitäten „offener Räume".

Die Werte der Moderne – Offenheit und Freiheit – und deren Systeme und Formen werden im Projekt einer „Zwischenstadt" weiterentwickelt. Methode und Leitbild als prozesshaft angestrebtes „Resultat" entsprechen der Realität von Stadt und Stadt-Werdung, d.h. der Dimension der Zeit. Dies betrifft die wiederentdeckte Qualität von Wahrnehmung und Bewegung: Hinkommen, Raumfolgen, Sequenzen von Wegen und Orten, in einer Einheit von Bildern und Bewegung, Wahrnehmung und Gebrauch.

So entstehen Ereignisse in einem Netz von Orten, in der Kombination von verschiedenartigen Schauplätzen vielfältiger Aktivitäten und Möglichkeiten. Anstelle formaler Modelle, welche die Gefahr funktions- und ereignisloser „toter" Räume enthalten, ist der Prozess der Stadt-Werdung zu organisieren.

„Ereigniswert" bedeutet das konkrete Vergnügen, das Stadt und Architektur durch überraschende Verbindung unterschiedlicher Nutzungen, Räume und Schnittstellen bieten. Diese Realität des modernen urbanen Alltags wird Charakteristik, Identität und Image der neuen „Zwischenstadt" bilden. Das Projekt Altes Flugfeld beruht auf der Definition von Regeln, die eine „Urbane Partitur" ergeben. Es entspricht einem Verständnis von Stadt und Stadtentwicklung, das auch für die historischen Städte und ihre jeweilige Ausprägung von Urbanität gilt: In der Vielfalt moderner Lebensweisen und ihres Wandels ist neue Urbanität nur in der Gleichzeitigkeit der Entwicklung verschiedener Systeme möglich.

Der Ort

Das Flugfeld zeigt sich als weit aufgespanntes, freies Feld, leicht verwundbar durch architektonische Eingriffe. Die Wege über das Feld verlieren sich am Horizont.

Die Wahrnehmung fokussiert sich ganz nah und ganz fern. Der Blick wechselt sprungweise vom dichten Bild des Bodens zum flüchtigen Rand des Horizonts. Und doch bietet dieser Horizont allein die Reihung der Orientierungspunkte, die die Verankerung der Blicke ermöglichen. Bezugslinien werden vorab visuell gespannt, zu den Bergen, den prägenden Gebäuden. Donauturm, Rinterzelt, Stephansdom tauchen auf, näher die Landmarken der Kirchen der alten Ortskerne sowie einige der größeren Siedlungen, die ihre Bezüge zum Rand noch zu suchen scheinen.

Diese Bezugslinien überlagern sich mit den vorhandenen Flurrichtungen sowie Weg- und Straßenverbindungen, die sich mit den bestehenden Netzen verknüpfen. Freiheit und Offenheit dieses Territoriums bilden den Leerraum, in den sich die neuen Strukturen einschreiben.

Die Lesbarkeit dieses Territoriums wird durch eine Methode der Annäherung erreicht: Das Verknüpfen mit dem Umland. Die Anwendung eines offenen Systems. Das Landen der Felder. Das Überlagern der Steuerungslinien, die sich aus Topos und Kontext formieren. Die horizontale und vertikale Differenzierung.

The Guiding Image

An urban district is inscribed in the Former Airfield, its topography and surrounding landscape, an urban quality of spaces for living with particular reference to this natural basis, to its attractive landscape and to the particular qualities offered by "open spaces" as regards life and leisure.

The values of modernism – openness and freedom – and the associated systems and forms are further developed in the project for a "city in-between." The method and guiding image – a process aiming at a "result" – are appropriate to the reality of the city and its development, i.e. the dimension of time. This applies to the rediscovered qualities of perception and movement: arriving, spatial series, sequences of routes and spaces in a unity of images and movement, perception and use.

In this way incidents develop within a network of places, in the combination of venues of different kinds, varied activities and possibilities. In place of formal models, which harbour the danger of "dead" spaces without functions or events, the aim is to organise the process of the development of a city. The "value of an event" means the concrete pleasure which the city and architecture can offer through surprising connections of different uses, spaces and interfaces. This reality of modern everyday life will form the character, identity and image of the new "city in-between." The Former Airfield project is based on the definition of rules that produce an "urban score." It conforms with an understanding of the city and urban development which is also applicable to historic cities and their particular form of urbanity: in the variety of modern ways of living and change a new urbanism is possible only if different systems can develop simultaneously.

The Place

The airfield is an extensive, free field easily susceptible to damage by architectural interventions. The paths across the field disappear at the horizon.

The perception focuses on what is very close or very far away. The gaze springs from the dense image of the ground to the hazy line of the horizon. And yet it is this horizon alone which offers an ordering of the orientation points that allows one to anchor ones gaze. Lines of reference are stretched visually: to the mountains, to the dominant buildings. The Donauturm, Rinterzelt, St. Stephen's cathedral emerge, closer the landmarks provided by the churches in the old village centers along with several of the larger housing estates, which appear to be still looking for their connection to the edge.

These lines of reference are overlaid with the existing country paths and pedestrian and road connections which link up with the existing networks. The freedom and openness of this territory offers an empty space in which new structures are inscribed.

The legibility of this territory is arrived at by a method of approximation: linking to the surroundings, the use of an open system, anchoring the fields, overlaying the controlling lines that are derived from the topos and the context, the horizontal and vertical differentiation.

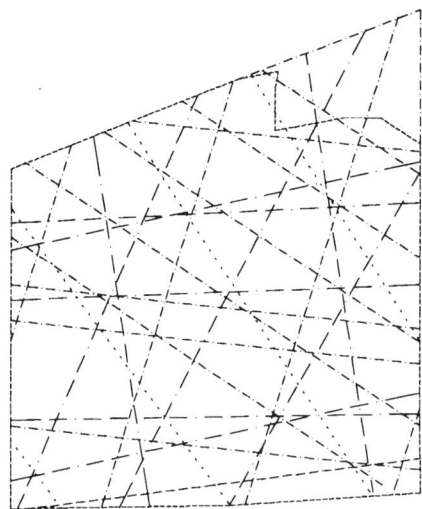

STRUCTURE GRID
For a concrete, varied, complex urban structure, rich in spatial and aesthetic qualities
STRUKTURRASTER
Für eine konkrete, vielgestaltige, komplexe städtische Struktur, reich an räumlichen und ästhetischen Qualitäten

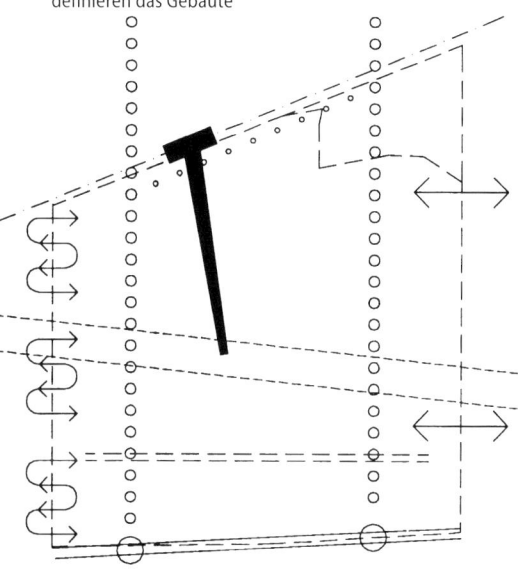

THE CONNECTION TO THE LOCATION / THE CONTEXT
Sight-lines
Lines of reference as controlling lines and regulating levels define the built substance
DIE ORTSBINDUNG / DER KONTEXT
Sichtlinien
Bezugslinien als Steuerungslinien und Regelungsebenen definieren das Gebaute

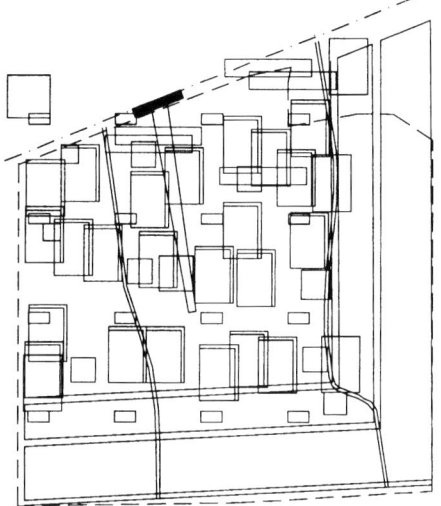

THE FIELDS
The measuring unit of the combinatorics as a variable and changeable basic unit
DIE FELDER
Maßeinheit der Kombinatorik als variable und mutierbare Grundeinheit

INNER STRUCTURE LINES
Edge references
INNERE STRUKTURLINIEN
Bezug der Ränder

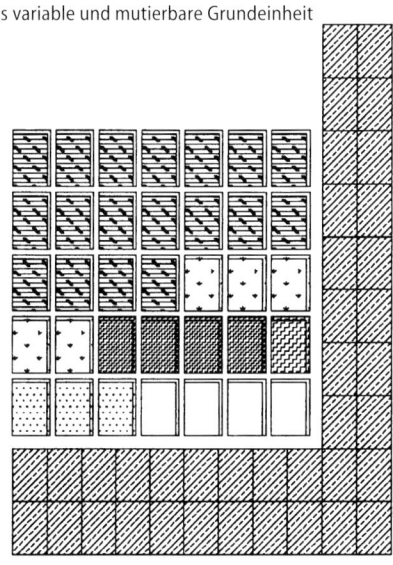

THE PROGRAMME
DAS PROGRAMM

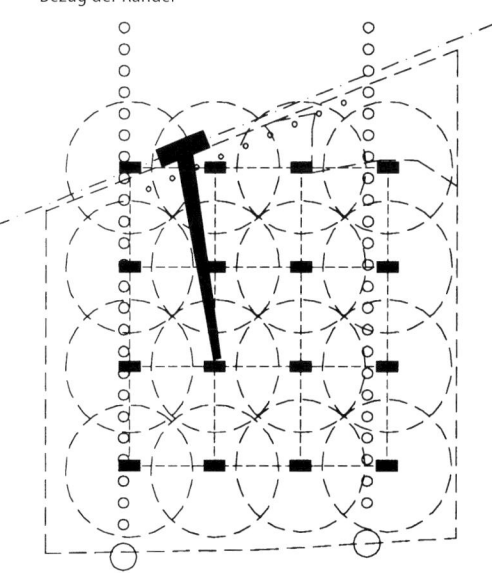

ARRIVING AND PARKING
Structure grid of the multi-storey car parks
ANKOMMEN UND ABSTELLEN
Strukturraster der Hochgaragen

Das Projektkonzept

Die Stadt ist bestimmt durch den gesellschaftlichen Gebrauch. Die Form ist Erläuterung.

Jede Stadtplanung ist charakteristisch für das im Moment dominierende Städtebaumodell. Der Wechsel dieser Modelle wird zu einer bewusstlosen Pendelbewegung, wobei eine Architekturdoktrin einige Jahre später von ihrem Gegenteil abgelöst wird (von der Gartenstadt über die Zeilen zu den Blöcken und wieder zurück). Der Effekt dieser Ja-Nein-Ja-Sequenzen ist anti-historisch, der Diskurs wird ersetzt durch eine nicht weiterentwickelbare Kette beziehungsloser Sentenzen. Die Regeln der klassischen Komposition entsprechen nicht mehr der gesellschaftlichen Realität, die Formen haben ihre Bedeutungskapazität verloren.

Forderungen, die die Stadt von heute an uns stellt, sind dagegen:
· das Verständnis der vielfältigen und heterogenen Anforderungen – dies geht weit über die Registrierung von Fakten hinaus.
· die Akzeptanz des Unvorhergesehenen, Unvorhersehbaren, Unwägbaren als wesentlichem Teil des urbanen Prozesses.

Es wird daher eine Methode zur Steuerung und Definition eines „offenen Systems" entwickelt.

Die urbane Partitur

Sie ermöglicht und fördert die Aneignungs- und Selbstentwicklungsprozesse. Definiert werden die „Regeln der Unregelmäßigkeit". Die verwendete Kombinatorik ermöglicht die Gleichzeitigkeit verschiedener Stadtentwicklungssysteme.

Bei diesem städtebaulichen Ansatz wird die Zukunft als eine gestaltbare Realität wahrgenommen. Die städtebaulichen Entscheidungen ergeben sich aus verschiedenen Interessenslagen von politischen Entscheidungen, Planern, Investoren und Bewohnern. Sie werden den Optimismus der Planer verifizieren oder falsifizieren.

Die Regeln

Um die notwendige, vielgestaltige, komplexe städtische Struktur zu sichern, die reich an räumlichen, sozialen und ästhetischen Qualitäten sein soll, wird ein Instrumentarium an Elementen erarbeitet, nach denen das Planungsgebiet entwickelt wird.
1. Die Ortsbindung, der Kontext. Bezugslinien und Sichtlinien zu bestehenden Stadtstrukturen und eine Regelung zwischen den Feldern.
2. Innere Strukturlinien. Das Einbinden und Kontrollieren der faktisch gegebenen Struktur des Ortes.
3. Ankommen und Abstellen. Die verkehrstechnische Logistik für die urbane Partitur mit parasitären Nutzungen für Verkehrsbauwerke.
4. Strukturraster. Eine Struktur als Bühne des sozialen Gebrauches: Regeln, welche als Steuerungsprozesse des architektonischen Systems einerseits den Mangel an Bedeutung üblicher städtebaulicher Modelle aufheben und andererseits unverständliche, sinnlose Entropie zu vermeiden suchen.
5. Die Felder. Eine Grundeinheit für die Bebauung als Maßeinheit und als variable und mutierbare Grundeinheit.

The Concept of the Project

The city is determined by social use. Its form is self-explanatory.

Each type of city planning is characteristic of the urban design model dominant at a particular time. The change in these models becomes an unconscious movement back and forth in the course of which one architectural doctrine is replaced, a few years later, by its opposite (from the garden city to the row to the block and back again). The effect of this yes-no-yes sequence is anti-historical, the discourse is replaced by a chain of unconnected sentences incapable of further development. The rules of classical composition are no longer appropriate to social reality, the forms have lost their capacity for meaning. The demands which the city today makes of us are on the other hand:
· an understanding of the varied and heterogeneous requirements that goes far beyond merely registering facts.
· the acceptance of the unexpected, unpredictable, unimaginable as a significant part of the urban process.

Therefore a method of steering and defining an "open system" must be developed.

The Urban Score

It allows and encourages the processes of assimilation and self-development. The "rules of irregularity" are defined. The combinatorics used allows the co-existence of different urban development systems.

In this urban approach the future is seen as a reality that can be shaped. Urban decisions result from the differently positioned interests of political decisions, planners, investors and residents. They will confirm or negate the optimism of the planners.

The Rules

To ensure the requisite varied, complex urban structure which should be rich in spatial, social and aesthetic qualities an instrumentarium of elements is worked out in accordance with which the planning area will be developed.
1. The linking to the place, the context: lines of reference and sight lines to existing urban structures and regulation between the fields.
2. Inner structural lines. The incorporation and control of the existing structure of the place.
3. Arriving and parking. The logistics of a traffic system for the urban score with parasitic uses for traffic structures.
4. Structural grid. A structure as a stage for social use: rules which, as steering processes of the architectural system, on the one hand neutralise the lack of meaning of standard urban models while, on the other, attempting to avoid an incomprehensible and meaningless entropy.
5. The fields. A basic unit for the development that is a unit of measurement and a variable and changeable standard unit.
6. The combinatorics of the fields, concentration. Distribution of the fields and infrastructure facilities according to the directional rules.

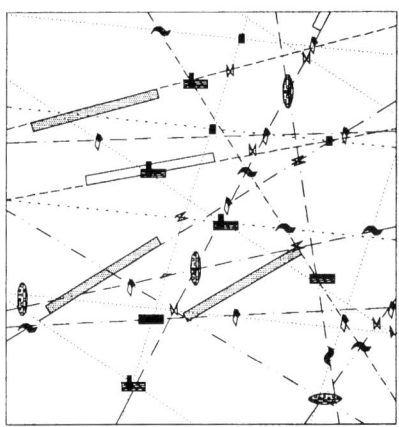

THE POINTS OF DEFINITION
determine the small-scale uses and define the surrounding empty space
DIE DEFINITIONSPUNKTE
bestimmen die kleinräumigen Nutzungen und definieren den umgebenden Leerraum

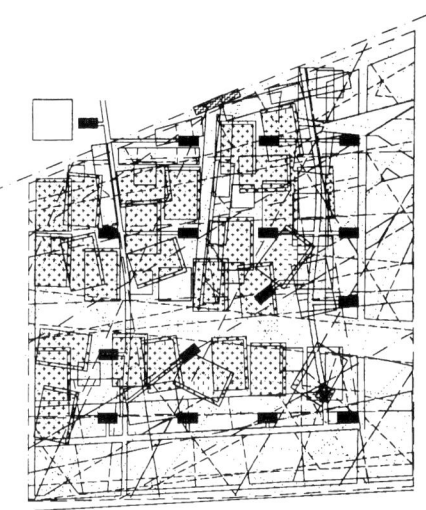

THE COMBINATIONS OF FIELDS/BUNDLES
Distribution of the fields and infrastructure facilities in accordance with the regulating rules
KOMBINATORIK DER FELDER/BÜNDEL
Verteilung der Felder und Infrastruktureinrichtungen entsprechend den Steuerungsregeln

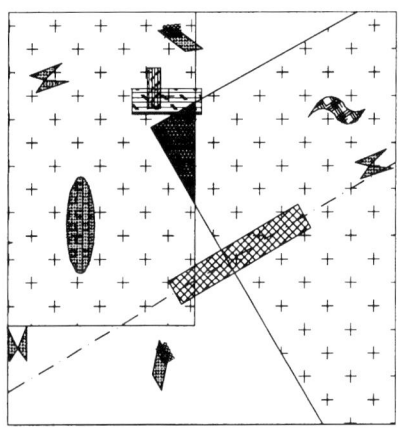

IMPRINT – "DEFINED POINTS"
Function spaces in the fine-mesh network
AUSPRÄGUNG – „DEFINIERTE STELLEN"
Funktionsräume im Feinnetz

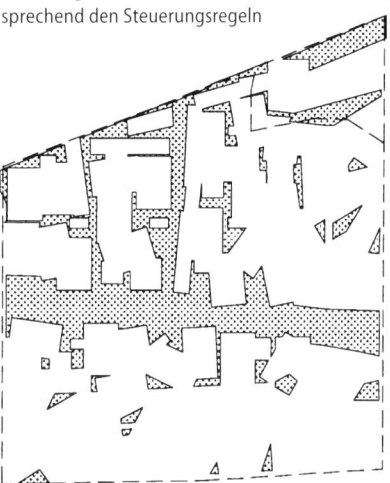

THE SPACES IN-BETWEEN
Activity space
Landscape "corridors" with differnt intensities of definition
DIE ZWISCHENRÄUME
Aktivitätsraum
Landschafts „korridore" verschiedener Definitionsstärke

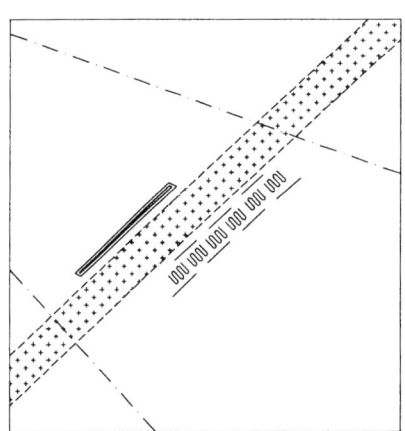

IMPRINT 1
Sight corridors and definition of the edges (hard, soft, osmotic etc.)
AUSPRÄGUNG 1
Sichtkorridore und Festlegung der Randbereiche (hart, weich, osmotisch etc.)

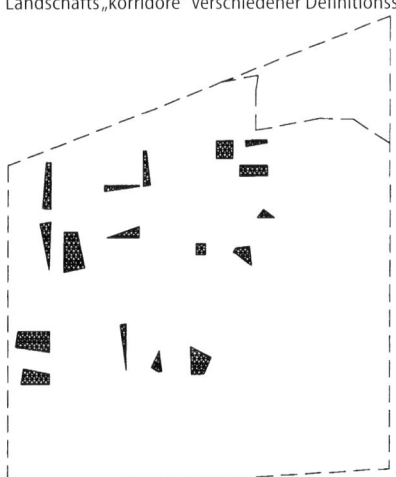

OVERLAPPING/"OPEN SPACE"
Open system areas for functions yet to be appropriated
ÜBERLAPPUNG/„OFFENER RAUM"
Offene Systembereiche für anzueignende Funktionen

6. Kombinatorik der Felder, Bündelung. Verteilung der Felder – Infrastruktureinrichtungen entsprechend den Steuerungsregeln.
7. Die Zwischenräume. Nichtbebaute Flächen mit Widmung für differenzierte Grünbereiche.
8. Aneignungsflächen. Der potentielle offene Nutzungsraum bezogen auf das Gesamtgebiet.
9. Definitionspunkte. Die Einschränkung der Felder bestimmt die Erweiterung der Möglichkeiten.

Auf diesen Elementen basiert das Regelwerk, das Grundlage für die Bebauung der Felder und Nutzung der Zwischenräume ist. Für jedes dieser Felder und die zugehörigen Zwischenbereiche wurden zusätzlich zum Bebauungsplan die spezifischen Regeln in einem „Handbuch" festgelegt. Diese Regeln bieten Entwicklungs- und Interpretationsmöglichkeiten. Die Festlegungen betreffen daher primär die Raum- und Gebrauchsqualität der Freiräume durch die angelagerte, gebaute Struktur. R.L.

7. The spaces in-between. Areas not built upon zoned as differentiated green areas.
8. Areas of appropriation. The potential open functional space applied to the entire district.
9. Points of definition. The restriction of the fields determines the expansion of the possibilities.

The standard work is based on these elements, it forms the foundation for the development of the fields and the use of the spaces in-between. For each of these fields and the associated intermediate areas specific rules, in addition to the development plan, were laid down in a "handbook." These rules allow flexibility of development and interpretation. The definitions thus affect primarily the spatial qualities and possibilities of use of the open spaces resulting from the addition of the built structure. R.L.

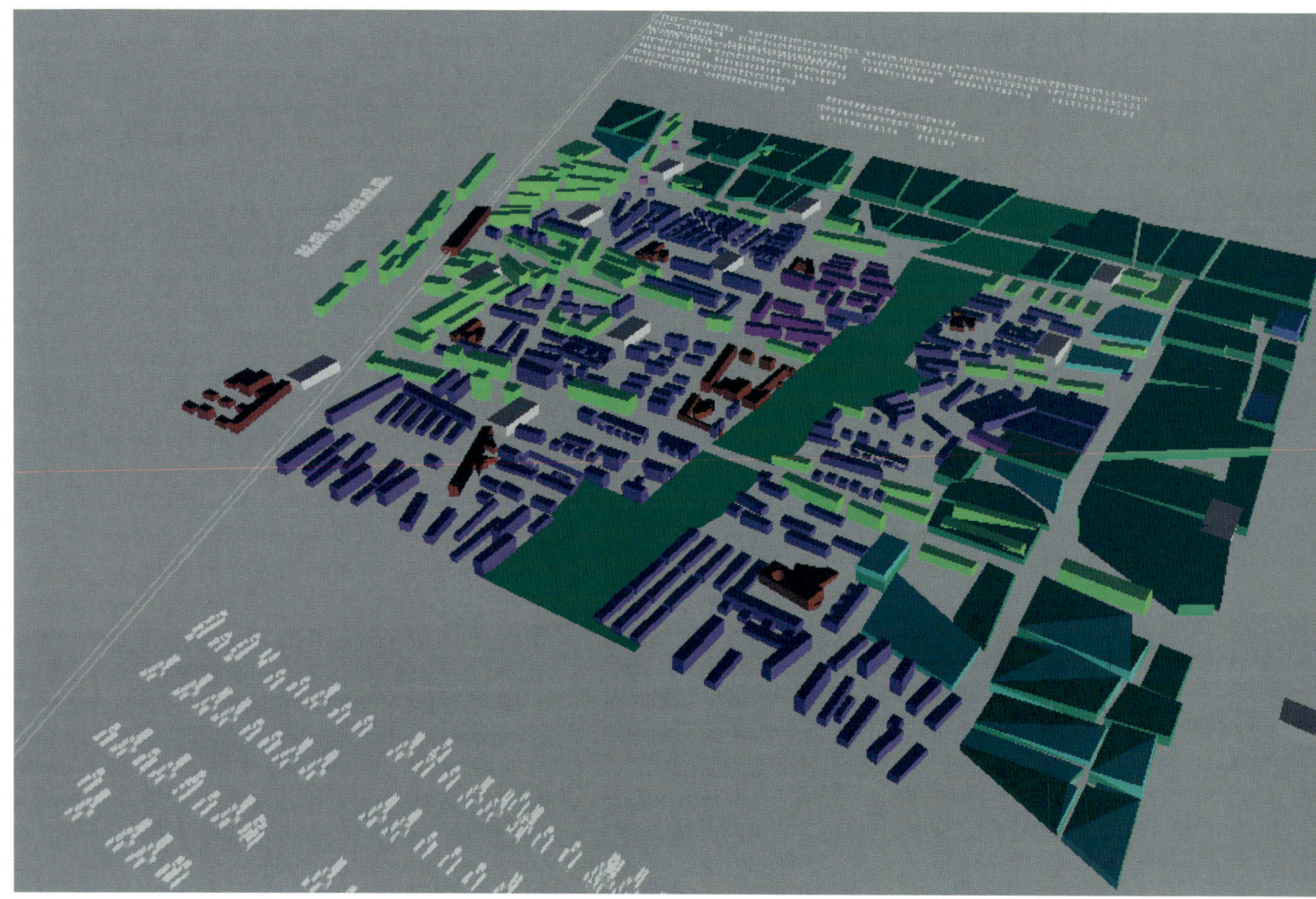

"INDUSTRIAL STRIP"

COMPRESSION IN THE INNER SPACE
KOMPRIMIERUNG IM INNEREN BEREICH

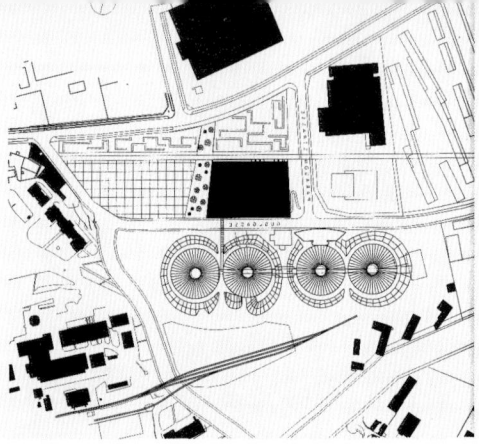

Umfeld Gasometer, Städtebauliches Strukturkonzept Wien–Landstraße, 1998/99

Das Umfeld der Gasometer in einer industriellen und gewerblichen Peripherie, aufgrund der U-Bahn aber in einer paradoxen Nähe zum Zentrum, schafft eine experimentelle Situation jenseits der Typen von Einkaufsmeile/Fußgängerzone/Wohnstraße oder museal eingefrorenen Platzbildungen und provoziert eine Neu-Definition von öffentlichen Räumen jenseits von Stadtmöblierung. Die Großform der Gasometer prägt die ehemalige Peripherie Erdberger Mais/Simmering: vier zylindrische Behälter des alten Gaswerks mit 70 Meter Höhe und 65 Meter Durchmesser. In diese Volumina wird eine multifunktionale Nutzung mit Wohnen, Büro, Shopping und Veranstaltungshalle implantiert. Der – gemessen am derzeitigen Umfeld – inselartige Charakter dieser neuen Entwicklungszone verlangt nach einer spezifischen Verdichtung und Nutzungsmischung sowie nach einer neuen Interpretation des Straßenraums nördlich der Gasometer.

Für die schrittweise Transformation der Nutzungen ist es dabei notwendig, von der vorgegebenen Besitzstruktur auszugehen, weil nur dadurch Anreize für Investitionen in eine selbsttätige Veränderung und Verdichtung gesetzt werden können. Die geforderte Nutzungsvielfalt und Nutzungsmischung führt zur Entwicklung einer Regelstruktur für die Gebäude bzw. Baublöcke, welche als Operator von einer horizontalen und vertikalen Schichtung ausgeht. Beide Schichtungen ermöglichen eine flexible und zugleich formgebende Anordnung der Funktionen innerhalb der Gebäudestrukturen mit einem Spielraum für Transformationen, selektive Umnutzungen und Verdichtungen.

Von Bedeutung ist die horizontale und vertikale Schichtung der Raumeinheiten auch für das Wechselspiel zwischen Gebäude und öffentlichem Raum: Die horizontale Schichtung ermöglicht eine Öffnung und/oder Schließung einzelner Nutzungen sowie eine neue Definition urbaner Qualitäten. Die „Fassade" wird selbst zum Außenraum des Innenraums – und zum Innenraum des Außenraums: Zum Transitorium für Wegeführungen von unterschiedlicher Öffentlichkeit, zur Vitrine als selektivem öffentlichen Raum, zu geschlossenen Bildwand (Billboard).

Urban Structural Concept for the Area to the North of the Gasometers, Vienna–Landstrasse, 1998/99

The area around the gasometers lies on an industrial and commercial periphery which, however, due to the Underground is in paradoxical proximity to the center, creates an experimental situation far beyond the shopping mile/pedestrian zone/residential street or antiquated, frigid spatial formations and provokes a new definition of public space that is far removed from urban furnishing. The major form of the gasometers dominates the former periphery Erdberger Mais/Simmering: the four cylindrical containers of the old gasworks are 70 metres high with a diameter of 65 metres. A multifunctional use is to be implanted in these volumes with housing, offices, shopping and a functions hall. The insular character of this new development zone – given the present surroundings – demands a specific increase in density and mix of use and also a new interpretation of the street spaces to the north of the gasometers.

In order to achieve a transformation of these uses in a series of steps it is necessary to take the existing ownership structure as a starting point. Only in this way can sufficient incentives for investment in spontaneous change and increase in density be created. The variety and mix of uses required leads to the development of a standard structure for the buildings or building blocks which as an "operator" starts from a system of horizontal and vertical layering. Both layerings allow a flexible and, at the same time, formative ordering of functions within the building structures that allows space for transformations, selective changes of function and increases in density.

The horizontal and vertical layering of the spatial units also plays a significant role in the alternating play between building and public space: the horizontal layering allows the opening and/or closure of individual functions and also a new definition of urban qualities. The "facade" itself becomes the external space of the interior and the interior of the outside space, a transitorium for the creation of path systems that are public to different degrees, a showcase as a selective public space, a closed screen (billboard).

UMFELD GASOMETER

 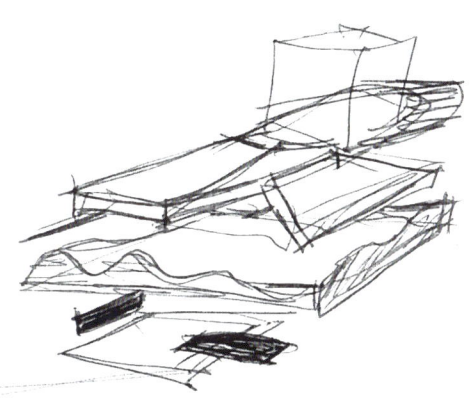 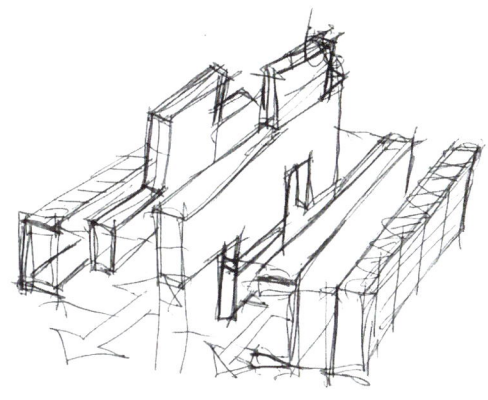

PRINCIPLE
LAYERING OF USES
Diversity of functions with minimal disturbance
PRINZIP
SCHICHTUNG DER NUTZUNGEN
Nutzungsvielfalt bei geringer Störung

HORIZONTAL LAYERING
Layering as a landscape element
"Topographical building"
HORIZONTALE SCHICHTUNG
Schichtung als Landschaftselement
„Topografische Gebäude"

VERTICAL LAYERING
Reference to the urban elements:
Changes in height, stepping;
Facade to the street/square
Buildings placed in front of the Gasometers
VERTIKALE SCHICHTUNG
Bezug auf die stadträumlichen Elemente:
Höhendifferenzierung, Abstufung;
Schauseite zu Straße/Platz
Gebäude lagern vor den Gasometern

Die für die Zone nördlich der Gasometer entwickelten Raumdefinitionen umfassen den „Vorplatz", das Proszenium der neuen urbanen Verdichtung (mit U-Bahnstation und Eingang in die Mall der Gasometer), den Kunstraum zwischen den Gasometern und den neuen multifunktionalen Ensembles. Der Aktionsraum Paragonplatz und der Kirschgarten trennen und verbinden die Baublöcke: In der Bandbreite zwischen Ereignisraum, Erlebnisraum, Erholungsraum und begrüntem Platz geben sie umrisshaft Raum für einen neuen urbanen Habitus.

Parallel zum Kunstraum führen innere Straßen, „Zeilen", die vielleicht auch an sehr alte Formen von Multifunktionalität und öffentlichem Leben auf Straßen und Plätzen anknüpfen: Vor den Geschäften, Lokalen, Werkstätten oder Ateliers überlagern sich Objekte, kleine Aktivitäten und ein Slow-Drive-Erschließungsverkehr.

Die starke Orientierung der Gebäude bzw. der Baublöcke auf die Vielfalt der Aktivitäten in den öffentlichen Räumen stellt zugleich die Null- oder Ausgangsebene für die vertikale Schichtung der städtebaulichen Struktur dar. Unterschiedliche Nutzungen auf Straßenniveau erfordern unterschiedlich hohe Eingangszonen. Sie werden überlagert von Bürogeschoßen, Parkdecks, Bildungs-, Kultur-, Sport- oder Freizeitnutzungen in ein, zwei oder drei Geschoßen. Darüber befindet sich ein neu gewonnener städtischer Freiraum von begrünten Dächern und aufgelockerten Wohnstrukturen, Ateliers oder repräsentativen Räumen der Unternehmen (Sitzungsräume, Tagungszentren, kleine Denkfabriken etc.).

Die Aufgabe, vielfältige Nutzungen sehr nahe aneinander zu rücken (wie die noch bestehenden Gewerbebetriebe, Lager etc. neben Büros, neuen Dienstleistungen oder Wohnen), hat es nahegelegt, mittels des Prinzips der Schichtung auch einen hybriden Zwischenraum zwischen divergierenden Nutzungen zu entwickeln: Die „Feuermauer" oder die alten Trennmauern oder Hoftrakte zwischen den Parzellen wurden als „Konverter", als eine neue Wand oder Mauer von einer gewissen Tiefe definiert, welche ergänzende Nutzungen von beiden Seiten her aufnehmen kann, die für die Bewohner, Betriebe bzw. Beschäftigten wichtig sind und auf dem Weg zu neuen städtischen Arbeits- und Lebensformen immer wichtiger werden: wohnungsnahe Gärten, von den Bewohnern betreute Glashäuser, Terrassen, Kinderspielplätze und Sitzplätze, Jugendtreffpunkte, Clubs, Ateliers, Installationen... Die horizontalen Schichtungen sind damit Medium der Kommunikation zwischen den städtischen Akteuren: den Unternehmen, Kulturschaffenden, Passanten, Bewohnern, Beschäftigten, städtischen Diensten.

Neue Lebensstile und Lebensformen werden sich in der Stadt nicht im Einkaufen, in hastigen Wegen zur U-Bahnstation oder zum Parkhaus, im Rückzug in ein Restaurant oder an die Theke von Fastfood erschöpfen. Für neue Gesten im öffentlichen Raum sind andere räumliche „Gelegenheiten" zu schaffen, nicht-konsumistische Impulse, Nischen entlang der abgelaufenen Muster von Straßen und Fußgängerzonen. R.L.

The spatial definitions developed for the area to the north of the gasometers enclose the "forecourt," the proscenium of the new urban intensity (with Underground station and entrance to the gasometer mall), the Kunstraum between the gasometers and the new multifunctional ensembles. The action space Paragonplatz and the cherry orchard separate and connect the building blocks. In a spectrum extending between event space, experience space, space for recreation and green space they provide the outlines of a space for a new urban disposition.

Parallel to the Kunstraum run internal streets or "rows" which are perhaps also related to extremely ancient forms of multifunctionalism and public life on streets and squares. In front of the shops, restaurants, workshops or ateliers objects are overlaid along with small-scale activities and slow-drive access traffic.

The pronounced orientation of the buildings or the building blocks to the variety of activities in the public space provides the zero or starting level for the vertical layering of the urban structure. Different uses at street level demand entrance zones of different heights. These are overlaid with office floors, car parking decks, education, culture and sport or leisure functions on one, two or three storeys. Above is a newly created urban outdoor space of planted roofs and relaxed residential structures, ateliers or impressive spaces for business companies (conference rooms, meeting centers, small think-tanks, etc.).

The task of moving very different uses very close to each other (such as the still existent businesses, warehouses, etc. beside offices, new service industries or flats) made it vital to also develop, using the principle of layering, a hybrid intermediate space between divergent uses. The "party wall" or the old dividing walls or courtyard wings between the plots were defined as "converters" as a new wall, load-bearing or not, with a certain depth that can absorb complementary uses from either side which are important for the residents, businesses or employees and will become increasingly more important on the path to new urban ways of working and living: gardens close to the apartments, glasshouses looked after by the residents, terraces, children's play areas and seating areas, youth centers, clubs, ateliers, installations... The horizontal layerings are thus the medium of communication between the urban protagonists: businesses, persons engaged in the cultural sector, passers-by, residents, employees, municipal services.

New life styles and forms of living will not be restricted in the city to shopping, the hasty route to the Underground or garage, to retiring to a restaurant or to the counter of a fast-food joint. Other spatial "opportunities" must be created to allow new gestures in public space: non-consumerist impulses, niches along the outdated patterns of streets and pedestrian zones. R.L.

THE URBAN PRINCIPLE
Intensified topological space with a variety
of urban functions
Differentiated landscape space

STÄDTEBAULICHES PRINZIP
Verdichteter topologischer Raum vielfältiger
urbaner Funktionen
Differenzierter Landschaftsraum

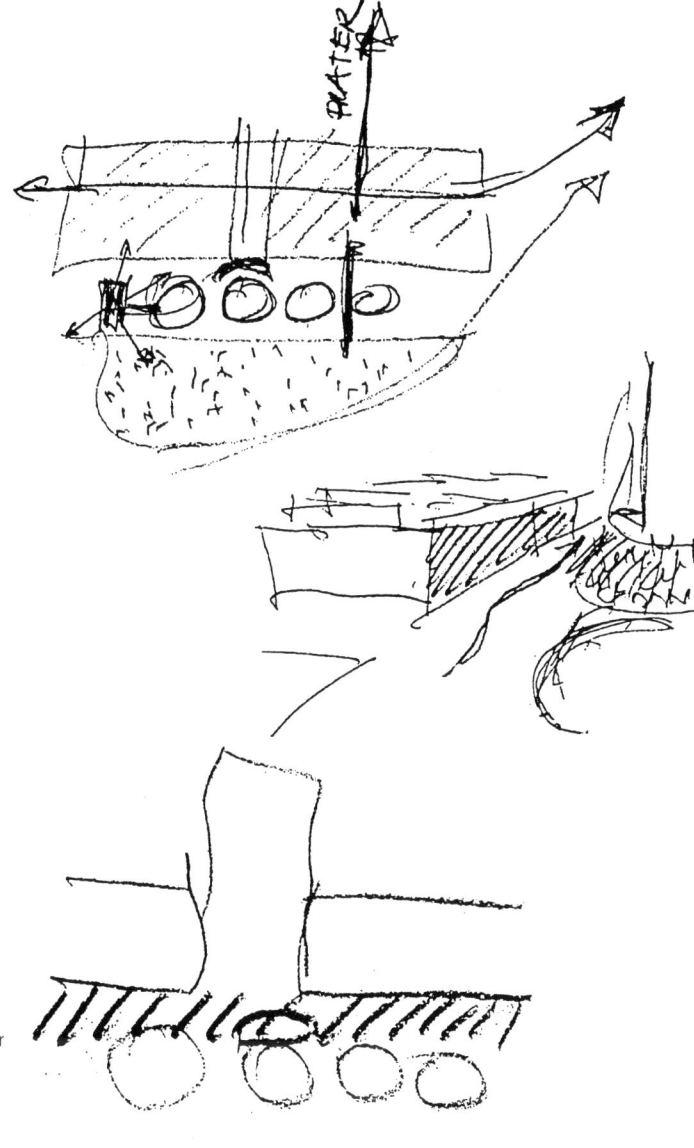

DEVELOPMENT OF GUGLGASSE
Emphasis of the street space between
natural planting and artificial wall

ENTWICKLUNG GUGLGASSE
Betonung des Straßenraumes zwischen natürlicher
Bepflanzung und künstlicher Wand

PARAGONSTRASSE MOVED TO THE FRONT
Urban square as a connecting space

VORGELAGERTE PARAGONSTRASSE
Urbaner Platzraum als Verknüpfungsraum

Longitudinal link of topological buildings
moved to the front

Längsverknüpfung vorgelagerter
topologischer Gebäude

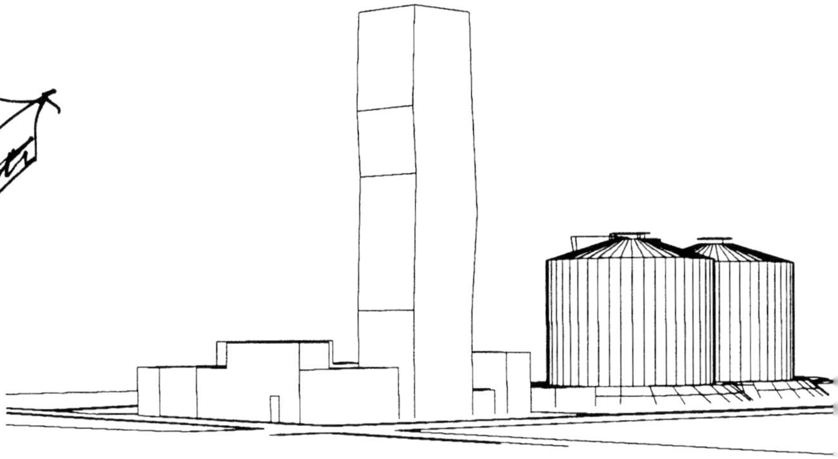

TYPOLOGY BLOCK GO-3 | TYPOLOGIE BLOCK GO-3
1:2000
Site area | Grundstücksfläche 9960 m²
Total gross floor area | gesamt BGF 60.000 m²
Density | Dichte 6,0

TYPOLOGY BLOCK E-3 | TYPOLOGIE BLOCK E-3
1:2000
Site area | Grundstücksfläche 6070 m²
Living | Wohnen 4.400 m²
44 apartments | Wohnungen
Commercial/offices | Gewerbe/Büros 10.000 m²
Garage | Garage 4000 m²
Total gross floor area | gesamt BGF 18.400 m²
Density | Dichte 3,0

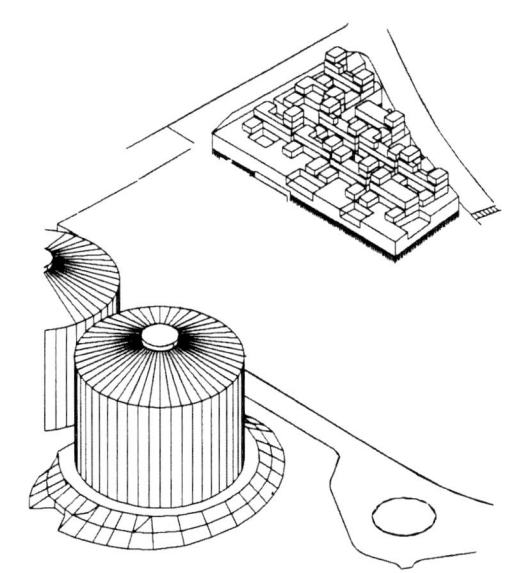

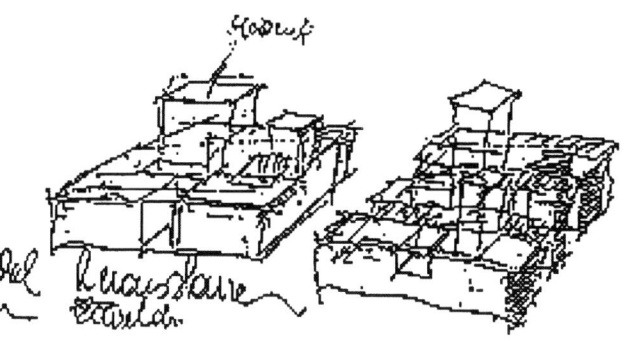
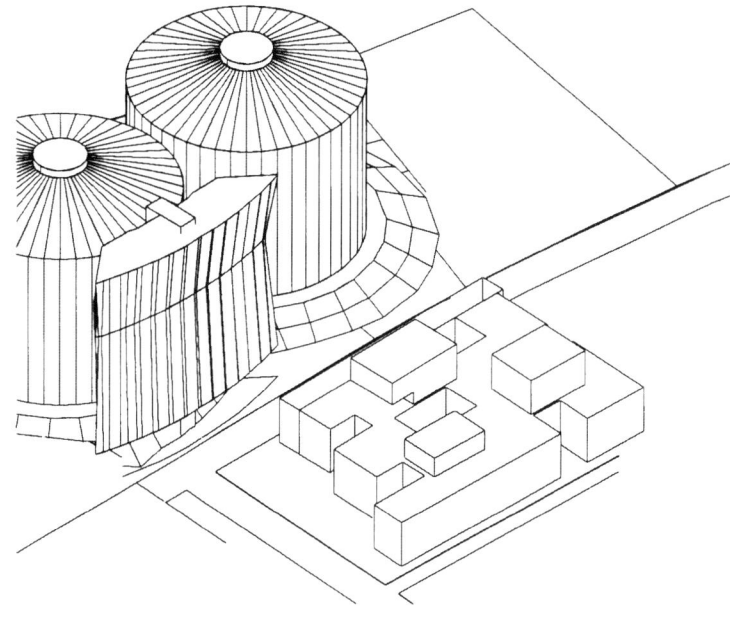

TYPOLOGY BLOCK K-3 | TYPOLOGIE BLOCK K-3
1:2000
Site area | Grundstücksfläche 7105 m²
Basis gross floor area | Basis BGF 15.600 m²
Towers gross floor area | Türme BGF 3.400 m²
Showcase gross floor area | Vitrine BGF 20.000 m²
Density | Dichte 2,8

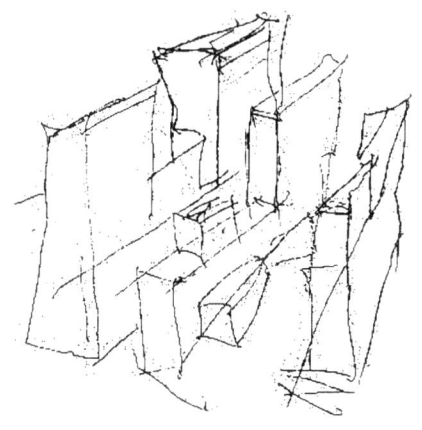
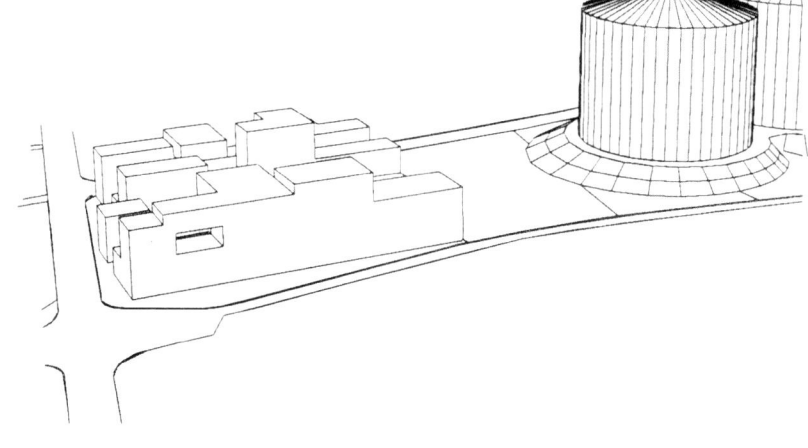

TYPOLOGY BLOCK GO-1 | TYPOLOGIE BLOCK GO-1
1:2000
Site area | Grundstücksfläche 9.960 m²
Basic gross floor area | Basis BGF 32.000 m²
Density | Dichte 3,2

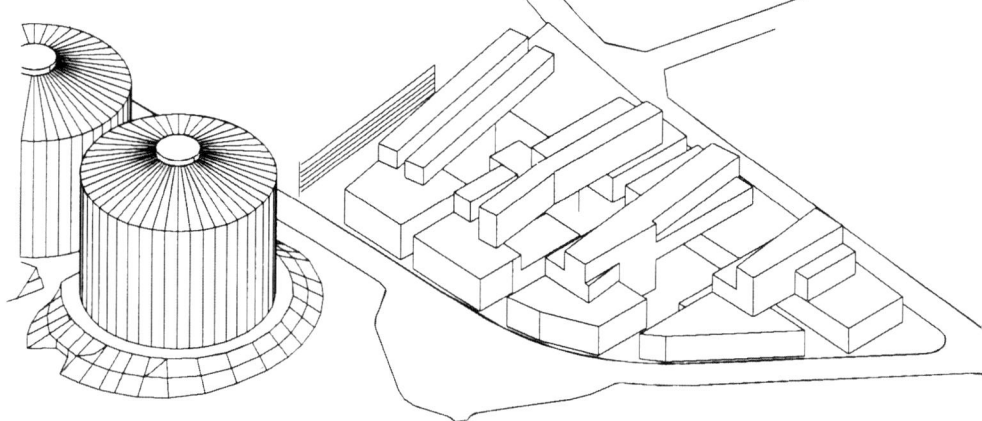

TYPOLOGY BLOCK E-4/K-4
TYPOLOGIE BLOCK E-4/K-4
1:2000
Site area | Grundstücksfläche 17.850 m²
Living | Wohnen 15.000 m²
150 apartments | Wohnungen
Commercial/offices | Gewerbe/Büro 22.500 m²
Garage | Garage 19.000 m²
Total gross floor area | gesamt BGF 32.000 m²
Density | Dichte 3,2

STRUCTURES/RULES | STRUKTUREN/REGELN
1:4000

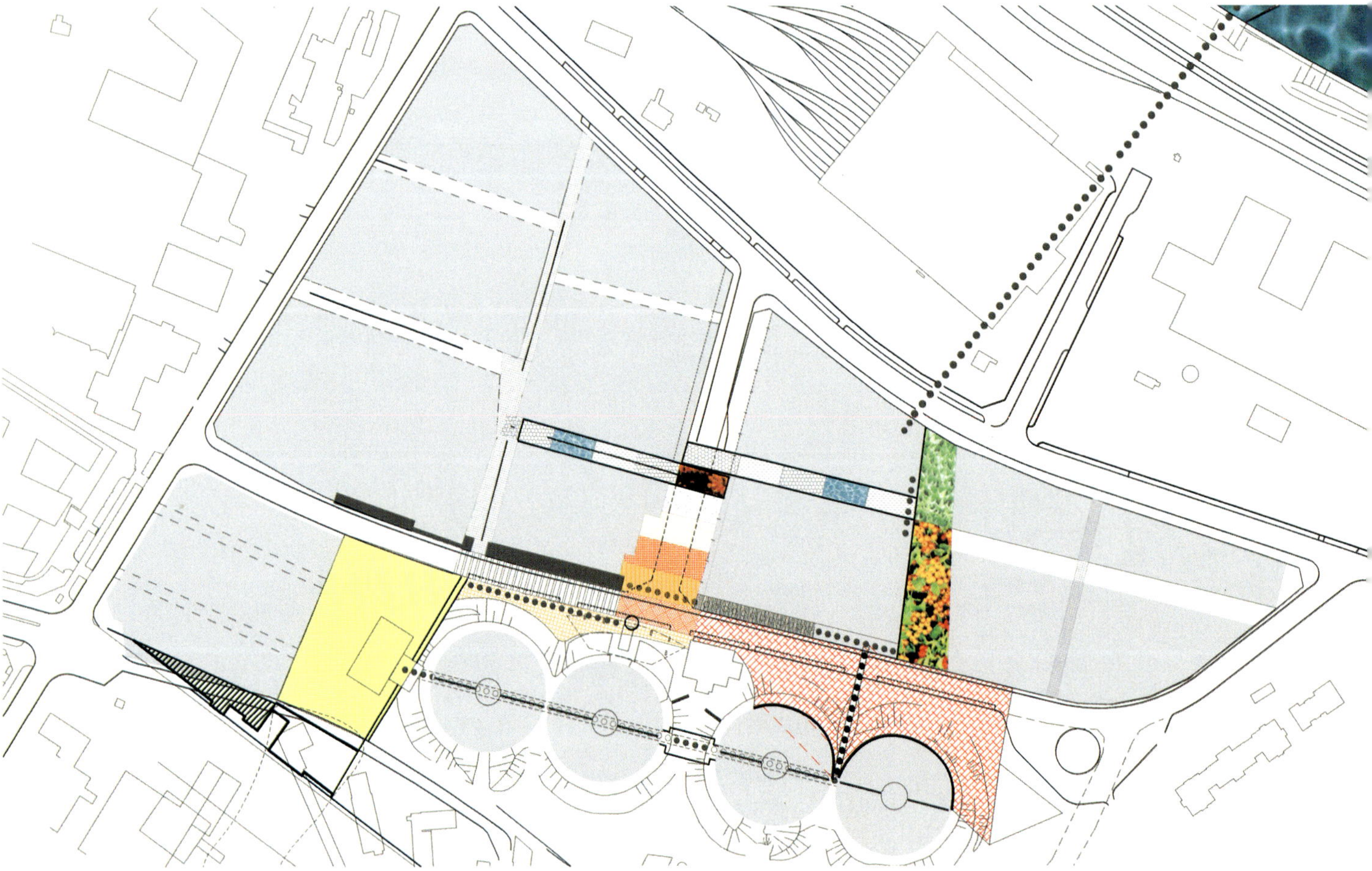

SPATIAL CATEGORIES/QUALITIES | RAUMKATEGORIEN/QUALITÄTEN
1:4000

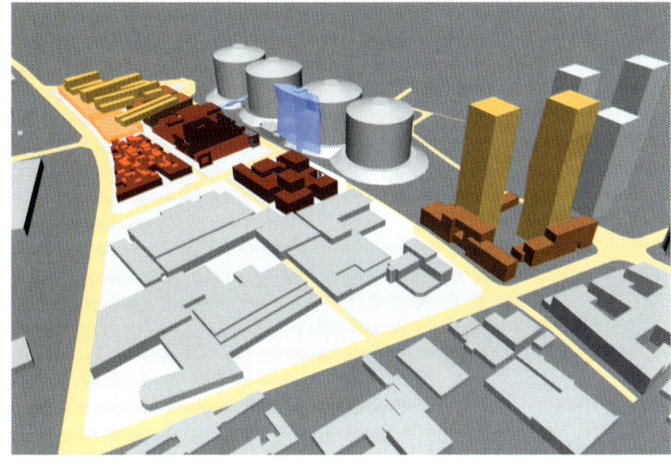
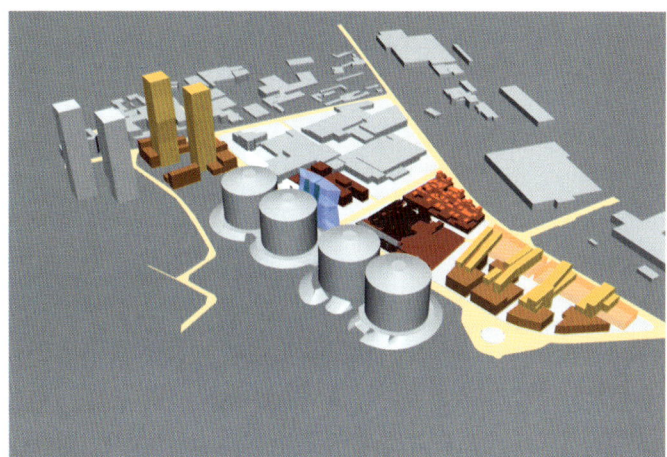

Die Wunderkammer

Die Wunderkammer ist Teil einer elektronischen Arbeitsumgebung. Sie wurde als eine multimediale 3D-Welt für das Archivieren, Sammeln, Ausstellen und Bearbeiten inspirationaler Objekte – Bilder, Musik, Video, 3D-Objekte – konzipiert. Die Metapher der Wunderkammer ist dem gleichnamigen Kuriositätenkabinett Rudolf II. am Prager Hof entlehnt.

Verständnis und konkreter Entwurf der Wunderkammer (in der Form eines System-Prototyps) stützen sich auf umfangreiche ethnographische Studien architektonischen Entwerfens und Planens. Dabei ging es sowohl darum, Praktiken des Sammelns, Archivierens und Mobilisierens inspirationaler Objekte im Entwurfsprozess zu identifizieren, als auch die zusätzlichen Möglichkeiten von 3D-Welten zu explorieren. Besucher der 3D-Wunderkammer in ihrer gegenwärtigen Form können in dieser navigieren und unterschiedliche Orte aufsuchen.

Entwurf und Inszenierung

Entwerfen erfordert die Konzeptualisierung von Vorstellungen, auf der Ebene von Bildern, Metaphern und Analogien, ihre Konfrontation mit den „Gegebenheiten", sowie den Umgang mit Gegensätzlichkeiten. Die Kunst des Entwerfens besteht darin, mit einer Fülle von Parametern zu jonglieren, sie wie durch ein Sieb zu schütteln, so dass ihre Beziehungen sich zwar nicht verfestigen, aber doch allmählich in ein Konzept fügen. Dieses Konzept muss in der Schwebe gehalten, mit immer neuen Eindrücken und Fakten konfrontiert werden.

The Wunderkammer (Chamber of Marvels)

The Wunderkammer is part of an electronic work environment that was conceived of as a multi-media 3D world for archiving, collecting, exhibiting and processing inspirational objects – images, music, videos and 3D objects. The metaphor of the Wunderkammer is borrowed from Rudolf II's curio gallery of the same name at his court in Prague.

The understanding and concrete design of the Wunderkammer (in the form of a system prototype) are based on comprehensive ethnographical studies of architectural design and planning. Here the issue was to identify practices of collecting, archiving and mobilising inspirational objects in the design process and also to explore the additional possibilities of 3D worlds. Visitors to the 3D Wunderkammer in its current form can navigate their way through it and visit different places.

Design and Staging

The act of designing demands the conceptualisation of ideas on the level of images, metaphors and analogies, confronting them with the "givens" and dealing with contradictions. The art of design consists of juggling a number of parameters, shaking them through a sieve so that the relationships between them, while not solidifying, are gradually arranged in a concept. This concept must be kept open and constantly confronted with new impressions and facts.

WUNDERKAMMER

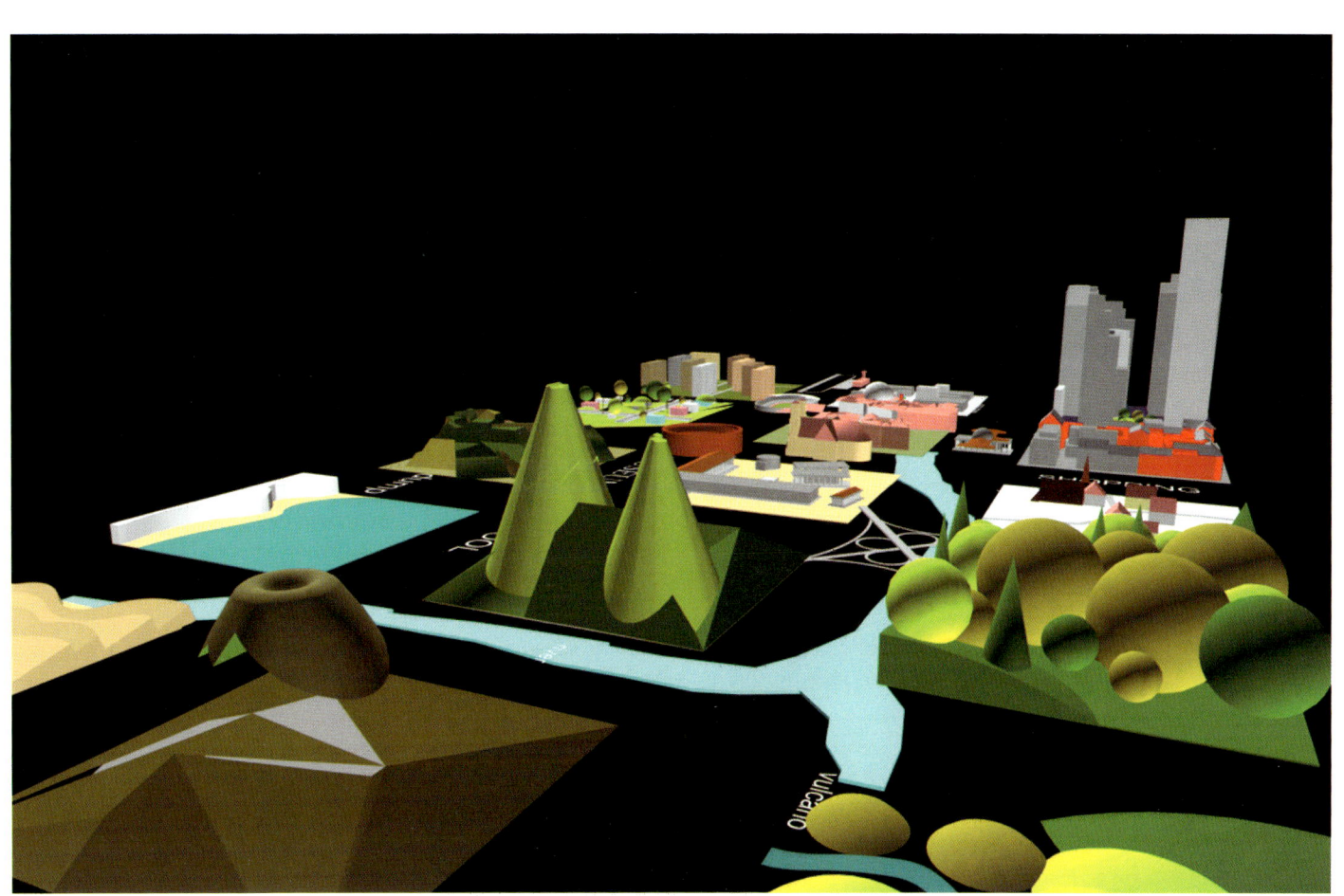

Die in diesem Prozess wirksamen inspirationalen Objekte sind vielfältig. Es sind dies zum einen Vorstellungsbilder von Ort und Kontext, unterstützt durch Pläne und Fotos, Bilder früherer oder verwandter Entwurfsprojekte, Objekte unterschiedlicher Qualität und Materialität. Eine entscheidende Rolle in diesem Prozess spielen Assoziationsbilder, Metaphern und Analogien. Wichtig ist sowohl die Vielfalt dieses Assoziationsmaterials als auch seine Unschärfe. Jede dieser Ressourcen mobilisiert den Entwurfsprozess auf eigene Weise. Bilder und Metaphern stellen eine reichhaltige Sprache dar, die hilft, Ideen zu formieren und Qualitäten auszudrücken.

Ein zentrales Problem ist die beschränkte Verfügbarkeit jener vielfältigen Ressourcen, die den Entwurfsprozess anregen und unterstützen. Spuren vergangener und gegenwärtiger Projekte sind im Architekturbüro selbst ausgestellt. In Regalen stapeln sich Bücher, Zeitschriften, Pläne, Kataloge, Broschüren und CDs. Materialien lagern auf dem Boden, Modelle von Projekten stehen auf den Tischen. Dennoch ist dieses Reservoir beschränkt. Vieles ist oft nur als schwaches Erinnerungsbild von Reisen, Stadtgängen, Kino- und Ausstellungsbesuchen, peripheren Fachgesprächen präsent und lässt sich nicht mehr mobilisieren. Außerdem sind bestehende Archivierungsmethoden in beschrifteten Boxen, Ordnern und Kisten unzureichend. Sie erfordern ein Aufbewahren von Gegenständen, deren Bedeutung sich laufend mit dem Kontext verändert, in „gefrorener Form". Die Wunderkammer versucht nun als technisches Objekt und als Instrument, die Formen des Aufbewahrens, Verfügbarmachens und Verwendens inspirationaler Ressourcen für den Entwurfsprozess zu flexibilisieren und zu erweitern.

Reisen und Sammeln

Die Kuriositätenkabinette der Vergangenheit lebten von Reisenden, die auf ihren Erkundungen der Natur, ferner Länder und fremder Kulturen Objekte mitbrachten. Damit verbunden ist die Vorstellung der „Welt als Ausstellungsraum", wie sie vor allem in den Zeiten des Kolonialismus präsent war und heute den modernen Bildungstourismus prägt.

Jene frühen Weltreisenden, die Rudolf II. Wunderkammer mit exotischen Objekten bereicherten, fanden eine Kammer vor: geschlossene Räume mit Regalen, Tischen und Truhen zum Verstauen und zum Zurschaustellen. Es entstand eine komprimierte, in Einzelstücken verdichtete Version der Welt des Inspirationalen. Ihre modernen Nachfolger reisen und sammeln ebenfalls. Jedoch reicht ihre Wunderkammer in weite Distanzen, sie selbst ist der Raum, den es zu bereisen und zu durchforschen gilt. Dies hängt mit den Möglichkeiten elektronischer Medien zusammen, die Welt selbst zu simulieren.

So ist die 3D-Welt als Stadt- und Landschaftsraum gestaltet. Sie enthält unterschiedliche Landschaftsformationen von der Wüste über das Bergland bis zu Küstengebieten sowie archetypische Stadt- und Siedlungsformen (Skyscraper City, mittelalterlicher Stadtkern, Agora, Dorf, Einfamilienhäuser, Gründerzeitviertel, die industrielle Peripherie, Wohnblocks der 60er Jahre, verödete Stadtrandgebiete). Verbindende Elemente wie Autobahnen, ein

The inspirational objects effective in this process are manifold. They include impressions of place and context supported by plans and photos, images of previous or related design projects, objects of different quality and materials. Images of association, metaphors and analogies play a decisive role in this process. Both the variety of this associative material and its blurred quality are important. Each of these resources mobilises the design process in its own way. Images and metaphors represent a rich language which helps to form ideas and express qualities.

A central problem is the restricted availability of the varied resources that stimulate and support the design process. Traces of past and current projects are displayed in architectural offices themselves. Books, newspapers, catalogues, brochures and CDs are stacked on shelves. Material samples lie on the floor, models of projects stand on the tables. Nevertheless this reservoir is limited. Often it exists only as a faint memory of travels, strolls through cities, visits to the cinema or exhibitions, marginal expert discussions and can no longer be mobilised. In addition, existing methods of archiving in titled boxes, files and crates are inadequate. They demand that objects, whose significance changes constantly depending on the context, be stored in a "frozen state." The Wunderkammer is a technical object and instrument that attempts to make flexible and expand the forms of preserving, rendering available and using inspirational resources for the design process.

Travelling and Collecting

In the past the cabinets of curiosities depended upon travellers who brought back objects from their explorations of nature, distant lands and foreign cultures. An associated idea is the concept of the "world as an exhibition space" found, above all, during the colonial period and which today characterises modern educational tourism.

The early world travellers who enriched Rudolf II's Wunderkammer with exotic objects found a chamber already in existence: defined spaces with shelves, tables and chests in which to store and present the objects. There resulted a compressed version of the inspirational world concentrated in individual objects. Their modern day successors also travel and collect, but their Wunderkammer extends into the far distance, it is itself the space to be explored and researched. This is a result of the possibilities offered by electronic media to simulate the world itself.

The 3D world is thus designed as an urban and landscape space. It contains different landscape formations from the desert by way of mountain ranges to coastal regions as well as archetypal forms of cities and settlements (Skyscraper City, mediaeval town core, agora, village, single-family house, Gründerzeit district, the industrial periphery, housing blocks from the 60s, desolate areas on the urban periphery) connecting elements such as motorways or a river as well as significant elements (amphitheatre, museum, cathedral, shopping center, airport) support the orientation. In this way the cabinet is transformed into a space that is, in principle, endless which invites one to reproduce travelling in

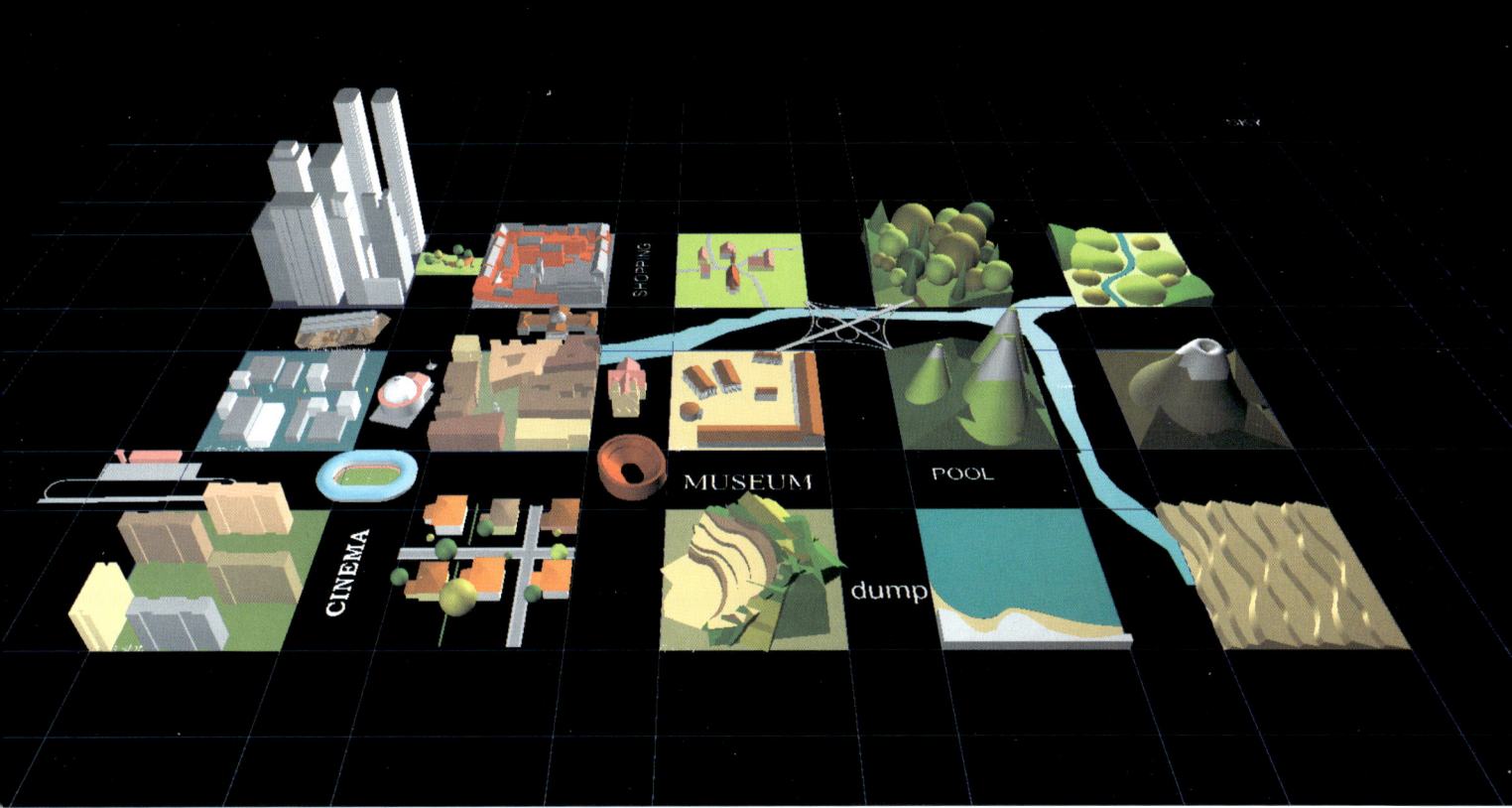

Fluss oder signifikante Objekte (Amphitheater, Museum, Kathedrale, Einkaufszentrum, Flughafen) unterstützen die Orientierung. Derart wird das Kabinett in einen im Prinzip unendlich ausgedehnten Raum verwandelt, der dazu einlädt, das Reisen in vielfachen Variationen zu reproduzieren, einschließlich des Sammelns. Unterschiedliche Reisegeschwindigkeiten und -modi sind möglich: vom Überfliegen bis zur Zugreise und dem Durchwandern.

Kategorisieren und Platzieren

Als Archiv- und Ausstellungsraum war die historische Wunderkammer neutral. Objekte waren entweder zufällig arrangiert und verstaut, sodass sich dem staunenden Besucher beim Öffnen eines Schranks oder im Vorbeigehen an einem Regal eine eigentümliche Mischung unterschiedlichster Gegenstände präsentierte. Doch setzten sich immer mehr chronologische Arrangements des gesammelten Materials, ihre Separierung in Genres und Medien sowie elaborierte Klassifikationsschemata durch.

Die moderne 3D-Wunderkammer erlaubt eine Rückkehr zu unscharfen und fließenden Formen des Kategorisierens. Ein Ort in der Wunderkammer ist nicht eindeutig beschrieben. Skyscraper City, zum Beispiel, evoziert kulturelle Konnotationen, die sich verbal oder bildlich ausdrücken lassen. Besucher der Wunderkammer mögen dort Bilder von Hochhäusern unterschiedlicher Perioden, Vistas, typischen Straßenmustern und Plazas erwarten, aber auch Objekte, die sie mit Attributen wie „schroff, dicht, ragend, zerklüftet, hektisch, rhythmisch" verbinden. Obwohl Orte in der Wunderkammer „erkennbar" sind, sind die Beziehungen zwischen Bild und Raum ausreichend offen und vielfältig, um unterschiedliche Assoziationen

manifold variations including collecting. Different speeds and methods of travel are possible, ranging from flying over to train travel and wandering through.

Cataloguing and Placing

The historical Wunderkammer was a neutral archive and exhibition space. The objects were either arranged and stacked arbitrarily so that, on opening a closet or passing by a shelf, an individual mixture of very different objects was presented to the amazed visitor. Gradually, however, the chronological arrangement of the collected material gained precedence. It was separated into genres and media and elaborate systems of classification were introduced.

The modern 3D Wunderkammer allows a return to the blurred, fluid forms of categorising. In this Wunderkammer a place is not described unambiguously. Skyscraper City, for example, evokes cultural connotations which can be expressed visually or verbally. Visitors to the Wunderkammer can expect images of sky scrapers from different periods, vistas, typical street patterns and plazas but also objects which they associate with the attributes "jagged, dense, projecting, fissured, hectic, rhythmic." Although places in the Wunderkammer are "recognisable" the relationships between image and space are sufficiently open and varied to allow different associations and placings. A picture by Delaunay may suit both the skyscraper city or the periphery of the mountain range. The particular creative potential of the 3D urban landscape lies not only in its fluid intuitive form of archiving through placing. Data bank and key-wording mechanisms make the images themselves moveable. As a visitor I can have all images in the colour "red" or

und Platzierungen zu ermöglichen. Ein Bild von Delaunay mag sowohl zur Wolkenkratzerstadt als auch an die Peripherie der Berge passen.

Das besondere inszenatorische Potential der 3D-Stadtlandschaft liegt nun nicht nur in dieser fließenden, intuitiven Form des Archivierens durch Platzieren. Datenbank und Keywording-Mechanismus machen die Bilder vielmehr selbst beweglich. Als Besucher kann ich alle Bilder mit der Farbe „rot" oder alle jene mit der Eigenschaft „labyrinthisch", „eng" und „geclustert" (dies mag ein Attribut sowohl des mittelalterlichen Stadtkerns als auch des Waldes sein) zu einer Ausstellung zusammenstellen lassen. Damit können aus dem Archiv in Sekundenschnelle spezifische Konfrontationen, Abfolgen und Zuordnungen inspirationalen Materials hergestellt werden.

Wiederfinden und Entdecken

Ein wesentliches Merkmal inspirationaler Objekte ist ihre oft nur periphere Präsenz. Sie werden flüchtig, im Vorbeifahren oder raschen Blättern, wahrgenommen, prägen sich als Erinnerungsspuren ein und vermögen doch Ideen und starke innere Bilder mitzugenerieren. Als Erinnerungsraum kann die Wunderkammer unterschiedliche Formen annehmen.

Ein Erinnerungsraum mag aus „erkennbaren" Plätzen mit relativ eindeutiger Zweckbestimmung gebaut sein. Dann ähnelt er den Ordnerarchiven auf der Grundlage eines mehr oder weniger ausgefeilten Klassifikationssystems. Er bietet die Sicherheit, die kostbare Sammlung von Steinen im Steinbruch oder jene von Flechtwerk im Volkskundemuseum wiederzufinden.

Das Gegenstück dazu ist Christian Boltanskis gekrümmter Archivraum „Registres". Es sind dort die über Jahre gesammelten Erinnerungsspuren an nicht mehr lebende Personen in kaum unterscheidbaren Blechboxen aufbewahrt: „Here, they are all presented on an equal footing, in the same format, and mixed up in an arbitrary way: the SS officer becomes a neighbour of a member of the Mickey Club, the child from the Lycée Chases is close to the Spanish criminal."[1] Boxen und die Personen, die sie repräsentieren, lassen sich beliebig kombinieren. Boltanskis Erinnerungsraum radikalisiert eine der Ideen der Wunderkammer als ein Raum, der es erlaubt, „to relate the unrelatable".

Wird die Wunderkammer kollektiv genutzt, von vielen, möglicherweise einander Unbekannten (beispielsweise über das Internet) möbliert und bereist, nehmen die Möglichkeiten des Entdeckens überraschender, vielleicht irritierender Formationen zusammenhangloser, widersprüchlicher Bilder, an einem Ort zu. Die Analogie zu dem, was Alison Landsberg „prosthetic memory" nennt, liegt nahe, Erinnerungen, die nicht selber durchlebt wurden, sondern kunstvoll kreiert, implantiert. Filme wie „Blade Runner" schaffen Erinnerungswelten, die nicht im eigentlichen Sinne „erlebbar" sind. Das elektronische Medium geht noch einen Schritt weiter als der Film, indem es die Beteiligung der Benutzer der Wunderkammer zur Konstruktion unterschiedlichster Erinnerungswelten- und formen verwendet. Alle Reisen durch die 3D-Welt, alle Platzierungen von Bildern, an den unterschiedlichsten Orten, alle Akte des

all those with the quality "labyrinthine," "narrow" or "lustered" (and this could be both an attribute of the mediaeval town center or of a forest) put together to form an exhibition. Within the space of seconds specific confrontations, sequences and attributions of inspirational materials can be assembled from the archive.

Discovering and finding again

It is the often only peripheral presence of inspirational objects that is an essential characteristic of inspirational objects. They are perceived fleetingly while driving by or leafing through, leaving just traces in the memory and yet can help generate ideas and powerful inner images. The Wunderkammer can adopt various forms as a memory space.

A memory space can be built from "recognisable" places with relatively unambiguous functions. In this case it resembles the archives of files based on a more or less sophisticated classification system. It offers the security of finding again the precious collection of stones in the quarry or the wicker-work collection in the folklore museum.

Christian Boltanski's curved archive space "Registres" forms a complete contrast to this. There the traces of memories of people no longer alive collected over the years are kept in metal boxes which can hardly be distinguished from each other. "Here they are all presented on an equal footing, in the same format and mixed up in an arbitrary way: the SS officer becomes a neighbour of a member of the Mickey club, the child from the Lycée Chases is close to the Spanish criminal."[1] Boxes and the people whom they represent can be combined as required. Boltanski's memory space radicalises one of the concepts of the Wunderkammer as a space which makes it possible, "to relate the unrelatable."

If the Wunderkammer is collectively used, furnished and travelled through by many people, who possibly do not know each other, (for example on Internet) the possibilities of discovering surprising, perhaps irritating formations of unrelated, contradictory images at a place increase. The analogy to what Alison Landsberg calls "prosthetic memory" is obvious, memories which are not personally experienced but artificially created and implanted. Films such as "Blade Runner" create worlds of memory which can not be experienced in the actual sense of the word. The electronic medium goes a step further than the film in that it employs the participation of the user of the Wunderkammer to construct very different forms and worlds of memory. All forms of travel through the 3D world, all placings of images at the most different locations, all acts of gathering and searching can be registered and combined to repeatedly form new, different landscapes of memory. Fragments of memory become movable, can be transported and combined as wished. "Electronic reproduction opens a wide, in principle uncontrollable, area for dislocations and recontextualisations. Relationships to people and places can be extinguished and created anew."[2]

Sammelns und Suchens können registriert und zu immer neuen und anderen Erinnerungslandschaften zusammengefügt werden. Erinnerungsstücke werden beweglich, transportierbar, beliebig kombinierbar: „Elektronische Reproduzierbarkeit eröffnet ein weites, im Prinzip unkontrollierbares Feld für Dislozierungen und Rekontextualisierungen. Beziehungen zu Personen und Orten können ausgelöscht, neue hergestellt werden."[2]

Kombinieren und Beleben

Eines der zentralen Merkmale der historischen Wunderkammer war, dass das zufällige oder neutrale Arragement der Objekte den Besuchern keine vorgedachten Beziehungen und Interpretationen nahelegte. Im Gegenteil, sie lud zum Entdecken von Beziehungen zwischen scheinbar unverbundenen Objekten ein. Auch die Besucher der modernen Wunderkammer werden eingeladen, ihre eigene kombinatorische Ästhetik zu praktizieren. Es mag gerade ein zufälliges Arrangement von Bildern und Fakten sein, das eine Entwurfsidee inspiriert.

Die Geschwindigkeit des Reisens verstärkt den Entdeckungseffekt. Der 3D-Raum erlaubt es, den fließenden schnellen Blick mit der Möglichkeit zu kombinieren, innezuhalten und ein Detail eines Bildes zu explorieren.

Schlussfolgerung

Die moderne Version der Wunderkammer simuliert das Reisen selbst, wenn auch in der merkwürdigen Form des Navigierens. Reisende können distante Ort erreichen, ohne je aufgebrochen zu sein. Kulturelle Distanz verliert ihren zeitlichen Aspekt.

Die Wunderkammer entsteht interaktiv. Benutzer legen ihre eigenen inspirationalen Objekte in ihr nieder und erzeugen durch ihre Erkundungen unterschiedlichste Erinnerungswelten, die wiederum von anderen bereist und verändert werden können.

Die in der 3D-Wunderkammer niedergelegten inspirationalen Objekte werden beweglich. Nicht nur können sie sich an vielen Orten gleichzeitig befinden. Die Konstellationen der Objekte zueinander und zum Raum werden über vielfältige Kombinationen dynamisiert. Darüber hinaus lassen sich Objekte beleben, vielfältig manipulieren und animieren, zu narrativen Fäden zusammenspinnen.

Schließlich lässt sich die moderne Wunderkammer in der technischen Arbeitsumgebung ihrer Benutzer installieren. Damit können diese ihr inszenatorisches Potential unmittelbar für die Entwurfsarbeit nutzen, etwa um die auf Imagination beruhenden, metaphorischen und narrativen Elemente eines Entwurfs zu kommunizieren. Rüdiger Lainer & Ina Wagner

1 Christian Boltanski, Dernières Années. Musée d'Art Moderne de la Ville de Paris, Paris 1998
2 Ina Wagner, Fließende Übergänge und Collagen. Ästhetische Produktion in
elektronischen Terrains. Alle möglichen Welten, M. Faßler (Ed.), München 1999

Combining and Animating

One of the central characteristics of the historic Wunderkammer was that the arbitrary or neutral arrangement of the objects did not impose preconceived relationships and interpretations on the visitors. On the contrary, they invited one to discover relationships between apparently unconnected objects. The visitors to the modern Wunderkammer are also invited to practice their own aesthetic of combinations. It may be an arbitrary arrangement of images and facts which inspires a design idea.

The speed of travel strengthens the effect of discovery. The 3D space makes it possible to combine the quick flowing glance with the possibility of combining standing still and exploring one detail of an image.

Conclusion

The modern version of the Wunderkammer simulates travel itself, albeit in the curious form of navigating. Travellers can reach distant places without ever setting out. Cultural distance loses its temporal aspect.

The Wunderkammer develops interactively. Users deposit their own inspirational objects in it and, through their exploration, produce highly different worlds of memory which can then be explored and altered by others.

The objects deposited in the 3D Wunderkammer become moveable. It is not only the fact that they can be found simultaneously in a number of places. The constellations of the objects to each other and towards space are dynamicised by means of various combinations. Above and beyond this objects can be stimulated, manipulated in a variety of ways and animated, spun into narrative threads.

Finally, the modern Wunderkammer can be installed in the user's technical work environment. In this way its dramatic potential can be used directly for design work – for example in order to communicate those metaphorical and narrative elements of a design that are based on imagination. Rüdiger Lainer & Ina Wagner

1 Christian Boltanski, Dernières Années. Musée d'Art Moderne de la Ville de Paris, Paris 1998
2 Ina Wagner, Fliessende Übergänge und Collagen. Ästhetische Produktion in
elektronischen Terrains. Alle möglichen Welten, Ed. M. Faßler, Munich 1999

**Steirische Landesausstellung
Jugendkulturen '68 – '98, Bad Radkersburg, 1998**

Im Süden der Steiermark, nahe dem Dreiländereck Österreich–Slowenien–Ungarn, liegt Bad Radkersburg, dessen schmucker Stadtkern noch heute von historischen Wallanlagen umgürtet und mit einem kleinen Glacis von der Umgebung abgesetzt ist. Am Hauptplatz spannte sich im Sommer 1998 vor der breiten Fassade des ehemaligen Rathauses ein roter „Screen", als läge dahinter eine Großbaustelle. In großen Lettern prangte darauf das Mischwort „YOUgend". Darunter stand „Jugendkulturen '68 – '98".

Für die Ausstellung wurde die Revitalisierung des historischen Gebäudes, mit der das Grazer Architektenteam Florian Riegler und Roger Riewe betraut war, im Rohbauzustand angehalten. Zwischen Altbausubstanz, bestehend aus einem Straßentrakt mit zwei Seitenflügeln, und einem neu hinzugefügten Quader aus Stahlbeton im hinteren Bereich des Grundstücks öffnet sich ein großzügiger Hof, der für die Zeit der Ausstellung mit einem provisorischen Dach überspannt war. In diese Struktur legten Rüdiger Lainer, Werner Silbermayr und der Grafik-Designer Erich Monitzer eine Ausstellungslandschaft, die über mehrere Ebenen führte. Als Rhythmusgeber dienten geschlossene thematische Stimmungsräume, auf die Vertiefungszonen folgten. Teils über offene Rampen und Stege, teils durch die Räume des Altbestands führte die Chronologie von den sechziger bis zu den neunziger Jahren.

**Styrian Federal State Exhibition
Youth Cultures '68 to '98, Bad Radkersburg, 1998**

Bad Radkersburg lies in the south of Styria, close to the point where Austria, Slovenia and Hungary meet. Its pretty town center is today still ringed by historic ramparts and separated from the surroundings by a small glacis. In the summer of 1998 a red "screen" was stretched in front of the broad facade of the former town hall as if a major building site lay behind. The English/German composite term "YOUgend" (youth) was printed on it in large letters, beneath stood "Jugendkulturen '68 –'98."

For the duration of the exhibition the revitalisation of the historic building – by the Graz team of architects, Florian Riegler and Roger Riewe – was stopped at an intermediate stage. A generous courtyard opens up between the old building substance, which consists of a street front tract and two side wings, and a newly added reinforced concrete block at the rear of the site. For the duration of the exhibition this courtyard was spanned by a provisional roof. Rüdiger Lainer, Werner Silbermayr and the graphic designer, Erich Monitzer, placed an exhibition landscape in this structure which led across a series of levels. Closed, thematic "mood spaces" served to establish a rhythm and were followed by zones intended to offer a deeper perception. The chronology led, partly along open ramps and footbridges, partly through the rooms of the old building, from the sixties to the nineties.

JUGENDKULTUREN

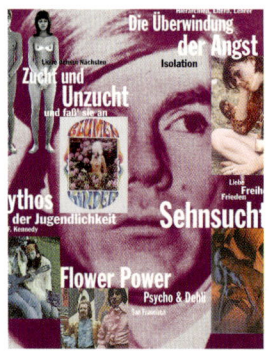  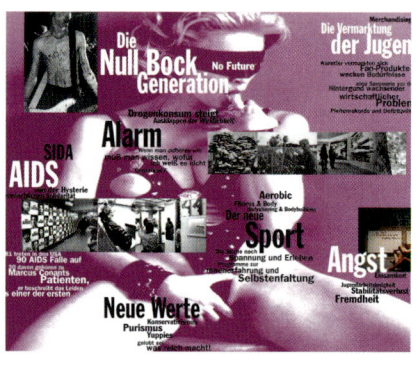 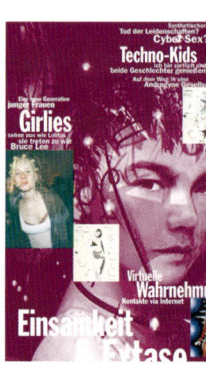

VIEWS OF THE ENCYCLOPAEDIC SHELVES "I"
ANSICHTEN DER ENZYKLOPÄDISCHEN REGALE „ICH"

Die Ausstellung war auf Schauen angelegt, weniger auf Lesen und Belehrung. Sie vermittelte vor allem Bilder, bewegte und statische, und natürlich Musik, jenes Medium, über das sich in den nachwachsenden Generationen seit Jahrzehnten die Gruppenzugehörigkeit definierte. Durch die lange Toreinfahrt erreichte man den Hof, der durch die Vorgaben der beiden Grazer Architekten eine leicht verwirrende „backstage"-Anmutung erhielt, was jedoch neugierig machte, vor die „Kulissen" zu schauen.

Der Zugang zur eigentlichen Ausstellung, die langsam und bedächtig oder schneller und überblicksmäßig zu begehen war, lag im Hintergrund des Hofes, von zwei leuchtenden Pfeilern angezeigt. Durch einen schmalen gebogenen Gang, der geschickt als Schallschleuse gestaltet war, geriet man unversehens in den ersten Stimmungsraum, der die sechziger Jahre thematisierte, und wurde von Musik- und Filmsequenzen aus dieser Zeit umfangen: Bonnie and Clyde von Schüssen durchsiebt, Charles Bronson unter der in die Stirn gezogenen Hutkrempe hervorglosend, ein erstaunlich junger Sean Connery, der den James-Bond-Mythos begründet, sowie Peter Fonda und Denis Hopper auf ihren „bikes". Manch anderes verwies in kürzesten „inserts" auf die Stimmung der endsechziger Jahre, jener Zeit des Aufbrechens ohne klares Ziel, doch mit überzeugter Absage an das Bestehende. Die visuelle und akustische Einstimmung mit Film, Dia, Licht und Ton nahm die Besucher gefangen, bis sich nach wenigen Minuten der unregelmäßig gerundete Raum aufhellte und ein projizierter Lichtpfeil zum Ausgang zeigte, wo eine weitere Schallschleuse zu einer gewundenen Rampe überleitete, an der entlang die erste thematische Vertiefung mit Objekten, Bildern, Namen, Schlag- und Stichworten zu sehen war. Nach der akustisch-visuellen „Druckkammer" des Stimmungsraumes kam es hier in räumlicher Hinsicht zur Entspannung. Die Rampe schraubte sich in die Höhe, es gab Blickbeziehungen in den Hofbereich hinunter, so dass nach dem „input" auf der Gefühlsebene die Orientierung wieder möglich wurde.

Die Materialisierung von Rampen und Raumhüllen erfolgte unter extremen „low cost"-Bedingungen: ein Handlauf aus dünnem Rundstahl, Geländerfüllungen aus roh belassenen Hartfaserplatten, die der Krümmung folgten. Auf der ersten Obergeschoßebene erreichten die Besucher den nächsten Stimmungsraum, der den siebziger Jahren galt. Die unregelmäßigen Volumen dieser Projektions- und Schallräume waren innenseitig teils akustisch ausgekleidet, teils als

The exhibition was based primarily on looking and less on reading or instructing. It communicated basically in terms of images, whether moving or static and, of course, music the medium by means of which identification with a certain group was, for decades, established for following generations. Through a long driveway you reached the courtyard which, as a result of the constraints imposed by the two Graz architects' design had a slightly confusing, "back-stage" feel to it which made one curious to take a look behind the "sets."

The approach to the exhibition itself, which could be traversed slowly and thoughtfully or more rapidly taking just a quick survey, was at the rear of the courtyard, indicated by two illuminated piers. Along a narrow curved corridor cleverly designed as a sound lock one entered unawares the first "mood space" that dealt thematically with the sixties where one was surrounded by music and film clips from this period: Bonnie and Clyde riddled by gunshots, Charles Bronson glaring from under the brim of a hat pulled down over his forehead, an amazingly youthful Sean Connery who established the James Bond myth as well as Peter Fonda and Dennis Hopper on their bikes. Further material referred, in very brief inserts, to the mood of the late sixties: a time of revolution without a definite goal but with a convinced rejection of the status quo. The visual and acoustic establishment of mood by means of film, slides, light and sound captivated the visitor until, after a few minutes, the irregularly rounded space was lit up and a projected arrow of light indicated the exit. From here a further sound lock led to a curving ramp along which the first thematic elaboration using objects, images, names, key words and catch phrases could be viewed. Following the acoustic and visual "pressure chamber" in the mood space, here, in spatial terms, a certain relaxation took place. The ramp wound upwards, visual relationships to the courtyard below were set up making it possible to orient oneself again.

The materials for the ramps and spatial shells were selected under the constraints imposed by an extremely low-cost budget: a hand-rail made from a thin round steel section, the panels for the balustrade made of untreated fibreboard which followed the curve. At first floor level the visitors reached the next mood space devoted to the seventies. The irregular volume of this sound and projection room was lined internally, partly with

 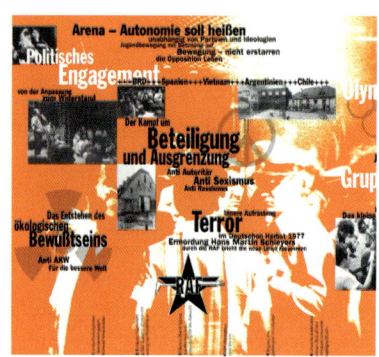 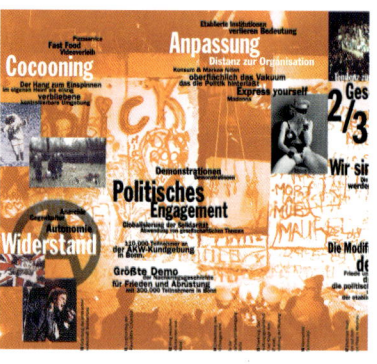 

VIEWS OF THE ENCYCLOPAEDIC SHELVES "WE"
ANSICHTEN DER ENZYKLOPÄDISCHEN REGALE „WIR"

Bildwände neutral geweißt. Außen war der gespachtelte Gipskarton dagegen farbig gestrichen. Damit konnte das „backstage-image" des Rohbaus relativiert werden, die großen klaren Farbflächen traten zeichenhaft strukturierend hervor und forderten das Besucherinteresse heraus.

Die Vertiefungsinstallationen und -collagen wurden nach den Begriffen „Ich", „Wir", „Hülle", „Sinne" und „Bildung" gegliedert. Bilder und Schlagworte aus Print- und elektronischen Medien, an die man sich vielleicht erinnerte oder die denen glichen, an die man sich zu erinnern meinte, riefen Bedeutungszusammenhänge auf. Einzelne Kultobjekte gaben Signale aus der jüngsten, bereits vom Vergessen erfaßten Vergangenheit, die bekanntlich rascher veraltet als das, was Jahrzehnte davor geschah.

Im weiteren Verlauf erreichte man einen mit psychedelisch weichen Formen ausgestalteten Entspannungsraum, der nicht zuletzt das Abhandenkommen von Inhalten und die Entpolitisierung Ende der siebziger Jahre symbolisierte, was sich dann am Anfang der achtziger Jahre in diffusen Gewaltaktionen entlud. Den Vertiefungszonen waren immer auch Kunstwerke aus dem entsprechenden Jahrzehnt zugeordnet. Naturgemäß standen dabei steirische Künstler und Werke aus den Sammlungen des Landes im Vordergrund. Bei der angestrebten Vermittlung der Zeitstimmung war Kunst im Original als Gegengewicht zum hohen Anteil reproduzierter Bilder unabdingbar.

Die Form des Stimmungsraumes für die achtziger Jahre war nicht mehr rund, sondern gezackt, und ein spiegelmäßig verdoppelter Arnold Schwarzenegger ballerte sich ohne ersichtlichen Grund durch eine Serie Gewaltszenen. Nach soviel filmischem Pulverdampf diente eine lange Rampe über dem Hof dazu, frische Luft zu schnappen, danach konnten die Besucher den Stimmungsraum der neunziger Jahre und eine komprimierte Technodisco besuchen.

Zum Ausklang folgte eine Serie offener Klangkabinen in neutralem Weiß, in denen Beispiele nebeneinander existierender zeitgenössischer Musikstile zu hören waren. Nach der kompakten Bilderflut wirkten die in der klösterlich anmutenden Raumstruktur vermittelten Inhalte umso einprägsamer. Ihre Leere machte deutlich, wie sehr die drei vergangenen Jahrzehnte von visuellen Medien mit ihrer Bilderflut beherrscht worden waren, wie anspruchsvoll es dagegen ist, ein Dutzend Musikstile nur mit dem Gehör zu differenzieren.

acoustic panels, partly with neutral white display surfaces, externally the rendered plasterboard was colourfully painted. This led to a modification of the "backstage" image of the half-completed building, the large, clear areas of colour emerged as a symbolic structuring element that provoked the visitors' attention.

The installations and collages intended to deepen one's perception were broken up according to the terms "I," "We," "Shell," "Meaning" and "Education." Images and phrases from the print and electronic media which, perhaps, you remembered or which were similar to those you believed you remembered, provoked associations of meaning, individual cult objects emitted signals from the very recent past already in the process of being forgotten. As everyone knows the recent past dates more quickly than what happened decades ago.

In the further course of the exhibition you reached a relaxation space with soft psychedelic forms, symbolising, not least of all, the loss of content and de-politicisation in the late seventies which then exploded in the eighties in diffuse acts of violence. The areas of intensification were, in each case, allotted art works from the appropriate decade. Naturally Styrian artists and works from the Styrian State Collection stood in the foreground. In the attempt to communicate the specific feeling of the time, original art formed a counter-balance to the high proportion of reproduced images.

The mood room for the eighties was not round but jagged. Arnold Schwarzenegger, multiplied by mirrors, banged his way without apparent reason through a series of violent scenes. After such an amount of cinematic gun-smoke a long ramp across the courtyard allowed one to take some fresh air, the visitors could then move on to the nineties mood space and a condensed techno-disco. The finale was provided by a series of open sound booths in neutral white in which examples of co-existent contemporary music styles could be heard. After the compact flood of images this material, communicated in an almost monastic spatial structure, seemed particularly effective. The emptiness made clear the extent to which the last three decades have been dominated by the visual media and their flood of images and how demanding it is, in comparison, to distinguish between a dozen styles of music using merely one's sense of hearing.

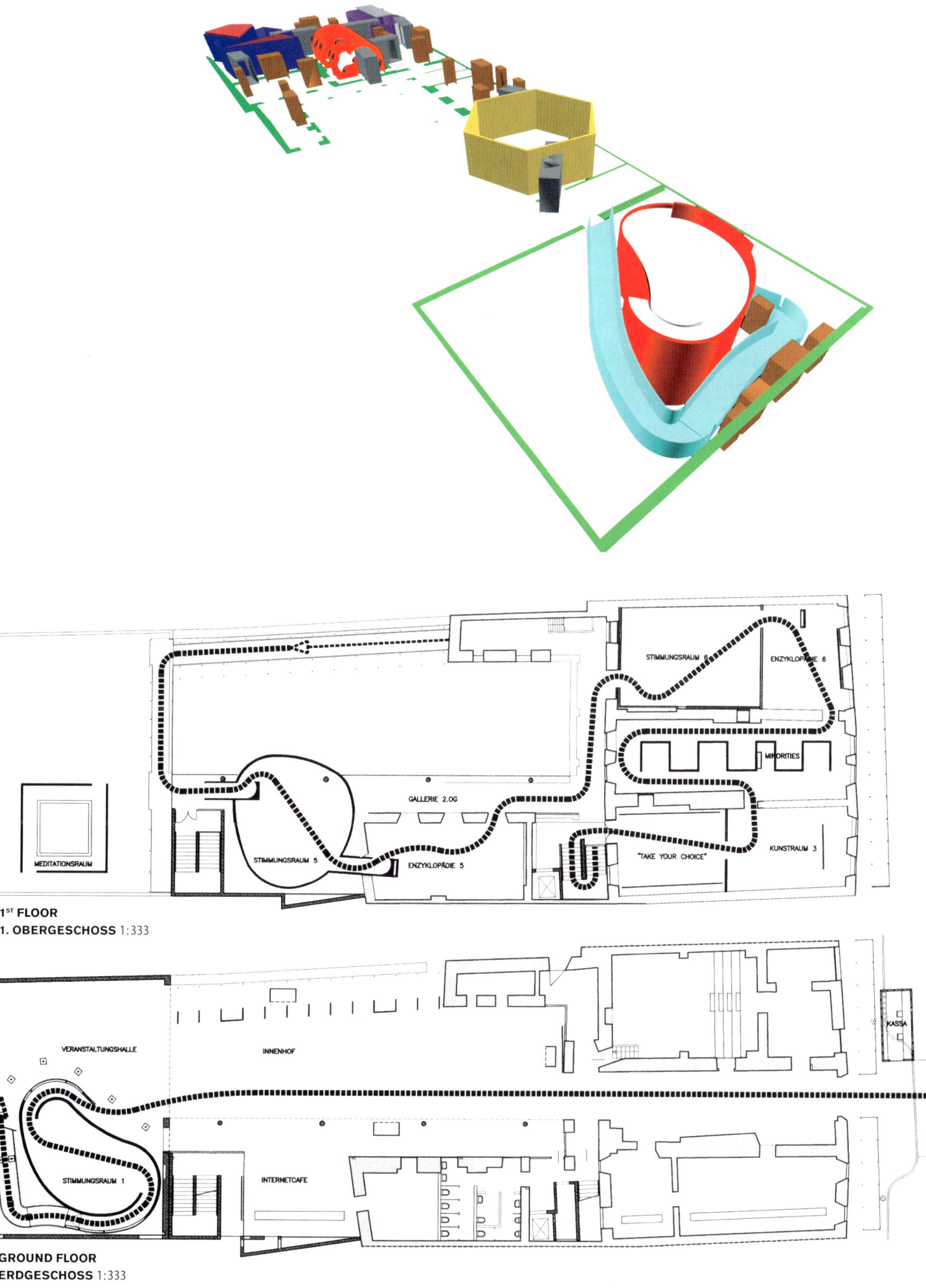

SHELL AND SPACE IN-BETWEEN

HÜLLE UND ZWISCHENRAUM

Aus dem Verhältnis von Hülle, innenliegenden Volumen und umfaßten Zwischenräumen entwickeln die folgenden Projekte ihre Spezifizität. Inhaltlich bleibt die Hülle als Schnittstelle Teil der architektonischen Konstruktion: ihre Funktion folgt der Form. Die innere Fassade entspricht der äußeren, als Oberfläche ist sie Träger zusätzlicher Funktionen wie auch Vermittler unterschiedlicher Stimmungen. Sie ermöglicht wechselnde Durchsicht, Transluzenz und Opazität.

Beim Projekt WIFI St. Pölten wird eigentlich ein Terrain durch die Umhüllung begrenzt. In diesem sind frei disponierte Volumen implantiert, innere Außenräume und äußere Innenräume umfasst. Der von der Hülle beschriebene Zwischenraum kann damit sowohl der Außen- wie der Innenwelt angehören. Durch das Einlegen changierender Zwischenschichten, das Einsetzen unterschiedlicher Materialien in und an eine Grundstruktur aus ein- bis mehrschichtigen Profilbaugläsern wird eine Vielfalt in der Einheit der Umhüllung angestrebt. Zum Beispiel wirken eingespannte Schlauchgewebe, deren inneres Algenwachstum den Schleier verändert, auch als Kollektor und Sonnenfilter.

Das Projekt ZMF Graz entwickelt einen Monolith aus den Kontextbedingungen. Aus dieser so objektivierten Form werden die Zwischenräume herausgeschnitten, der Körper wird perforiert. Die äußere poröse Hülle ist abgesetzt, sie bezieht ihre Energie aus der Art, wie sie die innere Form umspannt. Das vorgespannte Gewebe fungiert als Puffer und eine Art osmotischer Haut mit flächigen Kiemen. R.L.

SHELL AND SPACE IN-BETWEEN

The following projects derive their specific qualities from the relationship between the shell, internal volumes and enclosed spaces in-between. In terms of content the shell, as an interface, remains part of the architectural construction. Its function follows its form. The inner facade corresponds with the outer, as a surface it is the bearer of additional functions and mediator of different moods, it allows varying degrees of transparency, translucence and opacity.

In the WIFI St. Pölten project a terrain is defined by the shell. Freely disposed volumes are implanted in this shell, internal outdoor spaces and external interior spaces are contained. The space in-between that is described by the shell can thus belong to both the external and internal worlds. By inserting changing intermediate layers and using different materials in and at a basic structure that is made up of one or several layers of profiled construction glass an attempt is made to create variety within the unity of the shell. For example, stretched textile tubing with an internal growth of algae which changes the nature of the veil also functions as a collector and sun filter.

The ZMF project in Graz develops a monolith from contextual circumstances. The spaces in-between are cut out of this objectified form, the block is perforated. The external porous shell is detached, it derives its energy from the way in which it stretches around the inner form. The stretched material functions both as a buffer and a kind of osmotic skin with surface gills. R.L.

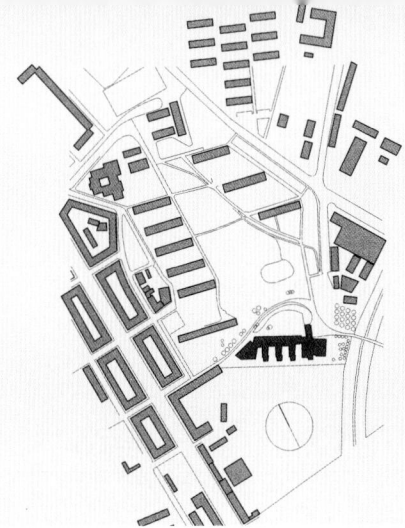

Hauptschule Absberggasse 50
Wien–Favoriten, 1994

Favoriten, der zehnte Wiener Gemeindebezirk, wird mehrseitig von Geleisebündeln umschnürt und von der Südosttangente durchschnitten. Nahe dieser Stadtautobahn endet ein Stadterweiterungsgebiet aus den sechziger Jahren mit zwölfgeschoßigen Scheibenhäusern, dessen Planung auf Roland Rainer zurückgeht. An der Südspitze lockert sich die Bebauung und lässt Raum für einen kleinen Park. Das neu hinzugefügte Bauwerk einer zwölfklassigen Hauptschule für zehn- bis sechzehnjährige Schülerinnen und Schüler bildet dessen Abschluss. Der lange ostwest-gerichtete, dreigeschoßige Basistrakt enthält die Bibliothek, Sammlungsräume, Sonderklassen und die Räume der Direktion. An seinen Enden docken Spezialräume an: Werkräume und Schulküche im Westen, im Osten die Mensa und die zwei übereinander angeordneten Turnsäle, die mit ihrer karg instrumentierten Flanke zur nahen Autobahn abschirmen. Dazwischen reihen sich kammartig drei kurze Klassentrakte mit je vier Klassen, jeweils zwei pro Geschoß, die einen dazwischengeschalteten Gruppenraum einschließen. Ein vierter, längerer Riegel mit sechs Klassenzimmern lagert hochgestemmt quer über dem Basistrakt, zum Park hin frech auf einer Zeile schlanker Rundstützen und einer einzelnen V-Stütze aufgestelzt, als Signal und Wetterschutz für den Eingang. Dieser nach Westen befensterte Trakt enthält die am Nachmittag genutzten Freizeitklassen. Die Erschließung im Erdgeschoß erscheint als lange, hallenartige Folge von Engnissen und Weitungen, zoniert von den unregelmäßigen Volumen der Bibliothek und des Mehrzweckraums, die sich auch nach außen durch die Fassadenebene hindurch bemerkbar machen.

Secondary School Absberggasse 50
Vienna–Favoriten, 1994

Favoriten, Vienna's tenth district, is laced on several sides by bunches of train tracks and severed by the South-East Tangent. Close to this city motorway an urban expansion area from the sixties terminates with twelve-storey panel system buildings, their planning going back to Roland Rainer. At its southern point the development loosens up allowing space for a small park. This newly added building, a twelve-class secondary school for ten to sixteen year old pupils of both sexes, forms the termination of the development. The east-west oriented, three-storey basic tract contains the library, rooms for collections of teaching aids, special purpose rooms and the school administration. Special rooms are attached at the ends: rooms for crafts and the school kitchen at the western end, at the east the lunch room and the two gyms placed one above the other, their severely designed flanks screening the nearby motorway. Between the ends three short classroom wings are arranged like the teeth on a comb each containing four classrooms, two on each floor enclosing a group room. A fourth, somewhat longer block with six classrooms is carried on struts above the basic tract, towards the park it is cheekily supported by a row of slender circular columns and a single, V-shaped strut and serving to signal the entrance and provide protection from inclement weather. This tract, its main windows facing west, contains the free-time rooms which are used in the afternoons. At ground floor level the circulation is a sequence of narrower and wider spaces zoned by the irregular volumes of the library and multi-purpose room which draw attention to themselves externally by penetrating the facade plane.

ABSBERGGASSE

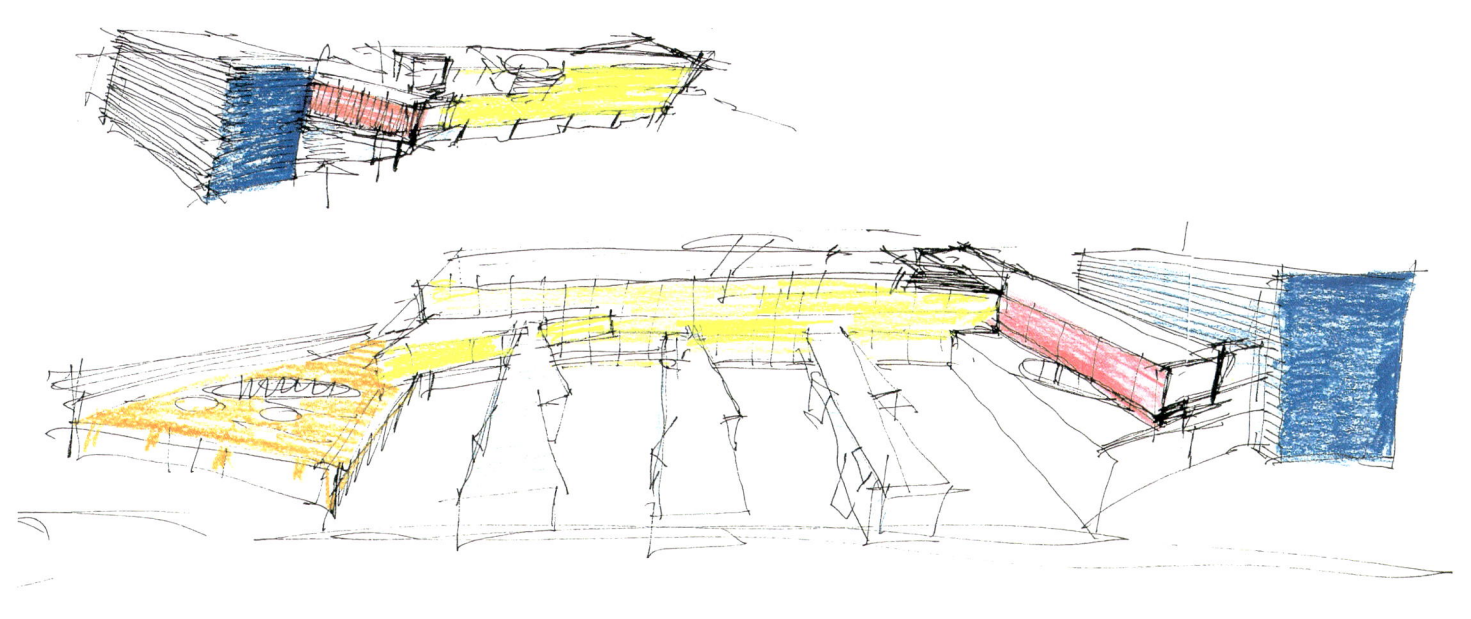

Dem Basistrakt ist nordseitig der Turnplatz vorgelagert. Er wird von einem langen bogenförmigen Teich umfangen, der den Park vom Schulbereich zaunlos abgrenzt. Nach Süden, zu den offenen Gartenhöfen zwischen den Klassentrakten spannen sich hohe Glaswände, vor denen die Vertikalverbindungen wie Stiege und Lift platziert sind und lebendiges Tropengrün hochgezogen wird. Von dieser abwechslungsreichen Allgemeinfläche führen Stichgänge mit Garderoben vor die Klassenzimmer. In den Obergeschoßen sind die Gänge schlanker, dennoch stoßen auch hier die Klassentrakte mit einer flachen Rundung weich in den Längsraum des Korridors vor. Hinter diesen Gelenkpunkten liegen die Toiletten – voll verglast der Waschraum bei den Buben; sollte einer dagegen bei den Mädchen durchs Türfenster kiebitzen, erblickt er im Frisierspiegel sein eigenes Gesicht.

Ein spezielles räumliches Erlebnis bietet jener Gang, der die Freizeitklassen im „Wolkenbügel" erschließt: Er liegt außen an der blauen Scheibe über dem Eingang, die von der V-Stütze getragen wird. Er ist als verglaster Laubengang konzipiert und verläuft den Kronen der nahen Parkbäume entlang, deren Laub und Geäst die Morgensonne filtert. Dieser spielerische Umgang mit den Erschließungsräumen, die auch Plätze und Bereiche zum Verweilen aufweisen, macht die Tagesschule zu einem prinzipiell angenehmen Aufenthaltsort. Wechselnde Zonierungen mit gemütlichen Nischen bei guter Übersicht und Erschließungsalternativen machen aus dem gegliederten Bauwerk eine kleine Stadt – wenn auch nur auf Zeit, so doch für die gesamte Hauptschulzeit.

Beim Flanieren durchs Haus stößt man auf zahlreiche einfühlsam festgelegte Details: da eine kleine Bank, dort ein Fenster für einen überraschenden Ausblick, der vor allem im obersten Geschoß weit über die Stadt reicht. Auf den Glastüren und Scheiben der transparenten Erdgeschoßbereiche finden sich eingeätzt Textfragmente aus Liedern, die zur Jugendkultur der vergangenen drei Jahrzehnte gehören. Rüdiger Lainer und sein Team nehmen die Schülerinnen und Schüler, die dem Kindesalter entwachsen, aber doch noch nicht erwachsen sind, ernst. Mit diesem Schulgebäude bieten sie eine temporäre Heimstatt an. Damit ist schon sehr viel erreicht. Alles weitere liegt bei den Lehrern und Schülern.

Die Farbgebung nach einem Konzept des Wiener konkreten Malers Oskar Putz baut auf warme, erdige Lilarot-, Rot-, Rotbraun-, Ocker- und Gelbtöne. Als Kontrapunkte sind einzelne tiefblaue Signale gesetzt, deren Widerschein dann und wann von außen in das weiß gehaltene Innere blitzt. Der Eingangsvorplatz wird von einer Mauerscheibe dominiert, die ein Schriftbild trägt. Ihr Inhalt: das Raum- und Funktionsprogramm einer Hauptschule der neunziger Jahre, ist letztlich mehr Programm als ein alle paar Jahre obsolet werdender ideologischer Sinnspruch. Das Schriftbild verweist darüber hinaus grundsätzlich auf eine Hauptleistung der menschlichen Kultur: Sprache und Schrift – und auf das schulische Angebot, sich im sprachlichen Ausdruck zu qualifizieren: zum Zweck einer guten Verständigung.

The sports area is placed in front of the basic tract on the north side, it is defined by a long, curving pond which separates the park from the school without requiring a fence. Towards the south, facing onto the open garden courtyards between the classroom wings, high glass walls are stretched behind which the vertical connections such as stairs and lifts are placed along with tropical plants striving upwards. Dead-end corridors with lockers in front of the classrooms lead from this varied communal area. On the upper floor the corridors are narrower, but here too the classroom wings protrude into the long main corridor space in the form of a shallow curve. The toilets lie behind these joints, the boys' washroom is entirely glazed, should someone try to spy through the opening in the door to the girls' washroom he is confronted with the reflection of his own face in a hairdresser's mirror.

The corridor leading to the free-time rooms in the "Wolkenbügel" offers a special spatial experience, it lies externally along the blue slab above the entrance that is carried by the V-shaped strut. It is designed as a glazed gallery and extends close to the tops of the trees in the nearby park, their branches and foliage filtering the morning sun. This playful treatment of the circulation system which offers spaces and areas to linger in makes the day school an essentially pleasant place to be. Alternating zonings with cosy niches, an easy comprehensibility, alternative circulation routes make the articulated building a small town, admittedly only for a time but at least for the entire school day.

On strolling through the building you encounter numerous sensitively executed details: a little bench, a window providing a surprising view which, above all on the top floor, extends far across the city. Fragments of song texts from the youth culture of the last three decades are engraved on the glass doors and panels of the transparent ground floor area. Rüdiger Lainer and his team take these boys and girls, emerging from childhood but not yet grown up, seriously. Their school offers a temporary home and this is a considerable achievement. Everything else remains up to the teachers and pupils.

The colour scheme derived from a concept by the Viennese concrete painter, Oskar Putz, is based on warm, earthy lilac-red, red, red-brown, ochre and yellow tones. Individual dark blue signals provide counter points, their reflection occasionally appearing in the white interior. The entrance forecourt is dominated by a wall slab bearing an inscription. It lists the spatial and functional brief of a secondary school in the nineties, this is, in the final analysis, more of a programme than some ideological phrase which becomes obsolete after a few years. The inscription is also an essential indication of one of the main achievements of human culture: language, writing and of the opportunity offered by the school of mastering the art of expressing oneself in order to make oneself understood.

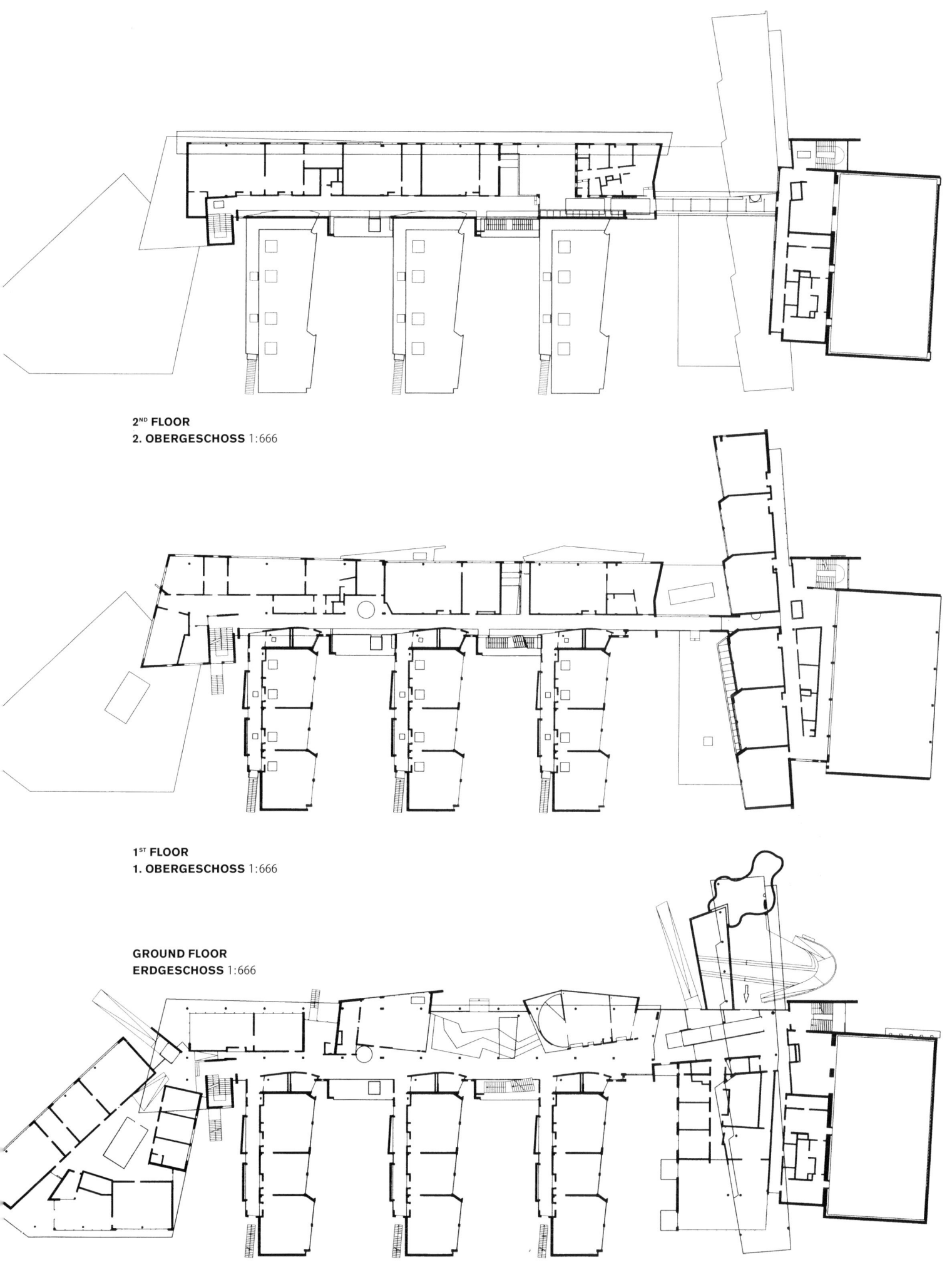

2ND FLOOR
2. OBERGESCHOSS 1:666

1ST FLOOR
1. OBERGESCHOSS 1:666

GROUND FLOOR
ERDGESCHOSS 1:666

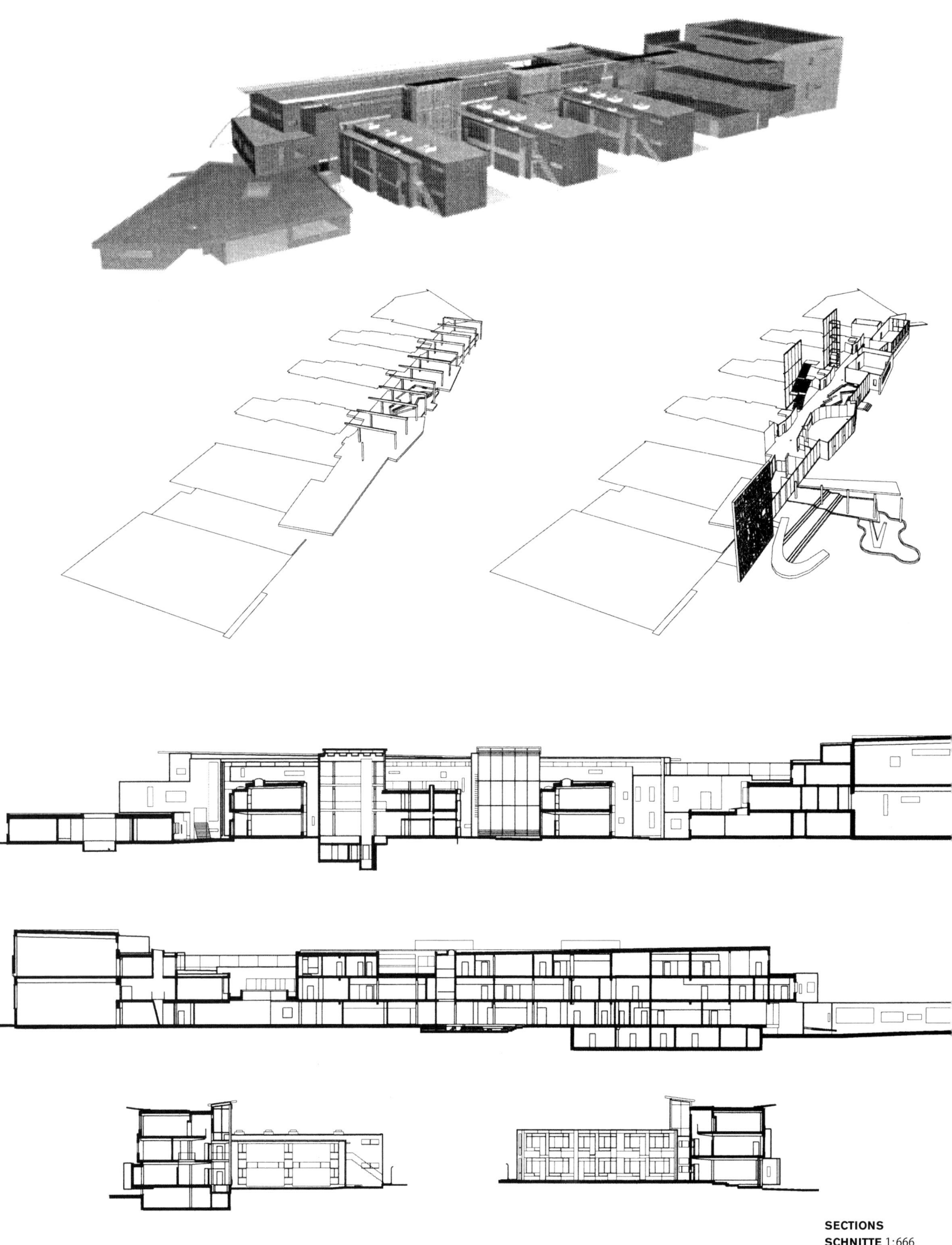

**SECTIONS
SCHNITTE** 1:666

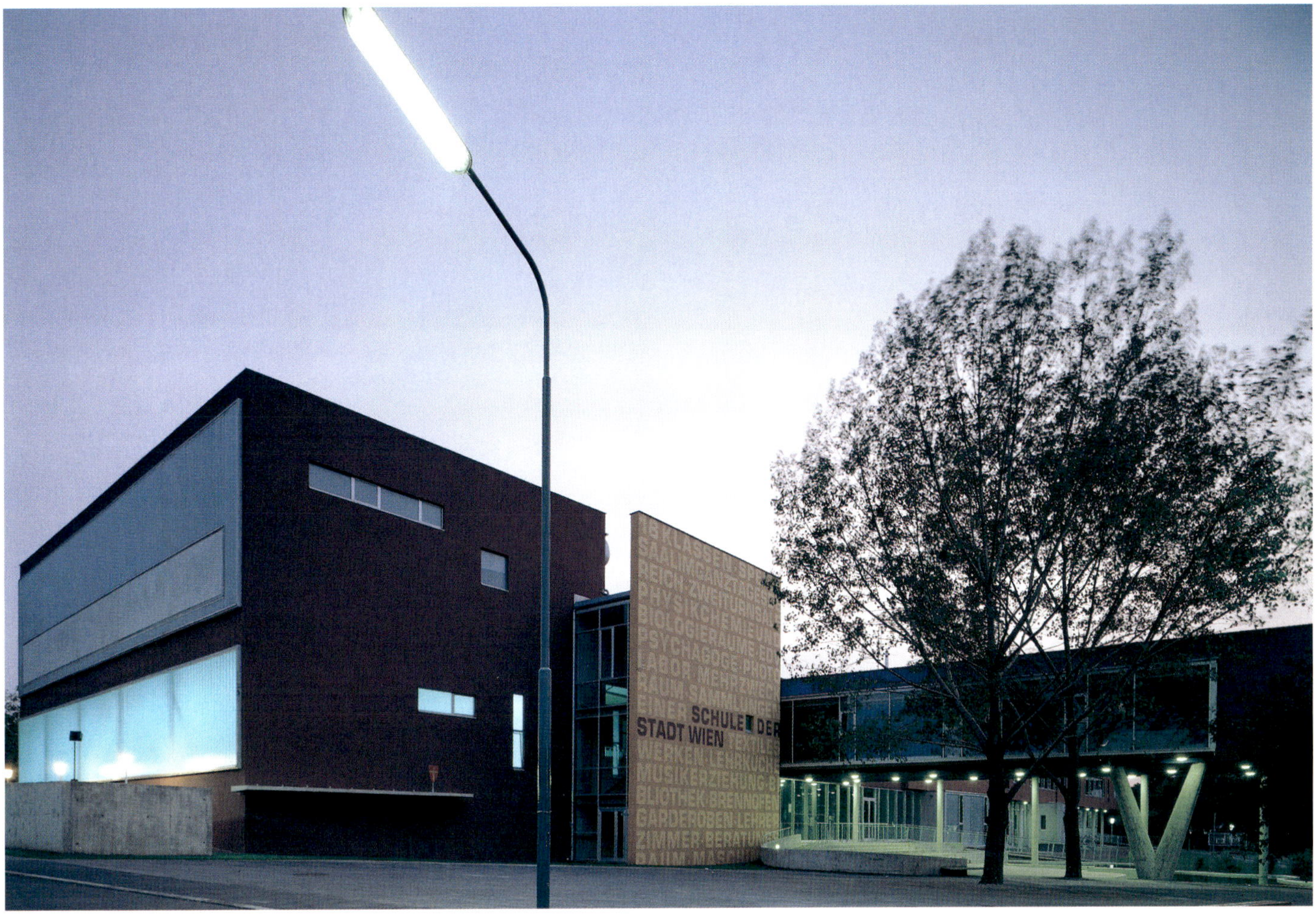
SCHULE DER
STADT WIEN

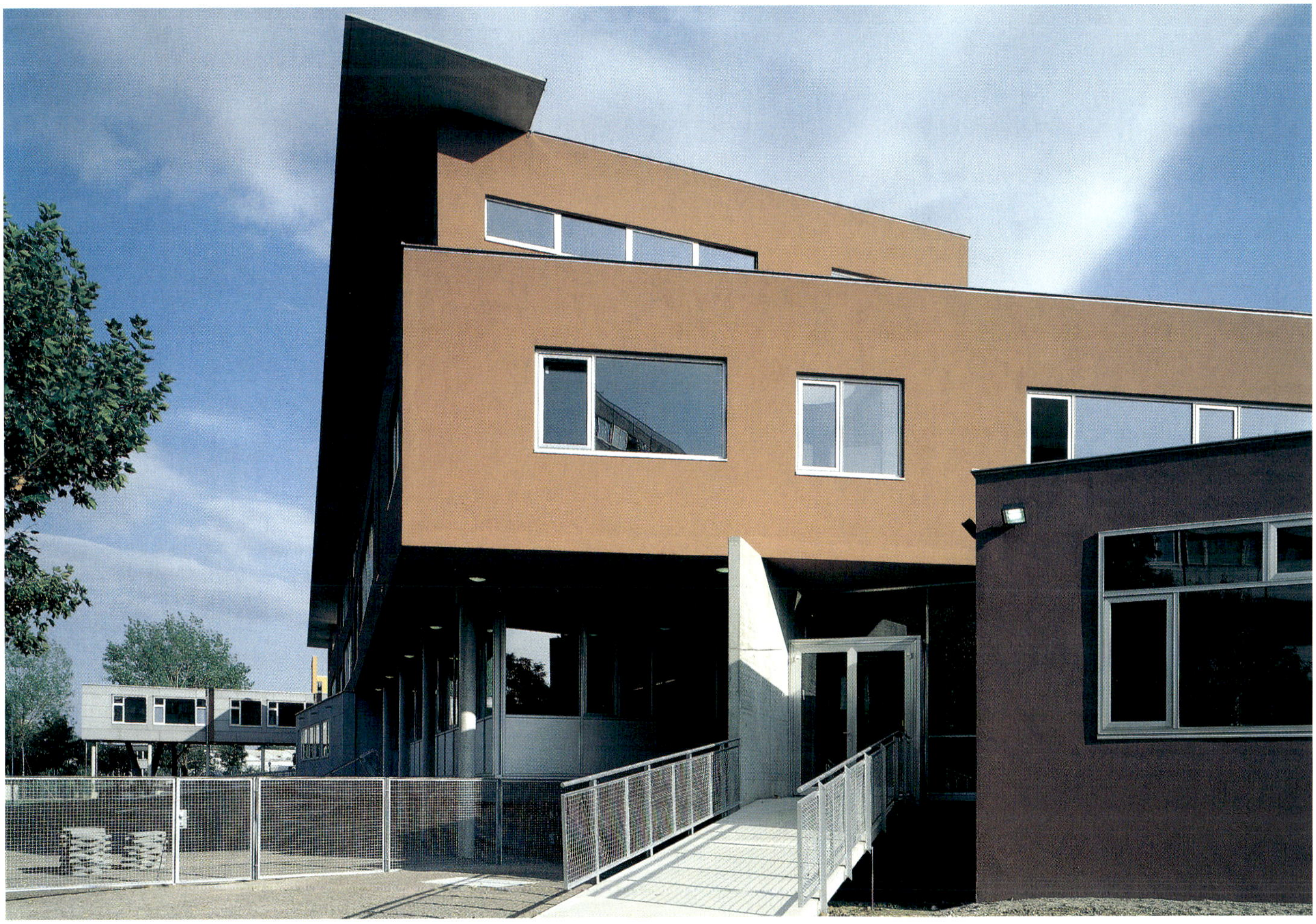

CLASSROOM COURTYARD | KLASSENHOF

COMMON ROOM IN-BETWEEN | GEMEINSAMER ZWISCHENRAUM

READING ROOM | LESERAUM

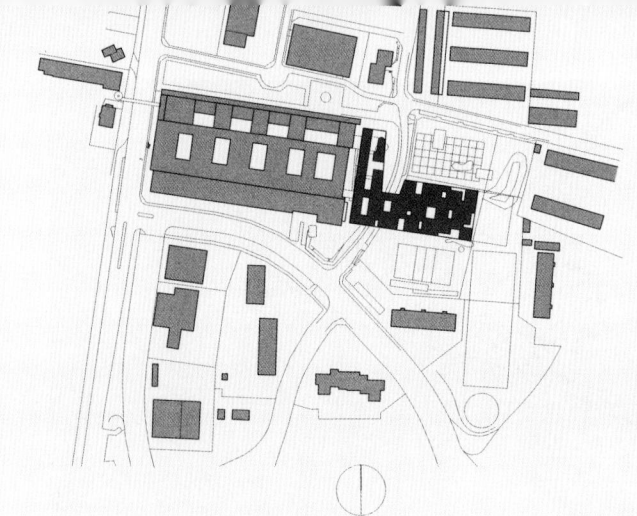

Erweiterungsbau WIFI Wirtschaftsförderungsinstitut St. Pölten, Wettbewerb, 1997

Die ausgedehnte Anlage – entworfen von Karl Schwanzer (1918–75) und 1972 fertiggestellt – weist eine nach außen plastisch gegliederte Form auf. Eine großzügige Leiterstruktur bestimmt den Grundriss. Fünf weiträumige Höfe werden von zwei langgestreckt-parallelen Ganghallen tangential eingeschlossen. Dieser introvertierte Charakter wird vom Vorschlag Rüdiger Lainers für eine Erweiterung aufgenommen, aber in anderer Form umgesetzt. Während der Verwaltungs- und Präsidialbereich mit bescheideneren Gängen und kleineren Höfen an den Bestand anschließt, entwickelt sich der clusterartige Teil mit den Lehrsälen, der auf der östlichen Seite der Steinfeldstraße ansetzt, etwas freier: Die Lehrsäle lösen sich aus der Rahmenstruktur und scheinen in dem von einer Fassaden-„haut" abgesteckten Feld zu „floaten". Die Zwischenräume verlieren ihren Korridorcharakter und variieren von schmalen Durchgängen zu nischenartigen Erweiterungen und offenen Ruhezonen. Diesem locker mit Raumkörpern und Zwischenräumen bestellten Feld werden, unregelmäßig verteilt, begrünte Lichthöfe überlagert, die den Außenraum von oben in den Cluster eindringen lassen. Die Lehrsäle erhalten auf diese Weise, trotz durchgehend gleicher Raumproportionen und innerer Ausstattung, über ihre Stellung im unregelmäßigen Gefüge von Körpern, Zwischenräumen und eingeschnittenen Höfen je einen individuellen Charakter. Zugleich bleibt die Anlage mit einem Dutzend Lehrsälen übersichtlich. Die integrierten Freiräume sind fix überdacht als Wintergärten und für den Sommer öffenbar mit transparentem Foliendach vorgesehen. Einer vorgefertigten Skelettbaustruktur aus Stützen, Scheiben, Trägern und Deckenplatten wird ein standardisiertes, auf drei Elemente reduziertes Fassadensystem für die Höfe eingeschrieben. Für die äußere Hülle ist Gussglas und Profilbauglas vorgesehen. Auf weitgehender Nachhaltigkeit basierende Konzepte werden für Haustechnik und Versorgung vorgeschlagen. Damit stehen bei diesem Projekt die spannende räumliche Vielfalt und eine klug eingesetzte Sparsamkeit in einem für die Architektur produktiven Verhältnis.

Extension to the Chamber of Commerce, St. Pölten Competition Entry, 1997

The extensive complex – designed by Karl Schwanzer (1918–75) – which was completed in 1972 has a form that is externally sculpturally articulated. The plan is based on a large-scale ladder structure. Five extensive courtyards are tangentially contained by two long, parallel corridor-halls. Rüdiger Lainer's suggestion for an extension adopts this introverted character but translates it into a different form. Whereas the administration and president's area with modest corridors and smaller courtyards adjoin the existing building, the cluster-like section with the lecture rooms which starts on the eastern side of Steinfeldstrasse is somewhat more free. The lecture rooms detach themselves from the structure of the frame appearing to float in a field defined within the facade skin. The spaces between lose their corridor character, varying from narrow passageways to niche-like extensions and open, quiet zones. Planted courtyards overlaid upon this field, which is loosely occupied by spatial elements and intervening spaces, allow external space to penetrate the cluster from above. As a result of their position in an irregular mesh that is made up of blocks, the spaces between them and incised courtyards, each of the lecture halls acquires an individual character despite the fact that they all have the same proportions and interior fittings. A further result is that the complex with a dozen lecture halls remains comprehensible. The integrated open spaces are envisaged with roofs that are fixed to create winter gardens or openable in summer with a roof of transparent sheeting. A standardised facade system reduced to three elements is inscribed into a pre-fabricated skeleton structure of supports, panels, beams and roof slabs. Float glass and profiled building glass is to form the external shell. The concepts suggested for building services and supplies were based on the idea of long durability. In this project an interesting spatial variety and an intelligent application of economy combine to establish a relationship that is productive in architectural terms.

WIFI ST. PÖLTEN

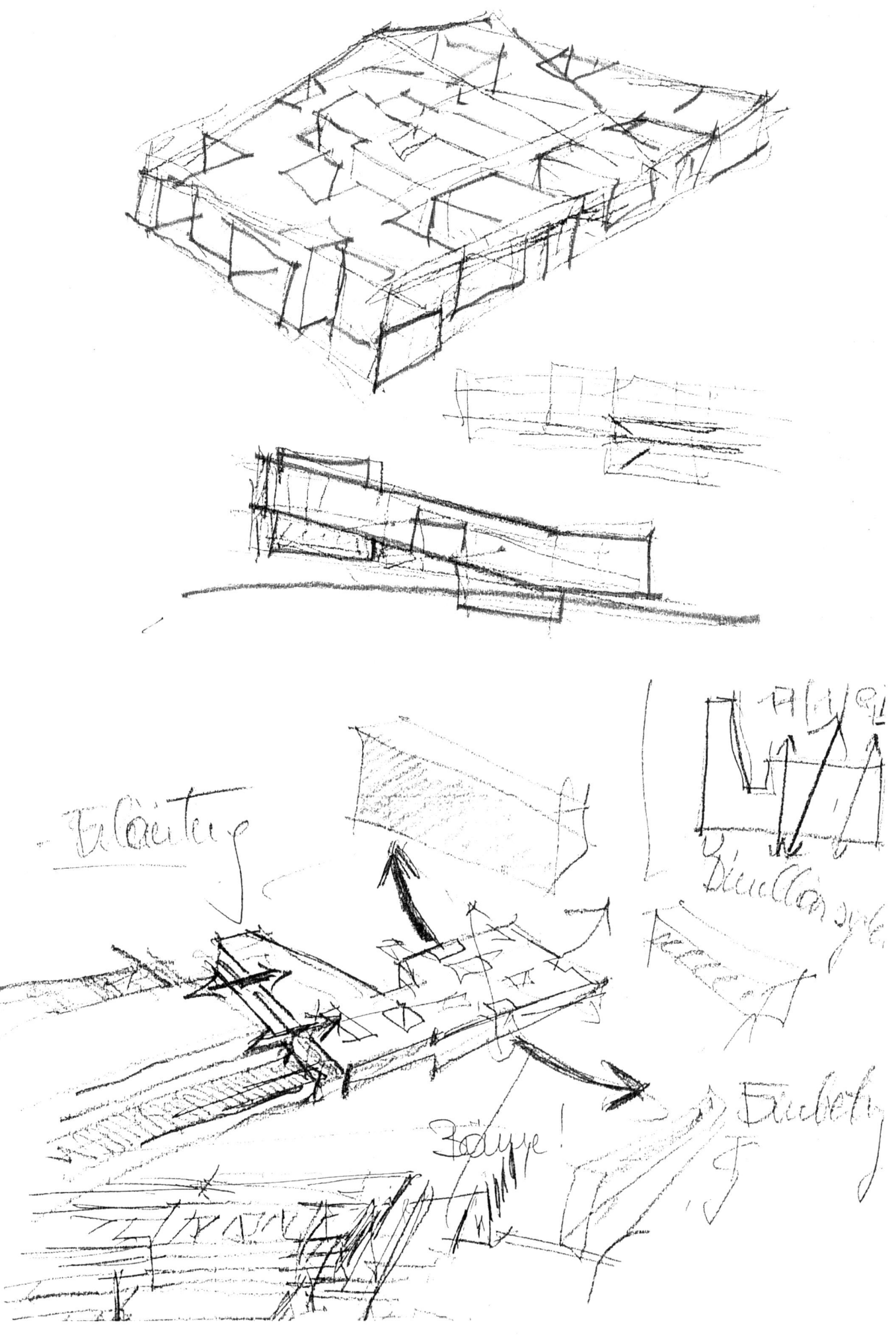

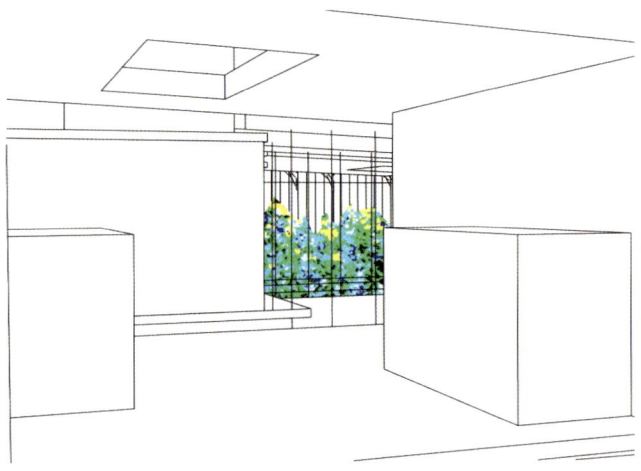

INTERIOR PERSPECTIVE | INNENPERSPEKTIVE

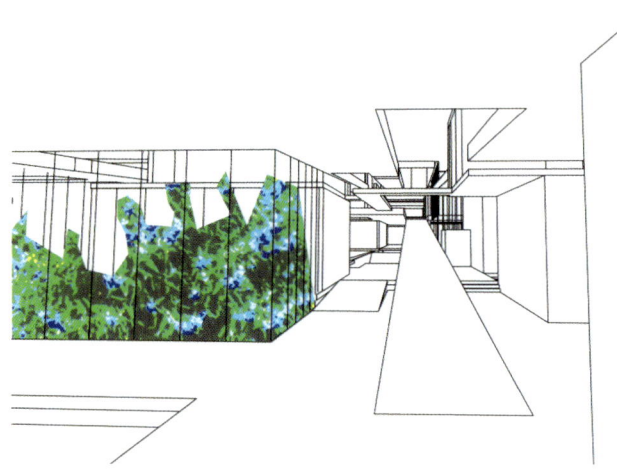

INTERIOR PERSPECTIVE | INNENPERSPEKTIVE

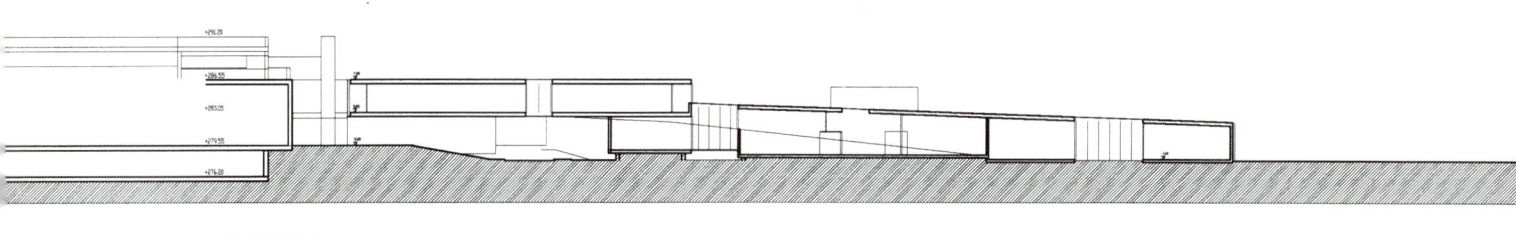

SECTION 1 – 1
SCHNITT 1 – 1 1:333

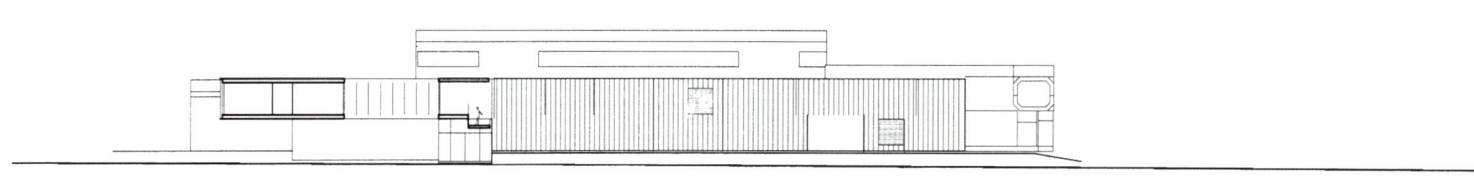

SECTION STEINFELDSTRASSE
SCHNITT STEINFELDSTRASSE 1:333

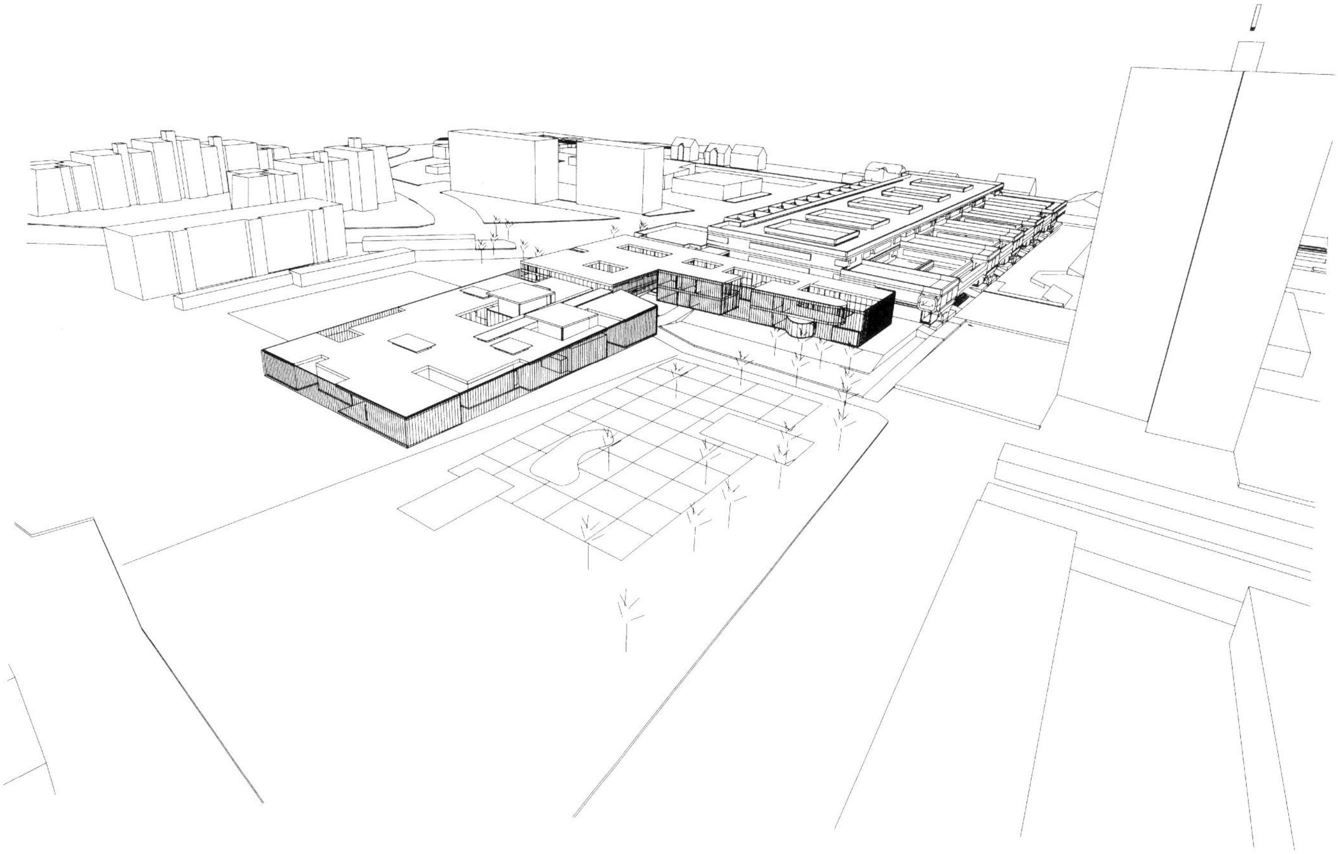

PERSPECTIVE
PERSPEKTIVE

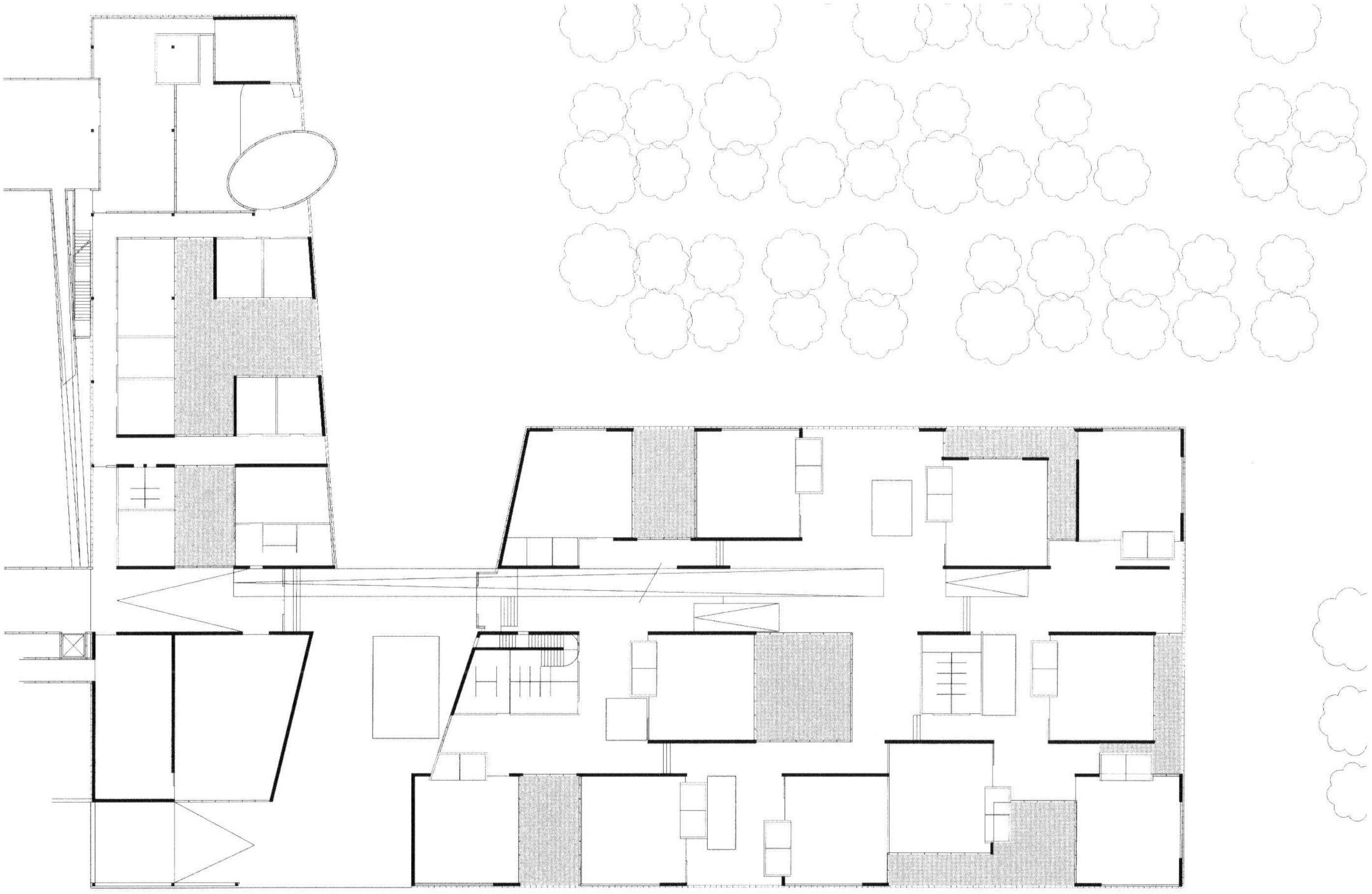

LEVEL 0
EBENE 0 1:333

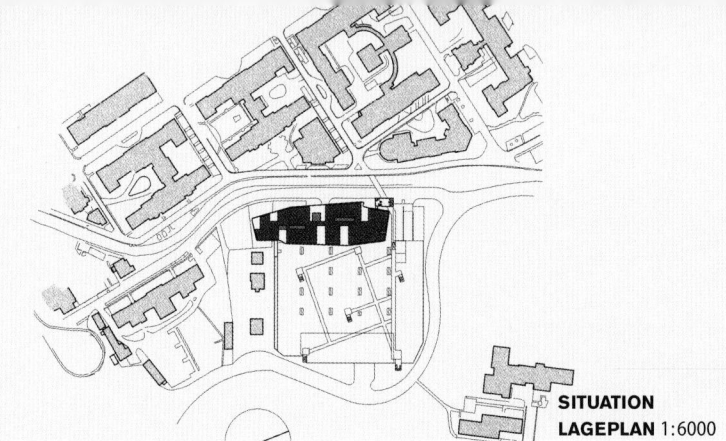

SITUATION
LAGEPLAN 1:6000

ZMF Zentrum für Medizinische Grundlagenforschung
Graz, Wettbewerb, 1998

Die Anlage des Grazer Landeskrankenhauses folgt dem Pavillonprinzip mit H-förmig angeordneten, nach den Himmelsrichtungen orientierten Trakten. Der östlich, auf der anderen Seite der Stiftingtalstraße anschließende Bauplatz für das Forschungszentrum wird von einer Schleife des Stiftingbachs eingefasst. Der Wettbewerbsentwurf für den Neubau löst sich aus der Rasterbindung und nimmt mit seiner Hauptrichtung Bezug auf die topographischen Elemente der Nachbarschaft und auf den Straßenverlauf, der bereits die benachbarte Kante des Krankenhausclusters beeinflusst hat. Die Großform des Baukörpers wirkt wie vom Wind erodiert, und tatsächlich fanden Versuche im Windkanal statt, um den aus Nordosten oder Südwesten in Talrichtung wehenden Wind für die Gebäudelüftung zu nutzen. Der unregelmäßigen Außenform, die durch eine von innen durchsichtige, von außen schleierartig gespannte Kunststoffmembran definiert wird, ist längs eine Erschließungshauptachse eingeschrieben, während die Zugänge zu den einzelnen Funktionsbereichen gleichsam mäandrierend erfolgen. Mehrere Lichthöfe sind in den Baukörper eingeschnitten, um die Arbeitsplätze mit natürlichem Licht zu versorgen. In diesen Lichthöfen sollte mit Begrünung und Bewässerung ein angenehmes Mikroklima erzeugt werden, so dass auch Fenster geöffnet werden könnten. Zwei weitere, im Kernbereich eingesetzte innere Lufträume dienen der visuellen Verbindung in Vertikalrichtung. Durch Überlagerung dieser verschiedenen räumlich-strukturalen Prinzipien entsteht hinter dem Schleier der Fassade ein dreidimensionaler Cluster, in den die Funktionsbereiche in einer logischen Ordnung eingeschrieben sind. Die Vielfalt der räumlichen Konstellationen und die zumindest zweiseitigen Erschließungen verleihen dem Forschungszentrum den Charakter eines kleinen urbanen Quartiers mit dem Zusatz der vertikalen Entwicklung. Mit diesem Entwurf wurde von einer starren Reihung und Funktionalisierung der Arbeitsräume Abstand genommen. Vielmehr folgt das Konzept im Sinne eines binnenstädtebaulichen Ansatzes den Erfahrungen, die bei der Planung der inneren Organisation von Wohnanlagen in den frühen neunziger Jahren gewonnen wurden.

ZMF Center for Basic Medical Research
Graz, Competition Entry, 1998

The complex of the Graz Federal State Hospital which is based on the pavilion principle has H-shaped tracts facing towards the principal points of the compass. The site for the research center, which lies towards the east on the other side of the Stiftingtalstrasse, is defined by a loop of the Stifting stream. The competition design for the new building frees itself from the established grid, its principal axis refers to topographical elements in the surroundings and to the line taken by the street which also influenced the neighbouring edge of the hospital cluster. The major form of the building seems as if it had been eroded by wind and, in fact, tests were carried out in a wind canal in order to exploit the breezes, which blow along the valley from the north-east or south-west, for the ventilation of the building. The irregular external shape, defined by a plastic membrane that is internally transparent and externally stretched like a veil, is inscribed along a main circulation axis whereas the approaches to the individual functional areas are meandering. Several courtyards are incised into the building to provide the work places with natural light. It is intended to create a pleasant micro-climate in these courtyards through the use of planting and water so that the windows facing onto them can be opened. Two further internal voids positioned in the core area serve to establish visual contact in the vertical dimension. The overlaying of different spatial structural principles creates a three-dimensional cluster behind the veil of the facade in which the functional zones are inscribed in a logical order. The variety of the spatial constellations and the access from (at least) two sides lend the research center the character of a small urban district with the additional quality of vertical development. In this design a departure was made from a rigid arrangement and mere functionalism of the work-rooms. The concept, much in the manner of an inner city approach, is derived from experiences acquired in planning the internal organisation of housing blocks in the early nineties.

ZMF GRAZ

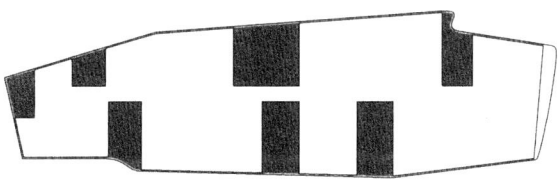

RELATIONSHIP TO OPEN SPACE
Visual; functional – natural ventilation; use of the specific micro-climate
BEZÜGE ZUM OFFENEN RAUM
Visuell; funktionell – natürliche Lüftung; Nutzung des spezifischen Mikroklimas

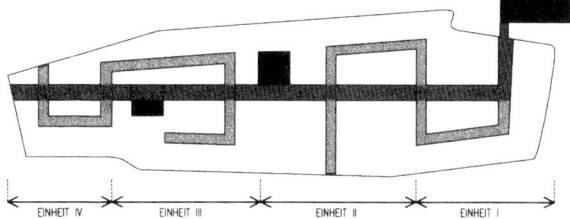

ROUTE SYSTEM
Linking the individual functional areas to form compact clusters
WEGEFÜHRUNG
Zusammenfassen der einzelnen Funktionsbereiche zu kompakten „Clusters"

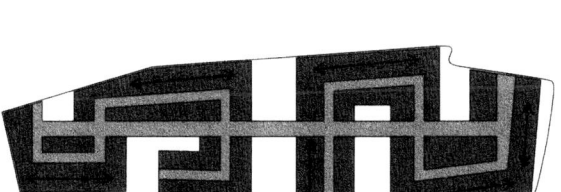

EXTENDED DEVELOPMENT
More spaces with natural light and ventilation: The serial nature and flexibility of the spaces
VERLÄNGERTE ABWICKLUNG
Mehr Räume an natürlichem Licht und Luft; Module: Serialität und Flexibilität der Räume

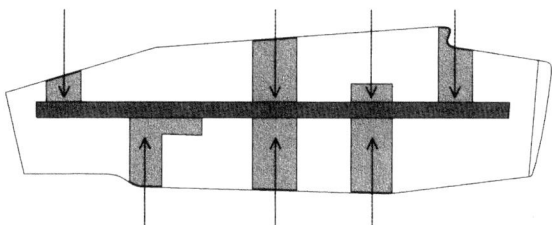

SPINE
Natural lighting and ventilation; the possibility of experiencing horizontality and verticality
RÜCKGRAT
Natürliche Belichtung und Belüftung; Orientierbarkeit; Erlebbarkeit von Horizontalität und Vertikalität

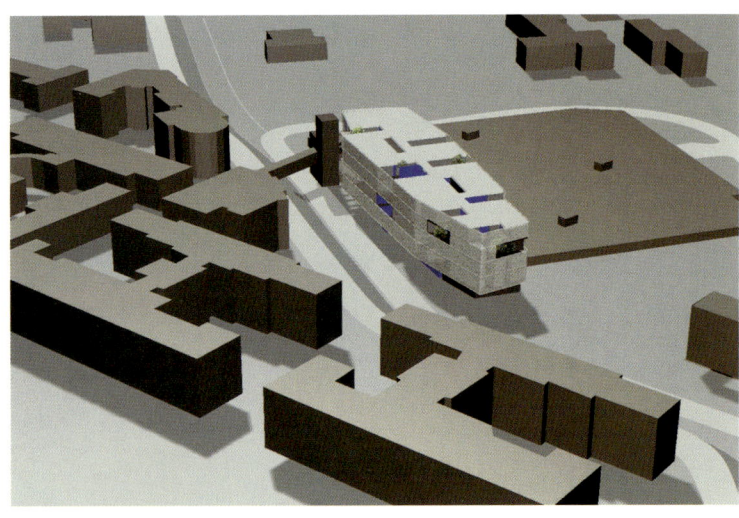
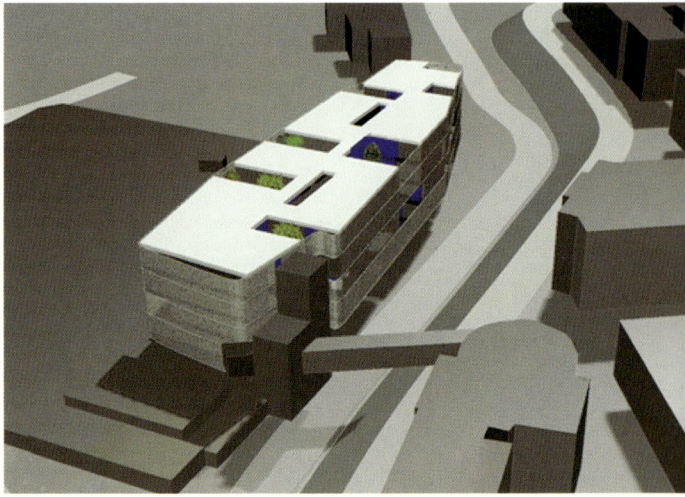

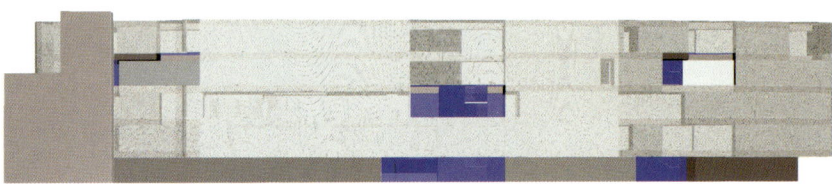
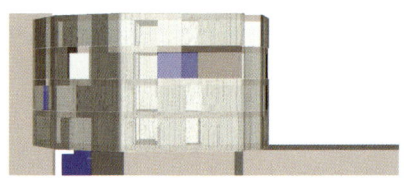

ELEVATION
ANSICHT 1:1000

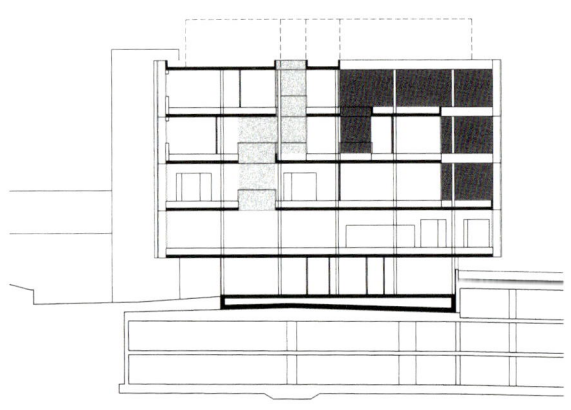
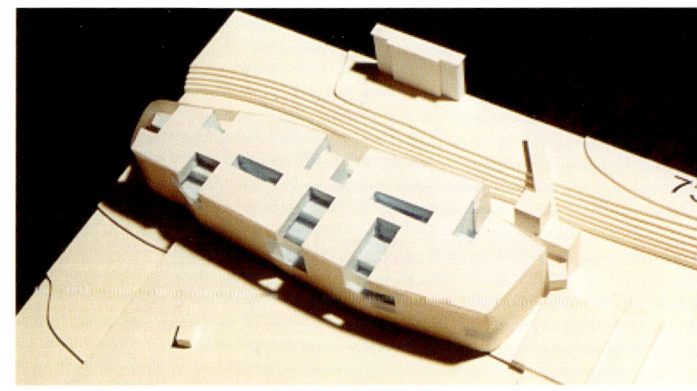

SECTION
SCHNITT 1:666

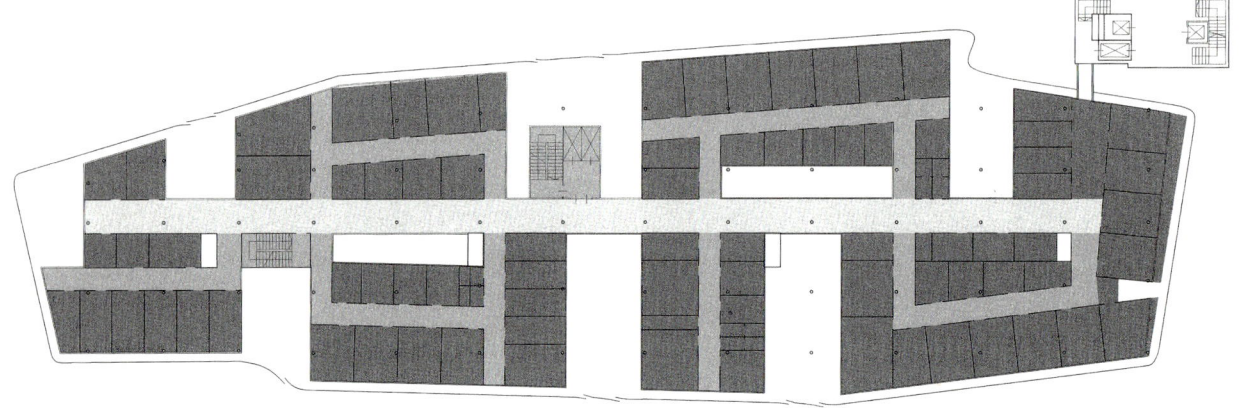

PLAN ILLUSTRATING THE PRINCIPLE
PRINZIPGRUNDRISS 1:666

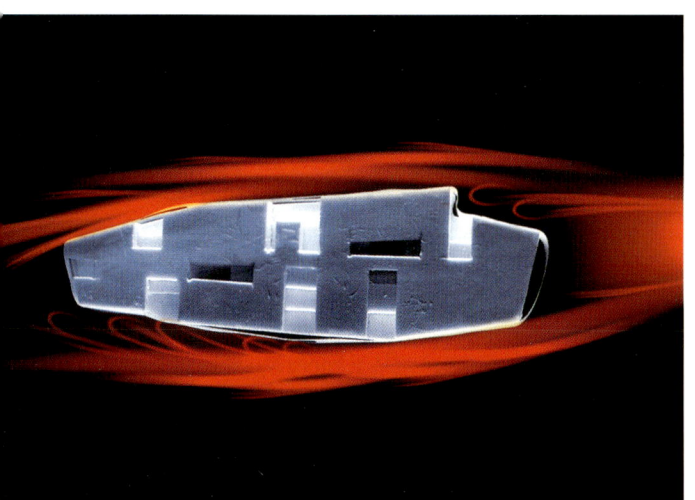
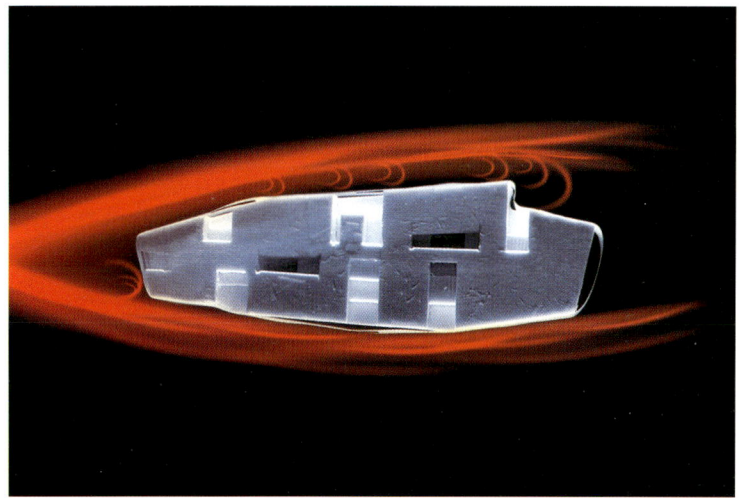

WORKING MODEL IN WIND-TUNNEL TEST EAST / WEST WIND
ARBEITSMODELL IM WINDKANAL-VERSUCH OST- BZW. WESTWIND

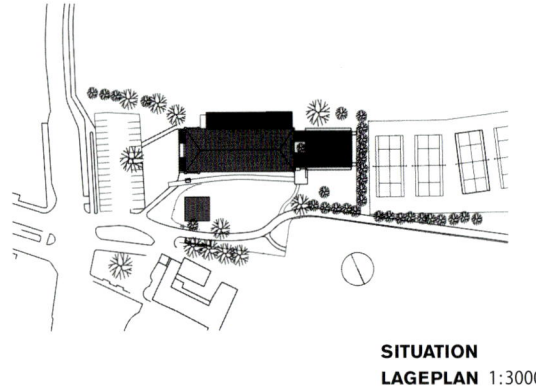 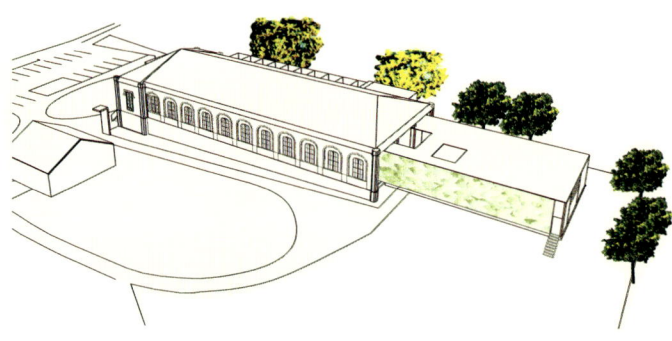

SITUATION
LAGEPLAN 1:3000

Veranstaltungszentrum Kaiserbahnhof
Laxenburg, 1998–

Die Halle des winzigen Kopfbahnhofs wurde Mitte des 19. Jahrhunderts für Sonderzüge des Kaisers errichtet. Später diente sie einem Industriebetrieb, hernach zu Reitzwecken und schließlich dem Tennissport. Mit dem für die Nutzung als Veranstaltungszentrum erforderlichen Zubau wird gestalterisch die früher offene Westseite neu interpretiert, indem der schachtelartige Neubauteil wenige Meter in den Bestand hineingreift, seitlich den Zugang offen lässt und über ein Atrium den Raumverschluss relativiert. Damit erhält das Bauwerk eine zweite Kopfsituation, die mit einer quer laufenden Treppenanlage abschließt, analog der allerdings symmetrischen Freitreppe an der bestehenden östlichen Stirnseite. Die neuen Nutzungen teilen sich die Halle, ohne in die Substanz einzugreifen. Den vorderen Teil belegt ein Restaurant mit Extrazimmer, Küche und zugeordneten Toilettenanlagen, wobei die neuen Baukörper unabhängig in den wesentlich größeren Binnenraum gestellt sind. Im Mittelteil, noch in der alten Halle, befindet sich der große Saal, der über bewegliche Elemente mit dem Restaurant räumlich verbunden werden kann. Der hereindrängende Neubauteil definiert mit der Mauerschale des Altbaus in der Überschubzone zugleich den Windfang – eine elegante Art, die Schnittstelle zwischen Alt und Neu zu thematisieren. In ähnlich gleitender Weise wirkt das Atrium im Neubauteil auf diesen räumlichen Übergang. Dabei vermag der Blick vom alten Eingang bei der Freitreppe her bei geöffneten Schiebeelementen und Sichtschutzvorhängen längs das gesamte Bauwerk und die vier Glaswände zu durchstoßen, die Räume und Raumzonen aufreihend wie ein Zigeunerspieß. An der Westseite zielt er durch die einzige Öffnung, ein breites Landschaftsfenster in der Richtung des längst entfernten Geleisestrangs. Der Neubauteil enthält Räumlichkeiten für Tischtennis sowie Sportkegeln und Badminton im Untergeschoß. Im Hochparterre sind ein Jugendraum und ein Clubzimmer nebst Garderoben und Nebenräumen für die Sportler vorgesehen. Die attraktive, nach Süden orientierte Längsseite wird mit einer Terrasse unter Pergolen aktiviert. Mit den differenziert eingesetzten Maßnahmen gelingt es, die denkmalgeschützte Hülle zu bewahren und darüber hinaus nachhaltig zu beleben.

Kaiserbahnhof Functions Center
Laxenburg, 1998–

The hall of this tiny railway terminus was built in the mid-19th century for special trains for the emperor. It later housed an industry, was then used as a riding arena and finally for tennis. The addition necessary for it to be used as a functions center represents a new interpretation of the previously open west side: the box-like new building reaches a few metres into the existing building, leaving the approach at the side open, and modifies the closure of the space with an atrium. The building is thus given a second end situation that concludes with a transverse staircase analogous to the external staircase on the existing eastern end of the building, which is, however, symmetrical. The new uses divide up the hall without disturbing the substance. A restaurant with a functions room, a kitchen and the necessary toilet facilities occupies the front part whereby the new elements are placed independently in the considerably larger interior. The major hall is in the central section, still within the old hall, and can be spatially connected with the restaurant by means of movable elements. Together with the wall shell of the old building the intruding new building defines the draught lobby in the transitional zone representing an elegant way of treating thematically the interface between new and old. The atrium in the new section affects this spatial transition in a similarly gradual manner. When the sliding elements and screening curtains are open the view from the old entrance beside the external staircase extends through the entire building and the four glass walls skewering together the spaces and spatial zones. On the west side the view is directed through the only opening, a wide panorama window, in the direction once taken by the train tracks which were removed a long time ago. The new section contains facilities for table tennis, bowling and badminton on the lower floor. On the main level a youth room and clubroom along with cloakrooms and ancillary rooms for the sports players are accommodated. The attractive, south-facing long side is enhanced by a terrace with pergola. The measures employed in a differentiated manner have made it possible to preserve the shell, which is under a conservation order, while giving it additional life.

KAISERBAHNHOF

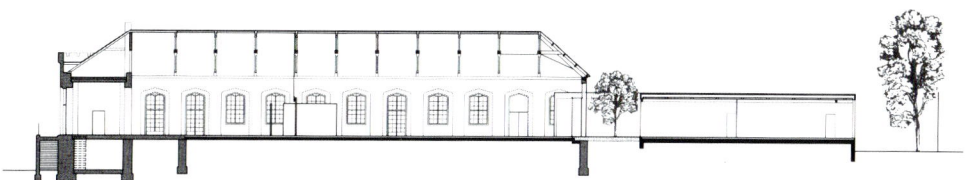

SECTION THROUGH THE EXISTING BUILDING AND THE EXTENSION
SCHNITT BESTAND UND ZUBAU 1:666

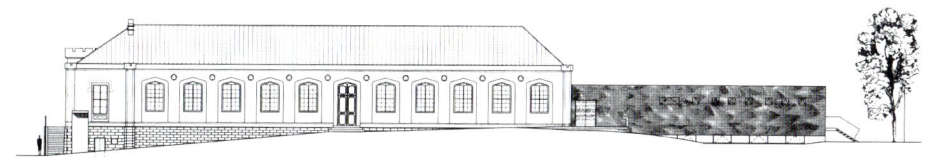

NORTH ELEVATION
ANSICHT NORD 1:666

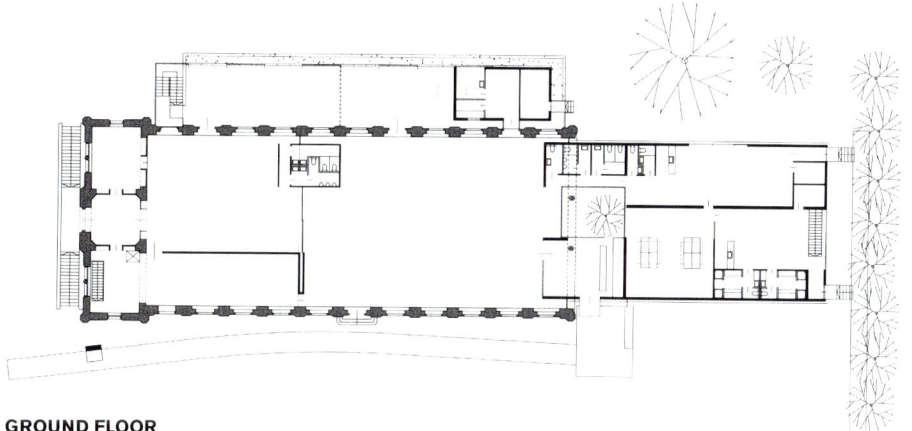

GROUND FLOOR
GRUNDRISS ERDGESCHOSS 1:666

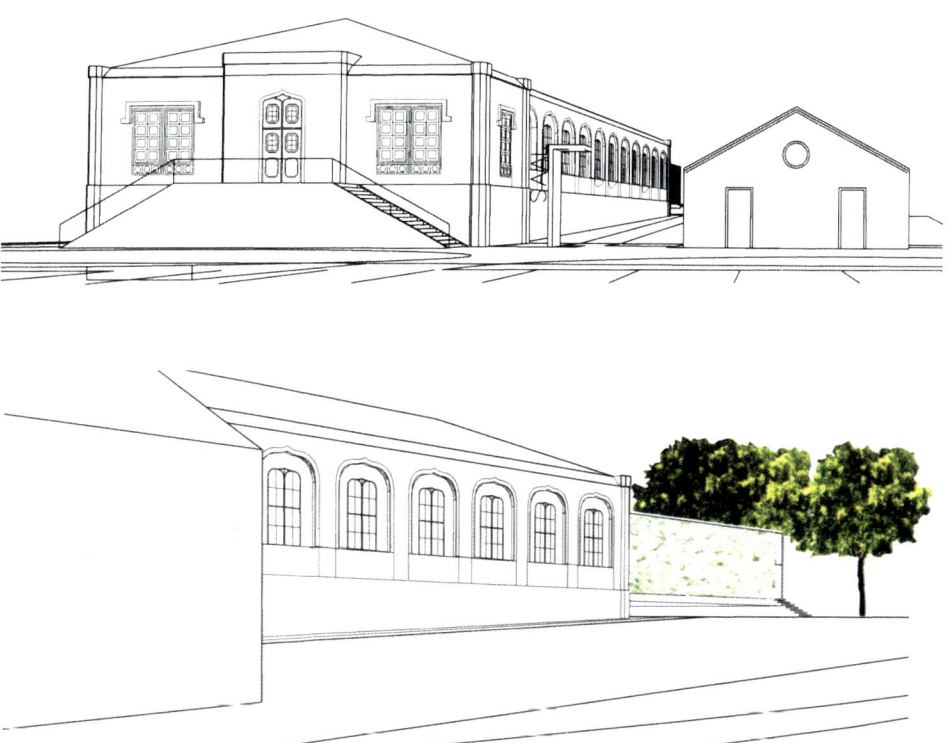

PICTORIAL WALL

SCHLEIER UND KÖRPER

Die äußere Schicht ist bei den vorhergehenden Projekten primär Mittler zwischen Innen und Außen. Sie ist sowohl Träger zusätzlicher Funktionen wie auch Vermittler unterschiedlicher Stimmungen.
Bei den Projekten Eurocity und Pleasure Dome[2] wächst die äußere Schicht nach innen, integriert Sequenzen des Innenraums und entwickelt damit variable Tiefe. Die Wand selbst wird zum Nutzungs- und Ereignisfeld, das beiden Welten angehört und deren Dichte nicht erkennbar ist. Die Hülle, die nun gleichzeitig Schleier und Körper sein kann, wird zum erzählenden Element, das in der Lage ist, sowohl Außen- wie auch Innenraum zu verändern.
Beim Projekt Eurocity ist die Hülle Bekleidung und Haut, die sich im Laufe des Tages fast unmerklich verändert. Durch Tönungen, Farbveränderungen wird aus einem hermetischen ein zart schimmernder Körper, der sich bei Ereignissen zur großen Collage entwickeln kann.
Der Pleasure Dome[2] wird von einer in Licht und Farbe getränkten Fassade umfasst, deren äußerste Schicht ein hochverdichtetes, langsam durchflossenes Aquarium evoziert. Diese Schicht ist abhängig von den dahinterliegenden Funktionen und Ereignissen – sie ist unterschiedlich im Material, in der Intensität und damit in der Wirkung.
Die Wahrnehmung der Fassade ist von innen und außen ähnlich, die gebaute Struktur grenzt sich nicht ab, sondern bindet sich an den öffentlichen Raum. R.L.

VEIL AND BODY

In the previous projects the external layer is primarily an intermediary between inside and outside. It is also the communicator of additional functions and mediator of different moods.
In the Eurocity and Pleasure Dome[2] projects the external layer grows inwards thus integrating sequences of the interior and developing a variable depth. The wall itself is a surface for use and events belonging to both worlds, its density not recognisable. The shell, which can now be simultaneously veil and body, becomes a narrative element that is in a position to alter external and internal space.
In the Eurocity project the shell is both clothing and skin, during the course of the day it changes almost imperceptibly. Through variations in hue and colour something hermetic becomes a gently shimmering block which, for specific events, can develop into a major collage.
The Pleasure Dome[2] is contained by a facade impregnated with light and colour, its outermost layer is evocative of a highly compressed aquarium with slowly flowing water. This layer is dependent on the functions and occurrences that lie behind it – it differs in material, intensity and therefore in effect.
The perception of the facade from inside and outside is similar, the built structure does not distance itself but is linked to public space. R.L.

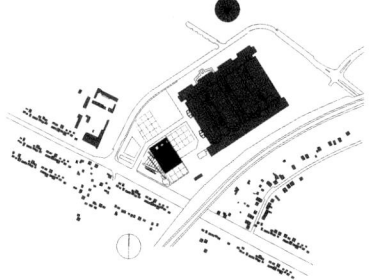

Betriebsgebäude Austria Email
Wien–Favoriten, Projekt 1996

Im Gebiet südlich des Meidlinger Bahnhofs, zwischen Sportflächen und Kleingartenanlagen, angelehnt an die Geleise der Verbindungsbahn, welche verschiedene Industriestandorte der Wiener Peripherie verknüpft, sind mehrere Betriebsanlagen eingestreut. Um haushälterisch mit der Grundfläche umzugehen, schlägt das Konzept eine Anlage auf zwei Ebenen vor, wobei unten Lager und oben Produktionsflächen vorgesehen sind. Insgesamt sollten 7000 m² Nettonutzfläche entstehen. Das weitmaschige Tragskelett erlaubt, an der Südwestseite drei niedrigere Geschoße zu Bürozwecken zu integrieren, die, unterbrochen von Lichthofeinschnitten, zu einer dreidimensionalen Bürolandschaft mit begrünten Binnenräumen gestaltet werden. An der nordwestlichen Längsseite des Gebäudes ist eine breite multifunktionale Serviceschicht angelagert – Lainer nennt sie eine sich „entwickelnde Wand". Hier befinden sich mehrere Hubplattformen, welche die Vertikalverbindung zwischen Lager- und Produktionsgeschoß sicherstellen. Die technische Infrastruktur wird in fünf vertikalen Kollektoren zusammengefaßt, von denen die beiden Geschoße über Deckenstränge versorgt werden. Neben Treppen und Personenliften enthält die nicht nur die senkrechten Beziehungen architektonisch interpretierende, sondern in jeder Hinsicht kommunikative Raumschicht außer einem begrünten Vertikalraum Reserve- und Verdichtungsflächen für betriebsbezogene Interaktionsmöglichkeiten. Mit mittelfristiger Perspektive lassen sich Elemente urbanen Charakters von außen andocken, die über Rampen und Gangways mit den Ebenen der „entwickelnden Wand" verknüpft sind. Damit versucht das Konzept den Produktionsbereich über die reinen Kundendienstaktivitäten hinaus mit städtischen Funktionen wie Galerie, Boardinghouse, Ateliers, Forschungs- und Denkzellen sowie Sozial- und Entspannungsräumen zu vernetzen, um der städtebaulich isolierten Situation entgegenzuwirken. Aber auch die öffentliche Kommunikation wird bewußt behandelt: Eine freistehende, mehrgeschoßige Großvitrine mit breiter Zugangsrampe dient Präsentations- und Repräsentationszwecken und bildet zur Eibesbrunnergasse ein riesiges Schaufenster. Die Konzeption nimmt so Elemente vorweg, die Ende der neunziger Jahre dem exklusiven Verkauf von Kleinstwagen dienen. Über das soziokulturell interaktive Konzept hinaus werden ökologische Aspekte bedacht: Das von den riesigen Dachflächen anfallende Regenwasser soll gesammelt, teils versickert und teils gefiltert, als Brauchwasser rückgeführt werden.

Austria Email (Austria-Enamel) Building
Vienna–Favoriten, Project, 1996

A number of industrial premises are scattered in the area to the south of Meidling railway station between playing fields and allotment gardens, adjoining the tracks of the Verbindungsbahn which connects the different industrial locations on the periphery of Vienna. In order to use the site economically the concept suggested a complex on two levels with the warehouse below and production above. The aim was to provide a total of 7000 m² net floor area. The wide-mesh, load-bearing skeletal frame allows the integration of three lower office storeys with green internal spaces on the south-west side. A broad, multi-functional service layer is attached to the north-western long side of the building, Lainer dubbed it "a wall in the process of developing." Several hub platforms located here ensure the vertical connection between storage and production levels. The technical infra-structure is contained in five vertical collectors which serve both floors by means of ceiling level ducting. As well as staircases and passenger lifts this spatial layer, which not only articulates the vertical connections but is in every sense communicative, contains a planted vertical space along with reserve and consolidation areas for possibilities of interaction related to the business. In the medium term perspective elements with urban character can be attached from outside, linked by ramps and gangways to the levels of the "developing wall." The concept attempts to counteract the isolated urban situation by going beyond the purely customer-oriented services and networking the production area with urban functions such as gallery, boarding house, ateliers, research and creative cells, social spaces and common rooms. The theme of public communication is also consciously handled. A large, free-standing showcase several storeys high with a broad approach ramp serves both presentation and representation and creates a giant "shop window" onto Eibesbrunnergasse. The concept anticipates many elements which, at the end of the nineties, are used to sell exclusive cars. In addition to the interactive socio-cultural concept ecological aspects are also considered. The rainwater running off the enormous areas of roof is to be collected, part then drained off and part filtered for further use.

AUSTRIA EMAIL

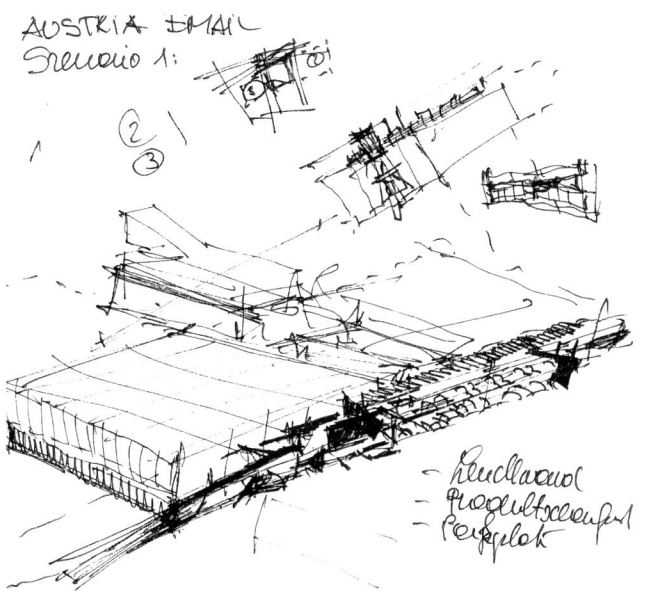

PRINZIP
Reduktion des Flächenverbrauchs
Mischung
Ökonomie der Ressourcen

PRINZIPLE
Reduction of the surface area used
Mixture
Economy of resources

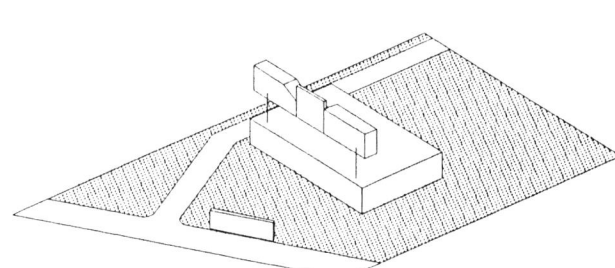

KONZEPT
Entwickelnde Wand
Große Vitrine
Schachtel

CONZEPT
Developing wall
Large showcase
Box

FLEXIBILITÄT
Neutrales Konstruktionssystem
Einbeziehung der Büroflächen in
das Konstruktionssystem
Technische Infrastruktur in seitlicher Wand, in
Kollektorgang und Vertikalschächten geführt

FLEXIBILITY
Neutral structural system
Incorporation of the office areas in the
structural system
Technical infrastructure in the sidewall, in the
collector passages, and in vertical ducts

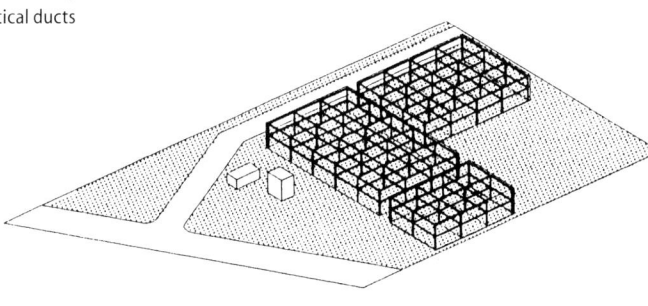

ERWEITERUNG
Innere Verdichtung

EXPANSION
Internal consolidation

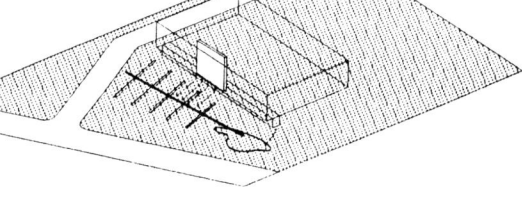

WASSERRECYCLING
Dach- und Oberflächenwässer
Vertikalbiotop
Sickergräben
Verbindungsstück
Teich
Rückführung Brauchwasser

WATER RECYCLING
Collection of roof and surface water
Vertical biotope
Drainage pits
Connecting element
Pond
Return of non-potable water

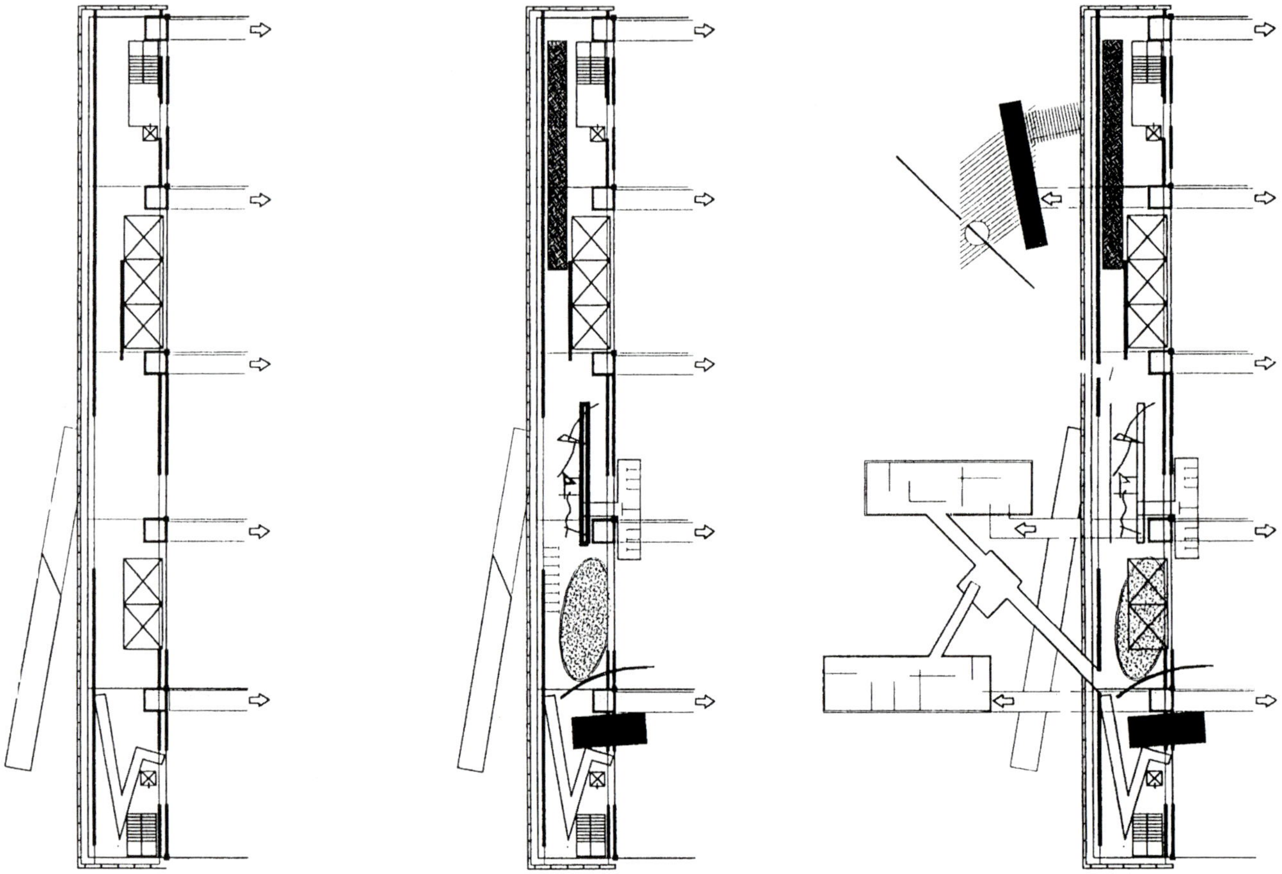

THE DEVELOPING WALL
DIE ENTWICKELNDE WAND 1:666

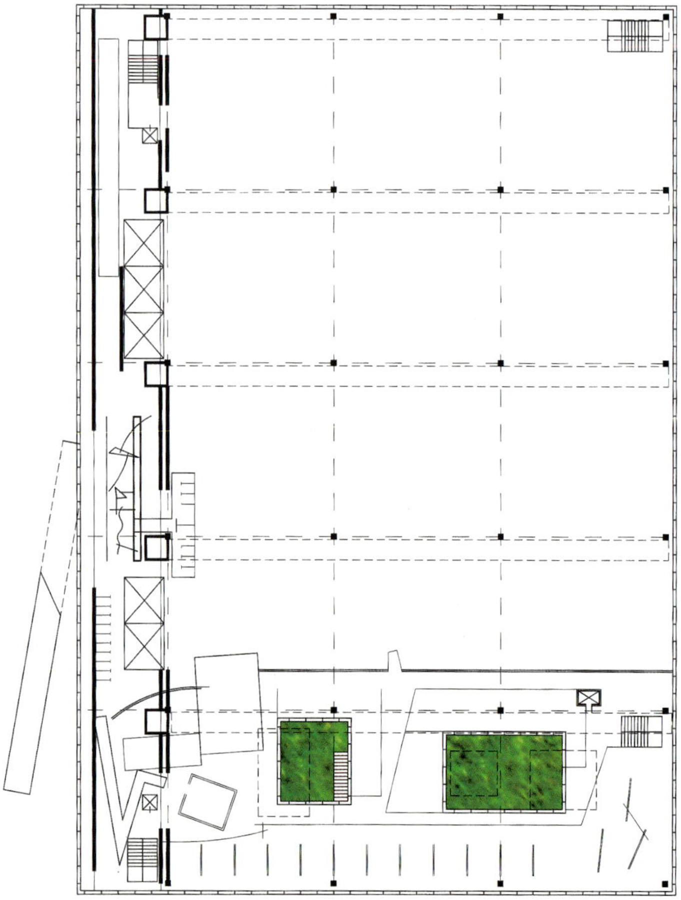

1ST FLOOR
1. OBERGESCHOSS 1:666

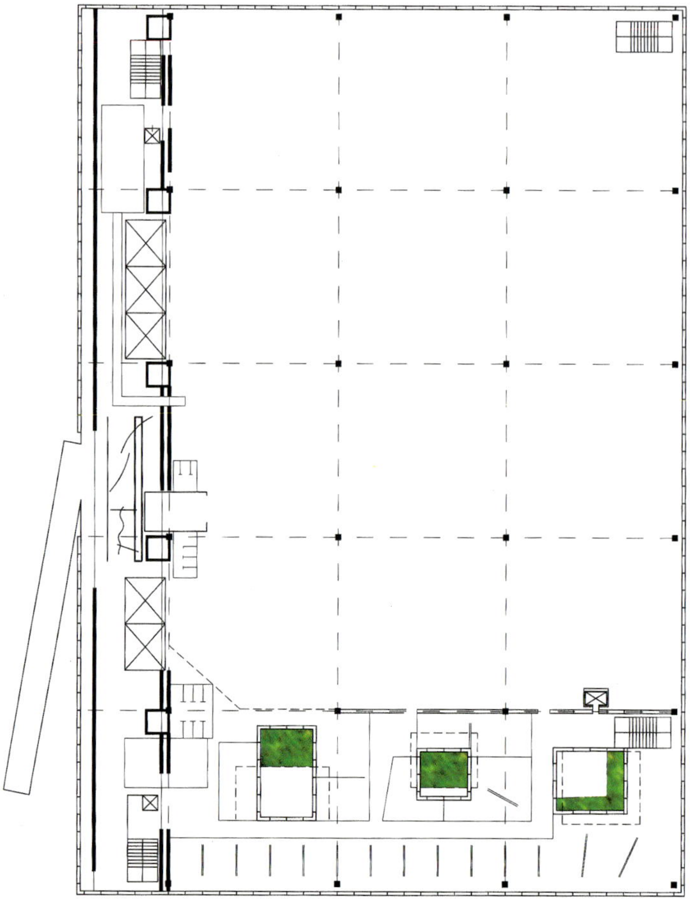

2ND FLOOR
2. OBERGESCHOSS 1:666

FACADE DEVELOPMENT
FASSADENABWICKLUNG

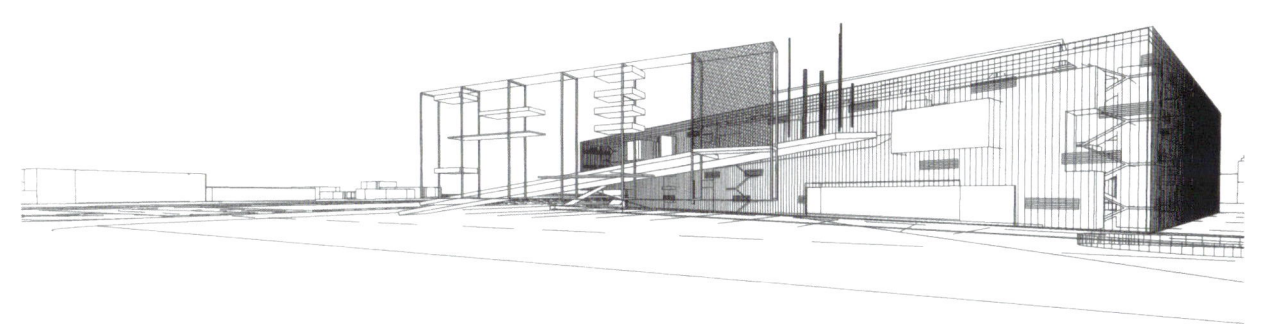

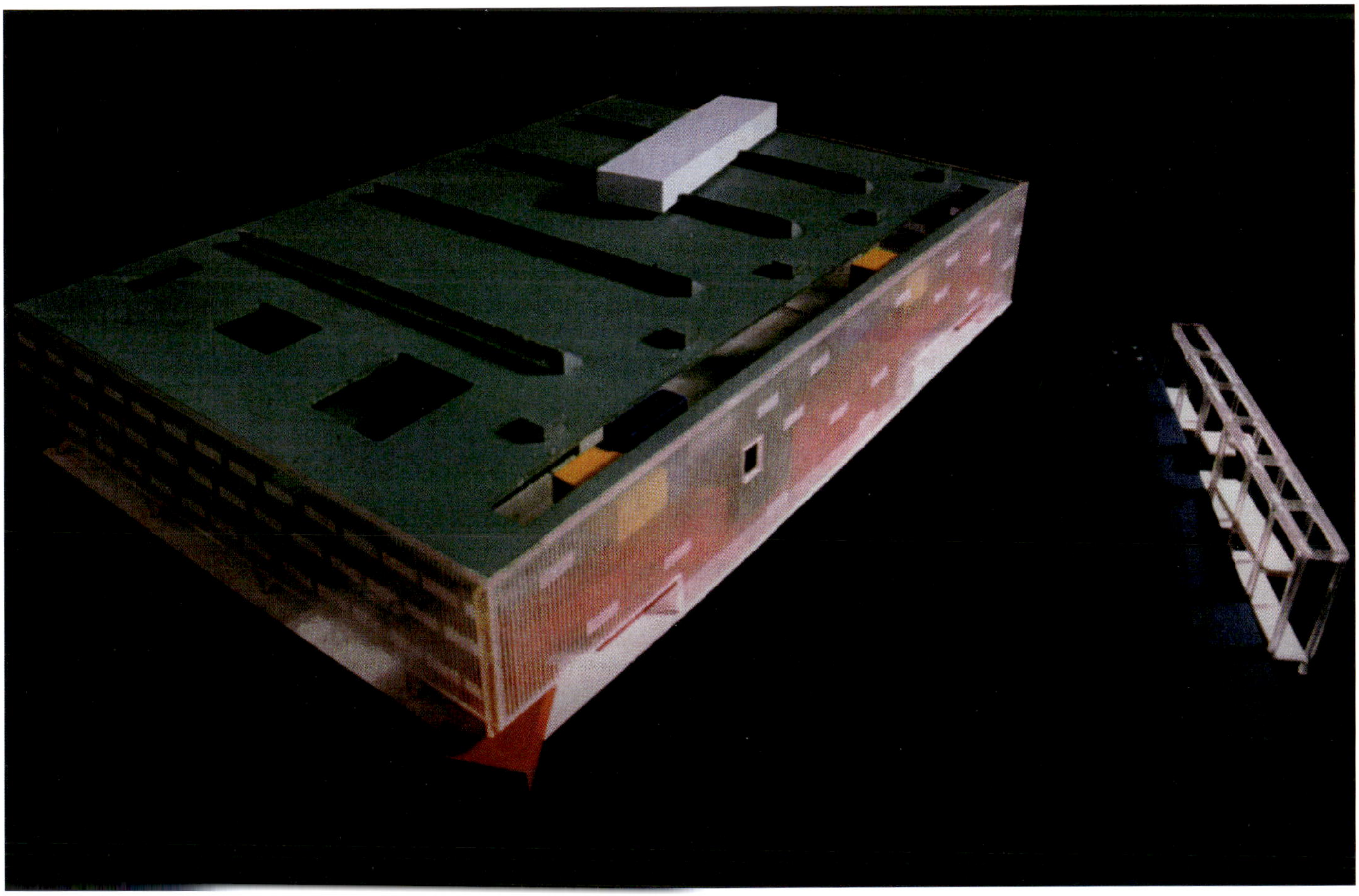

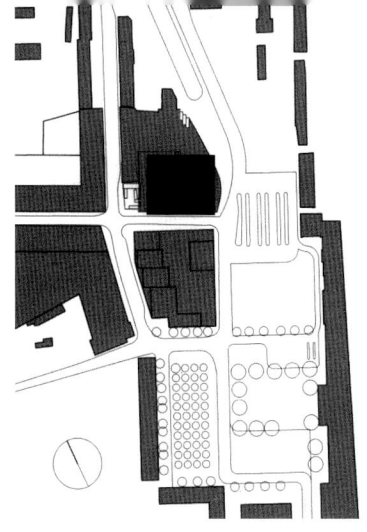

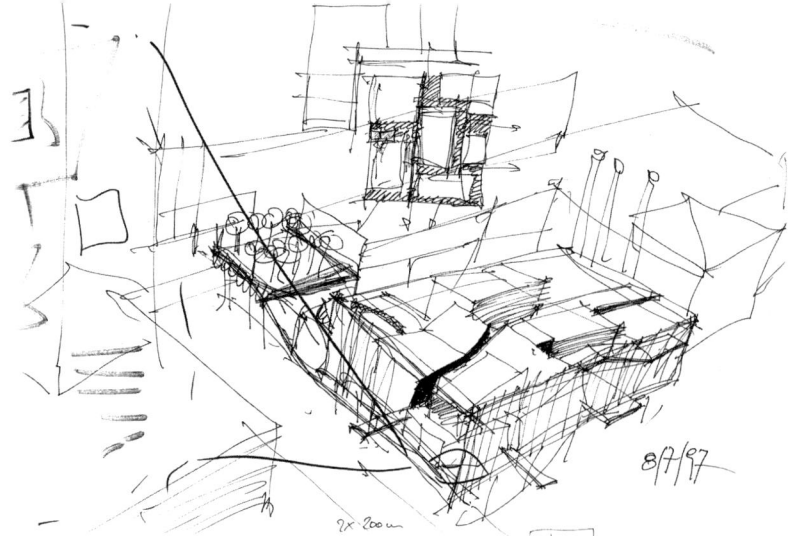

SITUATION
LAGEPLAN 1:6000

Eurocity Kino-Center
Salzburg, 1997–

Mit der klaren Großform eines liegenden Quaders, dessen Oberfläche mit Medien aktiv bespielbar ist, wird im nördlichen Teil des Bahnhofvorfeldes ein lebendiger städtebaulicher Akzent gesetzt, der, obwohl von solitärer Gestalt, das vorhandene, diffus gewordene Stadtgefüge kontextuell verdichtet.

Das Erdgeschoß und der angrenzende Altbestand eines ehemaligen Industriebaus von Hubert Gessner dient als Einkaufszentrum. In den Geschoßen darüber zieht sich vierseitig eine Raumschicht um die hohe Fassade. Sie enthält Erschließungen und die Hardware für die wechselnde Bespielung der Projektionsflächen mit Produktionen aller Art. Die schleierartige Hülle umfasst einen riesigen Binnenraum, in dem die Volumen der Kinosäle mit ihren signifikant ausladenden Unterseiten, die von den ansteigenden Sitzreihen herrühren, scheinbar lose gestapelt sind. Ihre Konstruktion ist in Stahlbeton vorgesehen, mit gestockten oder sandgestrahlten Oberflächen, die dadurch einen felsähnlichen Materialcharakter erhalten, was ihr blockartig-massives, geradezu asteroidenhaftes Wesen verstärkt. In den nicht unbeträchtlichen Zwischenräumen entwickeln sich Stiegenläufe und Stege nach oben und spannen sich galerieartig die Foyer- und Zugangsflächen von Körper zu Körper der Vorführsäle. Diagonale und vertikale Durchblicke erlauben es, den über 20 Meter hohen Raum als Ganzes zu erfassen. Der dreidimensional begehbare Foyer- und Wandelbereich verspricht ein differenziertes urbanes Erlebnis vor und nach dem Filmbesuch. Damit gelingt es, der Funktionalisierung, die mit dem Zusammenfassen mehrerer Kinosäle zu einem Multiplex-Kino einhergeht, eine spielerische Komponente einzuschreiben, deren Ausformung als vielfältig nutzbare Raumstruktur Offenheit und Wahlfreiheit zulässt. Dieser programmatische Aspekt bildet sich an der Fassade im Wechsel von Tag und Nacht, von Projektion und leichter Transparenz ab, so dass die urbane Belebung in changierenden Fassadenbildern ihre Entsprechung findet.

Eurocity Cinema Center
Salzburg, 1997–

A clear major form in the shape of a recumbent block, across the surfaces of which diverse media can be projected, places a living urban accent in the northern sector of the area in front of the railway station. Although it is an independent building it serves to intensify the somewhat diffuse urban mesh at this point. The ground floor and adjoining structure (a former industrial building designed by Hubert Gessner) serve as a shopping center. On the floors above a spatial layer extends around all four sides of the high facade. This zone contains the circulation and the hardware for the productions of various kinds that are played across the projection surfaces. The veil-like shell encloses an enormous internal space in which the volumes of the cinemas with their dramatically projecting undersides, a product of the ascending rows of seats inside, are apparently loosely stacked. It is intended to build these in reinforced concrete with a bush-hammered or sandblasted surface which will give them something of the character of a cliff face and will strengthen their massive, blocky, almost asteroid-like nature. In the not inconsiderable voids between these volumes staircases and footbridges develop upwards; the foyers and approaches span, like galleries, between the blocks containing the cinemas. Diagonal and vertical views allow one to grasp the space, which is more than 20 metres high, as an entity. The three dimensionally accessible foyer and spaces for promenading promise a differentiated urban experience both before and after the film. It here proves possible to inscribe a playful component in the primarily functionally motivated decision to combine several cinemas to form a multiplex cinema. The design is a spatial structure usable in a variety of ways allowing openness and freedom of choice. This programmatic aspect is illustrated on the facade in the change between day and night, between projection and light transparency so that the animating urban influence finds its reflection in the changing images of the facades.

EUROCITY SALZBURG

VERTICAL AND HORIZONTAL VIEWS
VERTIKALE UND HORIZONTALE DURCHBLICKE

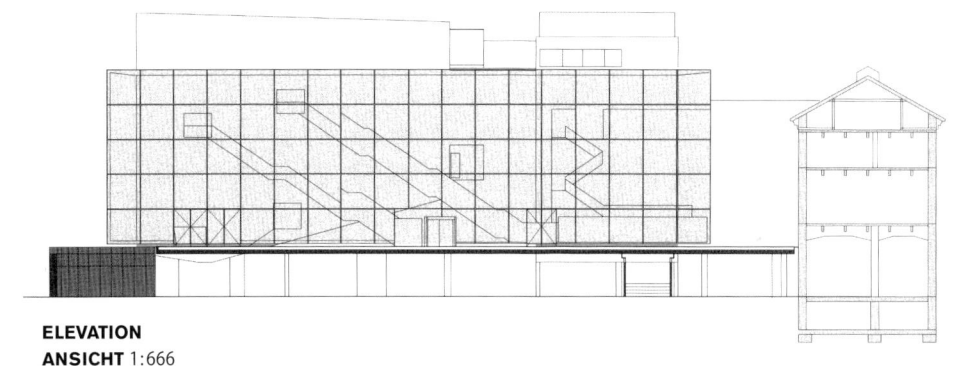

ELEVATION
ANSICHT 1:666

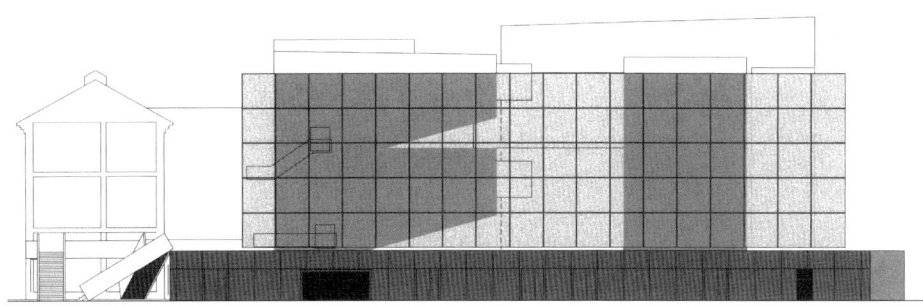

ELEVATION
ANSICHT 1:666

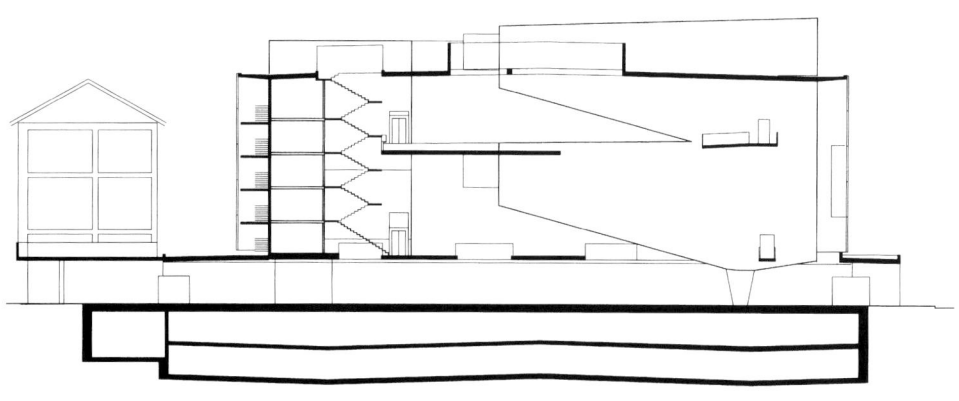

SECTION A
SCHNITT A 1:666

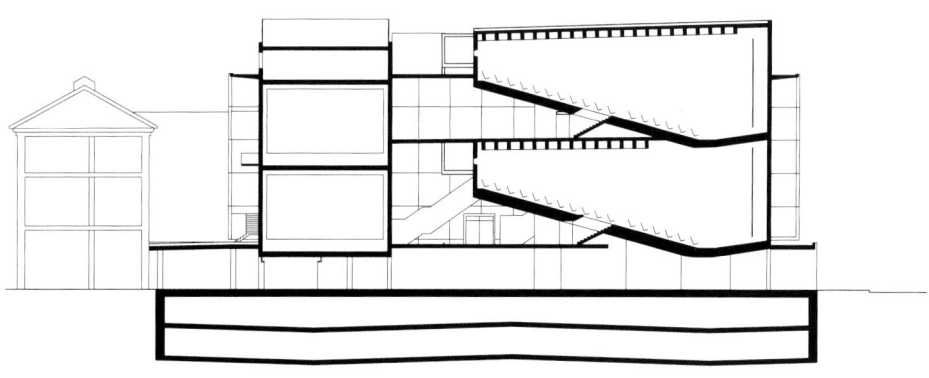

SECTION E
SCHNITT E 1:666

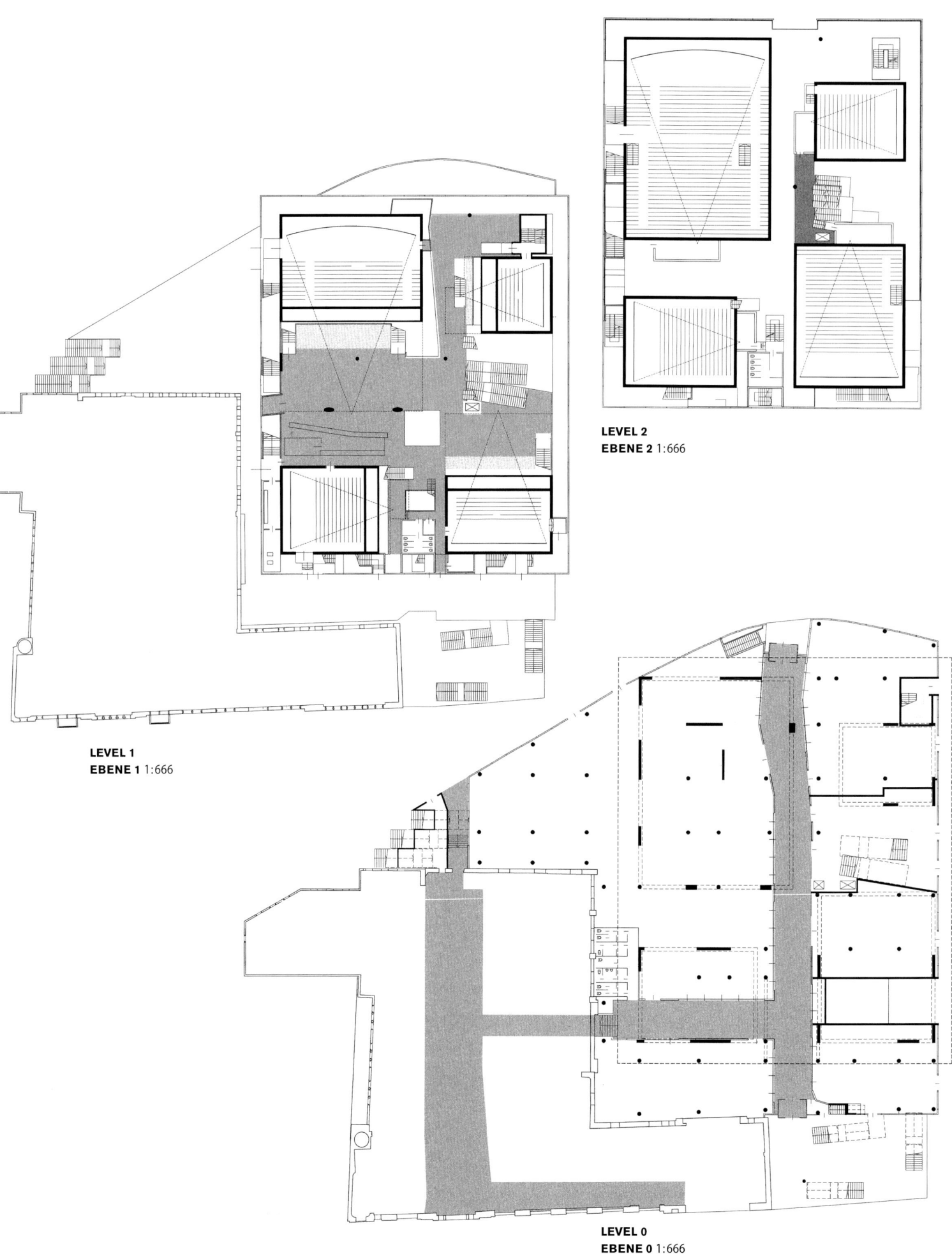

LEVEL 2
EBENE 2 1:666

LEVEL 1
EBENE 1 1:666

LEVEL 0
EBENE 0 1:666

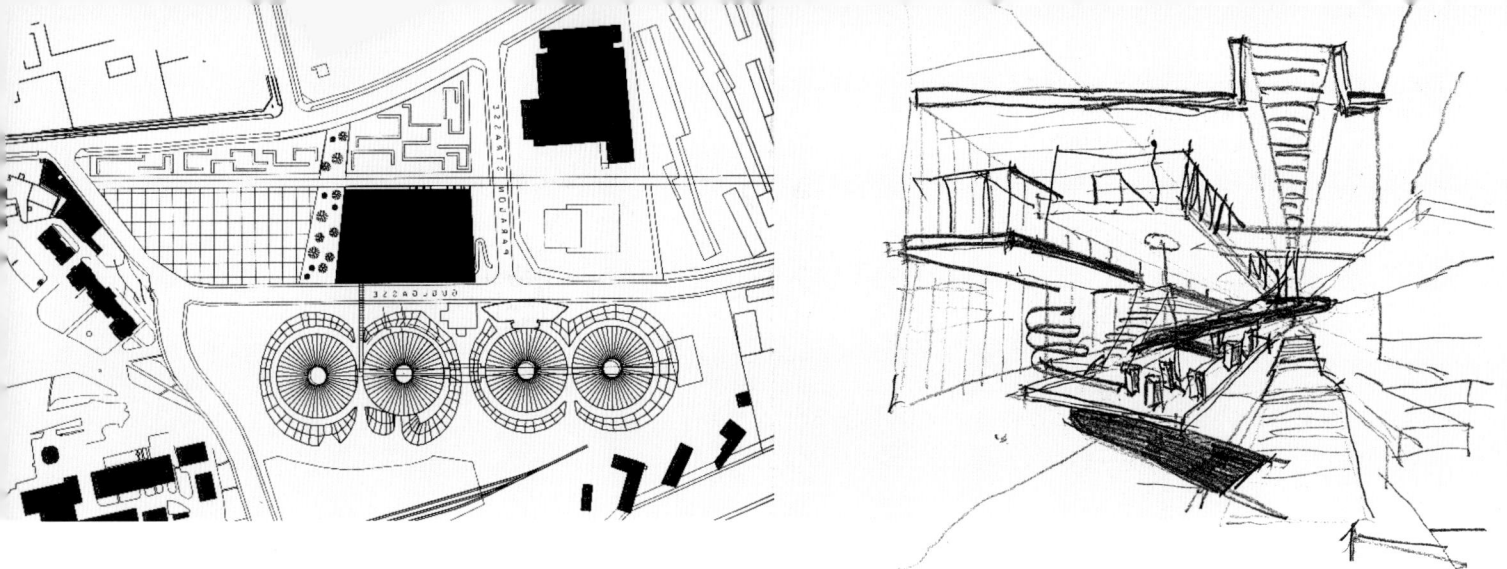

Pleasure Dome²
Wien–Landstraße, 1998–

Die vier Gasometer in Wien–Simmering sind europaweit als städtebauliches Superzeichen einzigartig. Ihre absolute Größenordnung wird erst erfassbar, wenn man sich vergegenwärtigt, dass in jeden einzelnen das ganze Wiener Riesenrad aus dem Prater hineingestellt werden könnte. Es ist derzeit vorgesehen, die gewaltigen Innenräume zu Wohnzwecken umzufunktionieren. Nördlich davon soll, basierend auf dem städtebaulichen Strukturkonzept von Rüdiger Lainer für das Gesamtumfeld, ein Unterhaltungszentrum mit einer großangelegten Freizeitinfrastruktur, Parkplätzen, Multiplex-Kino sowie spezifischen Einkaufsmöglichkeiten in einer auf mehreren Ebenen organisierten künstlichen Landschaft entstehen. Während die vier ehemaligen Gasometer auf relativ hohen, kegelförmig geböschten und grasbewachsenen Basements stehen, soll die Anlage der massenkulturellen Vergnügungen, darauf bezugnehmend, im unteren Bereich eine schürzenartig hüllende Konstruktion aufweisen. Die urbane Verdichtung populärkultureller Aktivitäten bildet einen Gegensatz zur Umgebung, die teils aus genutzten, teils aus brachliegenden Industrieanlagen besteht. Dieses städtebauliche Erwartungsgebiet bedingt, dass urbanisierende Interventionen eine kritische Größe übersteigen, damit sie insgesamt überlebensfähig werden. Das Konzept sieht im Unter-, im Erdgeschoß und auf zwei weiteren, die halbe Fläche des Bauwerks einnehmenden Ebenen gegen 1000 Parkplätze vor. Entlang der Guglgasse, welche die Anlage vom Gasometerquartett trennt, ist eine Raumschicht als Erschließungsstreifen vorgelagert, in dem sich, leicht seitlich ausschwingend, eine Straßenrampe hochzieht, Stiegen und Lifte sorgen für einen direkten Zugang. In der nicht von Parkplätzen besetzten Hälfte der Anlage befindet sich über den Parkebenen ein Ladezentrum mit Mall und Flächen für Unterhaltung und Spiel. Von dieser Höhe führt ein Steg zu den Gasometern hinüber, damit deren Shopping-Mall über einen kurzen Weg angebunden wird. Die höhenmäßig differenzierte Dachlandschaft ist begehbar und Teil der Unterhaltungsinfrastruktur.

Pleasure Dome²
Vienna–Landstrasse, 1998–

The four gasometers in Simmering are urban super symbols, unique in Europe. Their scale can only be appreciated when you realise that the Giant Ferris Wheel in the Prater could be placed inside each one. It is now intended to convert these powerful interiors to provide living accommodation. To the north, based on an urban structural concept by Rüdiger Lainer for the entire surrounding area, an entertainment center with a major leisure complex including car-parking spaces, a multiplex cinema and specific retail facilities in an artificial landscape organised on a series of levels is to be developed. The four former gasometers stand on relatively high, conical sloping basements which are planted with grass, in a reference to this the complex of the mass-cultural pleasure park will have an apron-like enveloping structure on the lower level. The urban intensification of popular cultural activities forms a contrast to the surrounding area that is composed of industrial premises, some still in use, some desolate. This district of urban expectations demands that urban interventions made here exceed a certain critical size in order to survive. Therefore the concept envisages approximately 1000 car-parking spaces on the lower level, ground floor and on two further levels which take up half the floor area of the building. Along Guglgasse, which separates the complex from the four gasometers, a spatial circulation zone is planned in which a street ramp rises, swinging out to the side in a relaxed fashion. Staircases and lifts provide a direct approach. In the half of the complex not occupied by the car-parking spaces a dozen cinemas of different sizes are stacked irregularly in two layers. The approaches and the platforms forming the foyers are spanned across high, canyon-like spaces that force their way between the blocky volumes of the cinemas. The other half of the complex contains a small shopping center with a mall and areas for sport and entertainment above the car-parking levels. The roofscape with its varying heights is accessible forming part of the entertainment infrastructure. A pedestrian footbridge leads through this section from the shopping mall, which extends under the four gasometers, to the leisure center and then onwards over the roofs of the nearby Viennese Transport Authority depot and other industrial premises into the green space of the Viennese Prater.

PLEASURE DOME²

STRUCTURE OF THE BUILDING | STRUKTUR DES GEBÄUDES
The artificial landscape as an imposed landscape
Die künstliche Landschaft als eingesetzte Landschaft

Crags | Felsen   Meadows | Wiesen
Base | Sockel

The building develops as an excavated landscape in different spaces
Das Gebäude entwickelt sich als ausgehöhlte Landschaft in vielfältigen Räumen

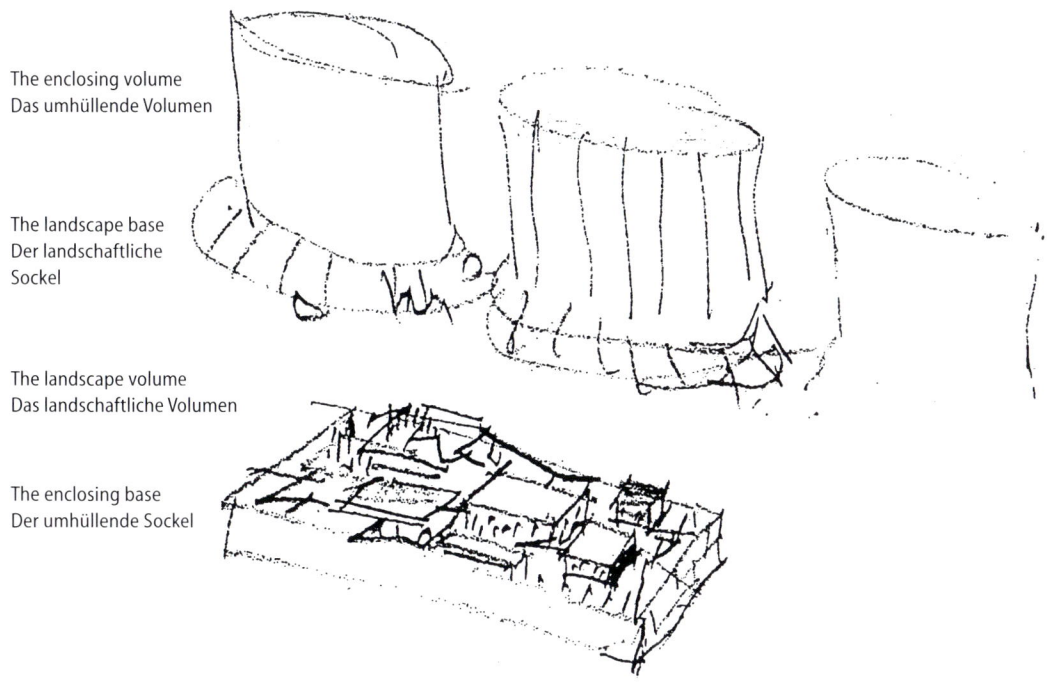

The enclosing volume
Das umhüllende Volumen

The landscape base
Der landschaftliche Sockel

The landscape volume
Das landschaftliche Volumen

The enclosing base
Der umhüllende Sockel

THE KUNSTRAUM
The connection between the Gasometers and the Pleasure Dome² as a juxta-positioning of art and nature
PERSPEKTIVE KUNSTRAUM
Die Verbindung von den Gasometern und Pleasure Dome² als Gegenüber von Kunst und Natur

THE MAJOR WALL
impregnated in light and colour (Chartres)
DIE GROSSE WAND
in Farbe und Licht getränkt (Chartres)

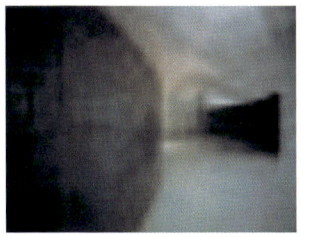 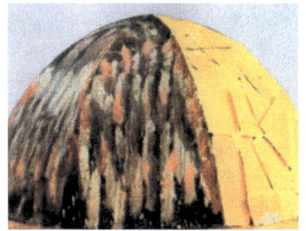

THE "MAJOR WALL" (Richard Serra) **ARTIFICIAL NATURE** (Mario Merz)
DIE „GROSSE WAND" (Richard Serra) **DIE KÜNSTLICHE NATUR** (Mario Merz)
Juxtapositioning of the elements | Gegenüberstellung der Elemente

NORTH VIEW
ANSICHT NORD

EAST VIEW
ANSICHT OST

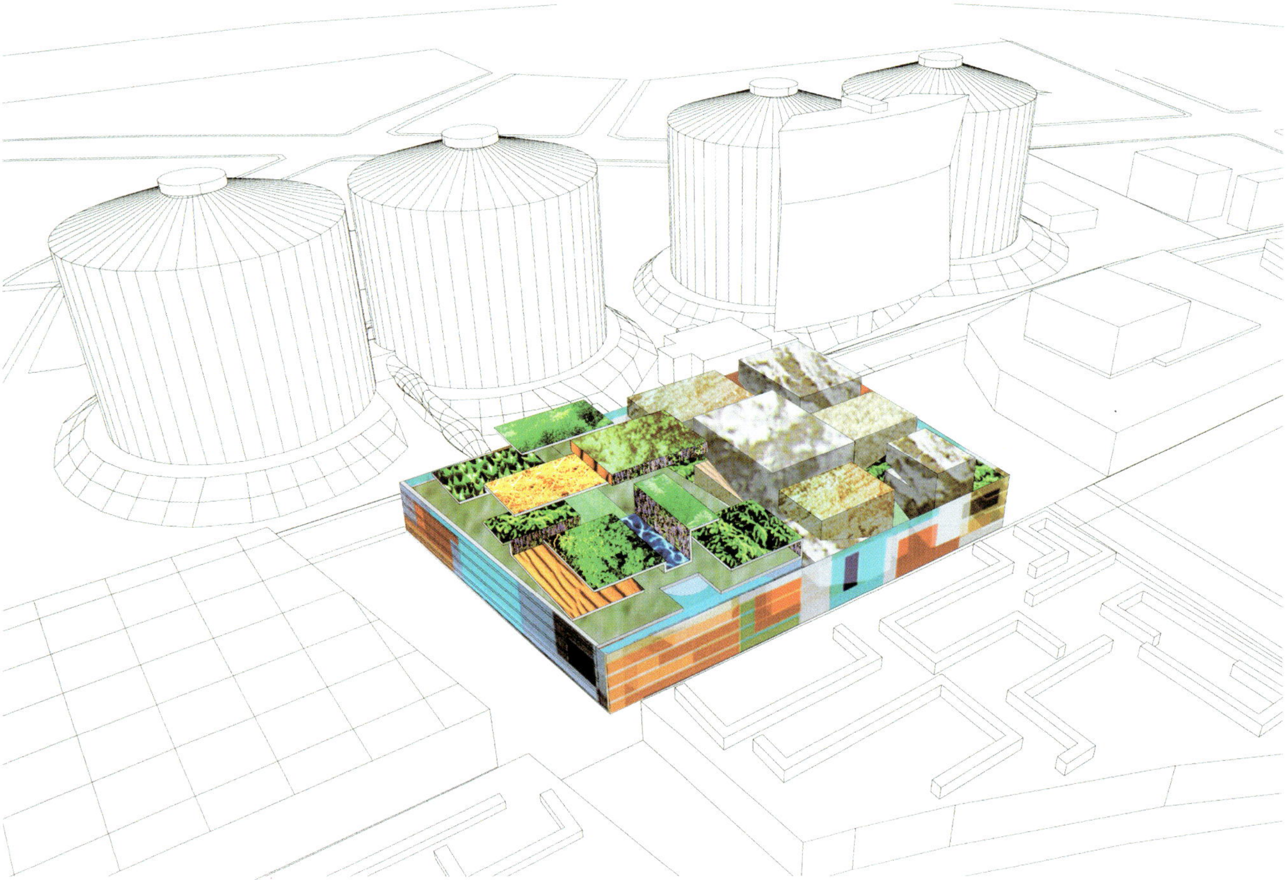

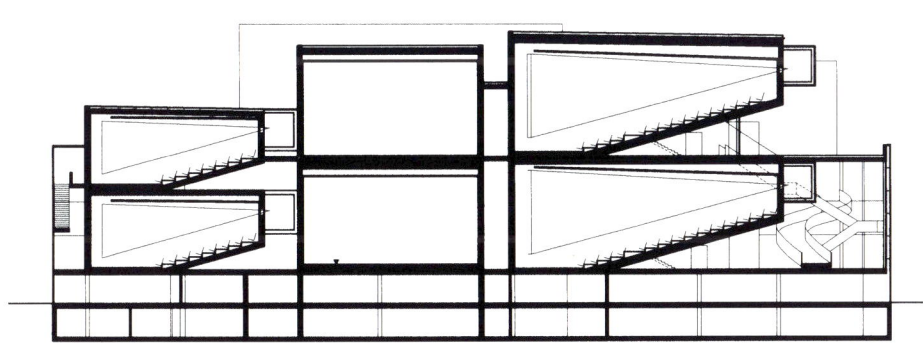

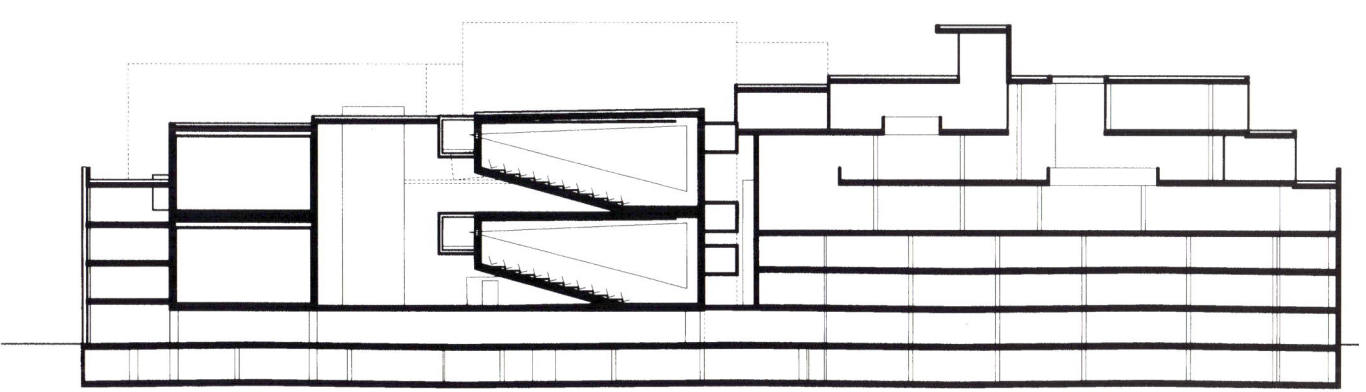

SECTION G – G
SCHNITT G – G 1:666

SECTION D – D
SCHNITT D – D 1:666

LEVEL 3
EBENE 3 1:666

LEVEL 1
EBENE 1 1:666

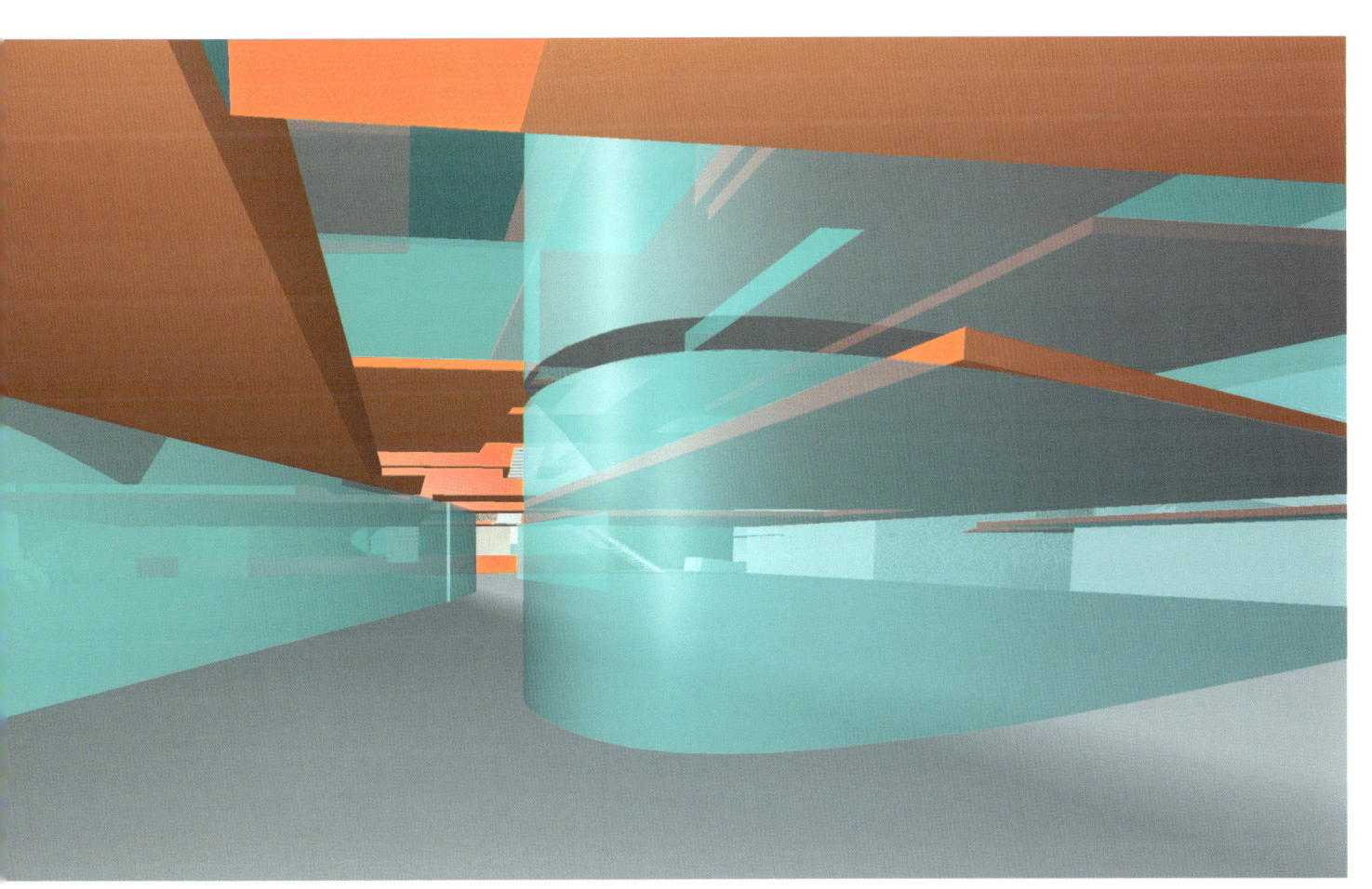

LEVEL 5
EBENE 5 1:666

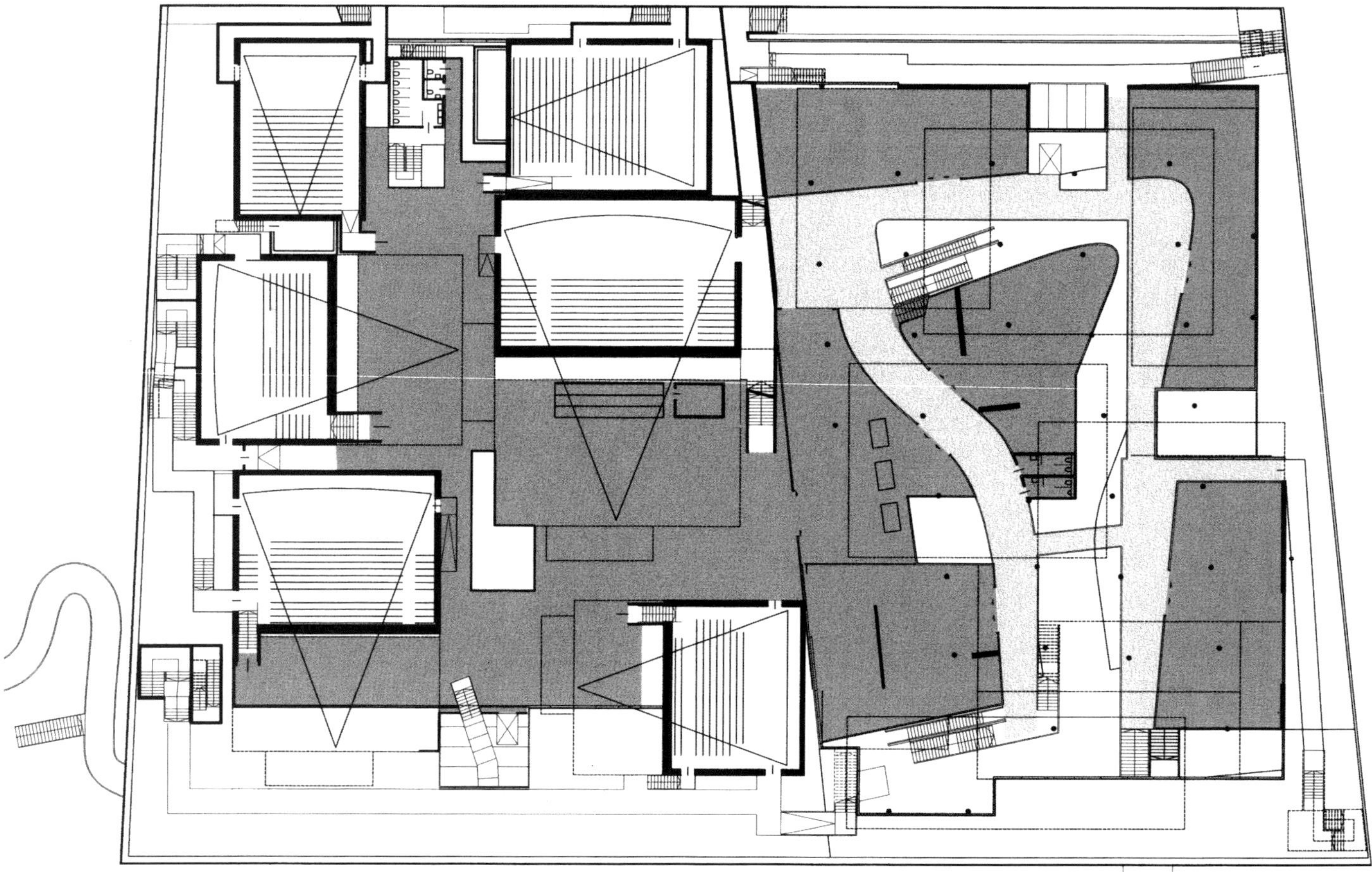

LEVEL 4
EBENE 4 1:666

PROJECT | PROJEKT
Location | Ort
Started/Completed | Planungsjahr/Realisierungsjahr
A   Associates | Partner
L   Project Leaders | Leitende Mitarbeiter
Co Consultants | Konsulenten
C   Clients | Auftraggeber

Buildings and projects dating from between 1983 and 1989 were carried out in partnership with Gertraud Auer.
Die Bauten und Projekte der Jahre 1983–1989 erfolgten in Partnerschaft mit Gertraud Auer.

UNESCO COMPETITION
WETTBEWERB UNESCO

Tomorrow's Habitat
Paris, 1983
Mention | Erwähnung

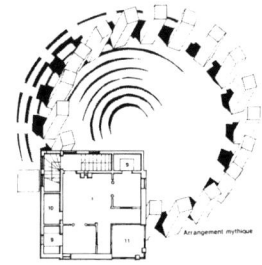

NEW BUILDING FACULTY OF HUMANITIES AND NATURAL SCIENCES | WETTBEWERB NEUBAU GEISTES- UND NATURWISSENSCHAFTLICHE FAKULTÄT KARL-FRANZENS-UNIVERSITÄT

Graz, 1984
2nd prize | 2. Preis
A Rainer Lalics

STUDY | STUDIE
HOTEL SHERATON

Linz, 1983

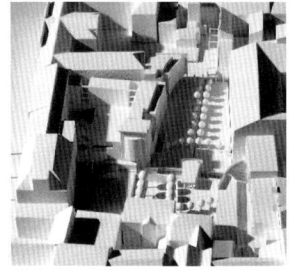

HOUSING AND URBAN RENEWAL COMPETITION | WETTBEWERB WOHNEN UND STADTERNEUERUNG

Engerthstraße, Wien 2, 1984
Purchased | Ankauf

COMPETITION NEW BUILDING INSTITUTE FOR BIOCHEMISTRY AND BIOTECHNOLOGY, UNIVERSITY OF TECHNOLOGY
WETTBEWERB INSTITUTSNEUBAU BIOCHEMIE UND BIOTECHNOLOGIE TECHNISCHE UNIVERSITÄT

Graz, 1983
Purchased | Ankauf

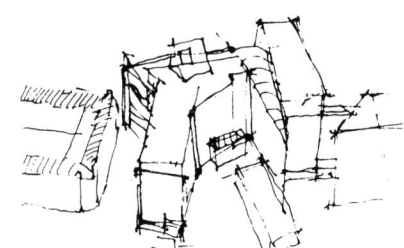

INLAND REVENUE OFFICE COMPETITION
WETTBEWERB FINANZAMT GRAZ

Graz, 1984
Purchased | Ankauf

LIST OF PROJECTS | WERKVERZEICHNIS

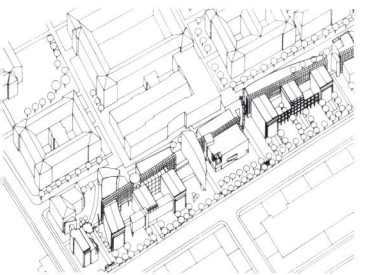

INSTITUTE BUILDINGS FACULTY OF LAW, SOCIAL AND ECONOMIC SCIENCES COMPETITION | WETTBEWERB INSTITUTSBAUTEN RECHTS-, SOZIAL- UND WIRSCHAFTSWISSENSCHAFTLICHE FAKULTÄT KARL-FRANZENS-UNIVERSITÄT

Graz, 1985
Purchased | Ankauf

CONVERSION | UMBAU GYROWETZGASSE 14

Wien 14, 1987/88
L Konrad Rautter
C Dörflinger/Langbein/Kernegger

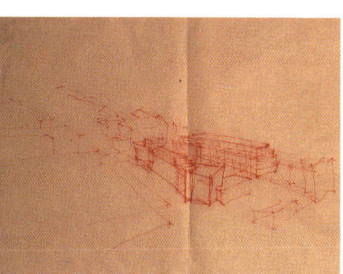

STUDY FOR A NEW HOTEL BUILDING STUDIE HOTELNEUBAU

Neutorstraße, Salzburg, 1985

OFFICE, SOUND STUDIO AND APARTMENTS CONVERSION | UMBAU BÜRO, TONSTUDIO UND WOHNUNGEN

Haberlgasse 85, Wien 16, 1987/88
C Adolf Tögel

KARMELITERVIERTEL COMPETITION WETTBEWERB KARMELITERVIERTEL

Wien 2, 1985

CONVERSION | UMBAU HERMANNGASSE 29

Wien 7, 1988–90
L Peter Tremba, Hannes Schild
    Bernhard Moos, Konrad Rautter
Co Helmuth Locher, Jochen Käferhaus
C Miteigentümergemeinschaft

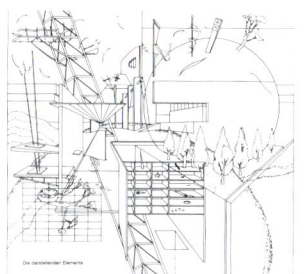

SECONDARY SCHOOL COMPETITION WETTBEWERB AHS ALLGEMEINBILDENDE HÖHERE SCHULE

Graz, 1986

HOUSING DEVELOPMENT | WOHNBAU WAIDHAUSENSTRASSE 24

Wien 14, 1988–91
L Inge Andritz, Hannes Schild
C Wohnungseigentum Wien

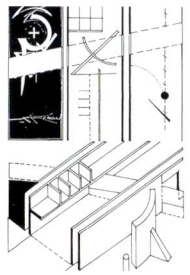

FORMER IMPERIAL STABLES COMPETITION | WETTBEWERB MESSEPLATZ, AREAL DER EHEMALIGEN HOFSTALLUNGEN MESSEPALAST

Wien 1, 1986

HOUSING DEVELOPMENT WOHNHAUSANLAGE SIEGESPLATZ 21/BENJOWSKIGASSE

Aspern, Wien 22, 1988–91
L Hannes Schild
C SEG Wien

LIST OF PROJECTS | WERKVERZEICHNIS

TRADE FAIR STAND | MESSESTAND

Chamber of Engineers and Architects, Vienna
Ingenieur- und Architektenkammer, Wien
1989, 1990

**HOUSING DEVELOPMENT
WOHNHAUSANLAGE
ROTHENBURGSTRASSE 2**

Wien 12, 1989–92
L   Konrad Rautter
Co Helmuth Locher
C   SEG, Wien

**CONGRESS AND EXHIBITION CENTER
COMPETITION | WETTBEWERB KON-
GRESS- UND AUSSTELLUNGSZENTRUM**

Linz, 1989
Purchased | Ankauf

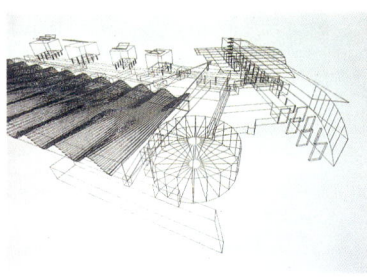

**WALL LAMP | WANDLEUCHTE
„EINFACH"**

1990

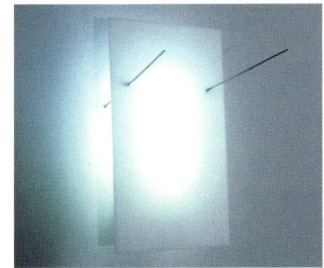

**HOUSING COMPETITION
WETTBEWERB WOHNBAU
TRAVIATAGASSE**

Wien 23, 1989

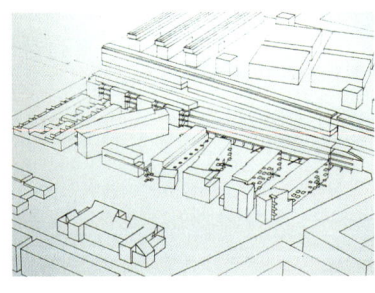

**FEDERAL OFFICE BUILDING
COMPETITION | WETTBEWERB
BUNDESAMTSGEBÄUDE**

Deutschlandsberg, Steiermark, 1990
2nd prize | 2. Preis

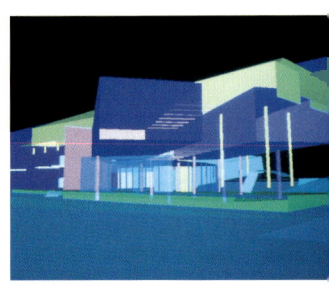

**CONVERSION | UMBAU
ÖLZELTGASSE 4**

Wien 3, 1989/90
C Kosesnik-Wehrle

**HOUSING DEVELOPMENT COMPETITION
WETTBEWERB WOHNBEBAUUNG
ST. PETER-OST**

Salzburg, 1990
Purchased | Ankauf

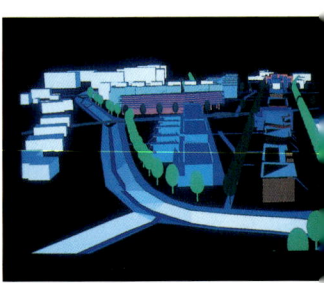

VIVRE. MILENA JESENSKÁ

Center Georges Pompidou, Paris, Wiener
Festwochen, Messepalast, Wien, Manes, Prag
Exhibition conception | Ausstellungs-
konzeption 1989–91
Concept | Konzept Gertraud Auer

**KAGRAN ICE-SKATING RINK
COMPETITION | WETTBEWERB
EISSPORTHALLE KAGRAN**

Wien 22, 1990
Prize | Preis

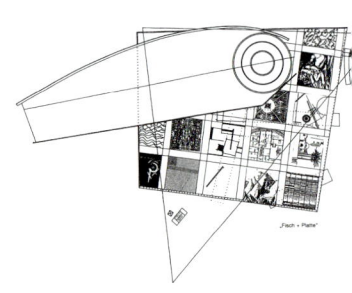

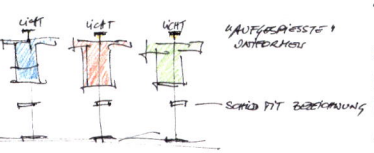

**ON AN ELEGY OF COLLECTING
ZUR ELEGIE DES SAMMELNS**

Museum Schloß Loosdorf, Niederösterreich
Exhibition conception | Ausstellungskonzeption
Project | Projekt 1990
A Konrad Rautter
C Verena Piatti

**PENTHOUSE
SEILERGASSE 16**

Wien 1, 1991–95
L Stephen Bidwell, Hannes Schild
Co Helmuth Locher, Introplan
C Martin Schwanzer

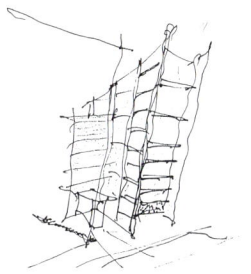

**APARTMENT AND OFFICE BUILDING
WOHN- UND BÜROHAUS
ALSZEILE**

Wien 17
Project | Projekt 1990–97
L Konrad Rautter
C Sigma Bau

**HOUSING DEVELOPMENT
WOHNBEBAUUNG
GASSMANNSTRASSE 41**

Wien 12, 1992–95
L Bernhard Moos
C Stadt Wien

**CONVERSION APARTMENT BUILDING
UMBAU MEHRFAMILIENHAUS**

Grein, Niederösterreich, 1991/92
L Hannes Schild
C C. u. T. Huemer

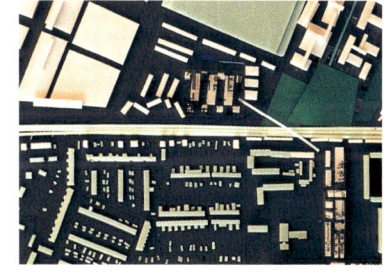

**URBAN DEVELOPMENT STUDY
STÄDTEBAULICHE STUDIE
ENTWICKLUNGSGEBIET S 80/B 3D**

Wien, 1993
1st prize | 1. Preis

**SECONDARY SCHOOL OF THE CITY OF
VIENNA | HAUPTSCHULE DER STADT
WIEN**

Absberggasse 50, Wien 10, 1991–94
L Karin Krummlauf, Hannes Schild
Co Helmuth Locher, Jochen Käferhaus
    Hans Dworak
    Anna Detzlhofer, Oskar Putz
C Stadt Wien, GSD Wien

**URBAN GUIDELINE PROJECT FORMER
ASPERN AIRFIELD | STÄDTEBAULICHES
LEITPROJEKT ALTES FLUGFELD
ASPERN**

Wien, 1993–95
International competition 1st prize
Internationaler Wettbewerb 1. Preis, 1992
L Suki Sangha, Bernhard Moos
    Markus Tomaselli
Co Roman Ivancsics, Werner Rosinak
C Stadt Wien, WWFF

**HOUSING DEVELOPMENT | WOHN-
BEBAUUNG
RADEGUNDERSTRASSE**

Graz, 1991–94
Project | Projekt
L Karin Krummlauf, Petra Gruber
C Neue Heimat Graz

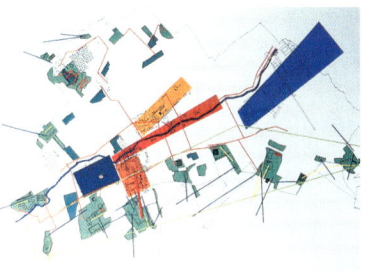

**URBAN DEVELOPMENT COMPETITION
STÄDTEBAULICHER WETTBEWERB**

Weiz, Steiermark, 1994
2nd prize | 2. Preis
P Claudio Blazica, Laura Spinadel

LIST OF PROJECTS | WERKVERZEICHNIS

**HEALTH CENTER
GESUNDHEITSZENTRUM
ANTONIGASSE**

Wien 18, 1994
Project | Projekt
L   Bernhard Moos
C   Martin Schwanzer

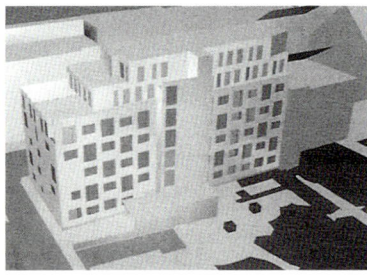

**TOMBSTONE FOR KARL SCHWANZER
GRABMAL KARL SCHWANZER**

Wien 19, 1995
L   Agnes Stryjewska

**AUSTRIA EMAIL WORKS BUILDING
BETRIEBSGEBÄUDE AUSTRIA EMAIL**

Eibesbrunnergasse, Wien 10
Competition 1st prize | Wettbewerb 1. Preis
Project | Projekt 1994–96
L   Suki Sangha
Co Anna Detzlhofer, Helmuth Locher
C   Herbert M. Liaunig

**INTERNATIONAL COMPETITION
SCOTTISH ARCHITECTURE AND DESIGN
CENTER | INTERNATIONALER WETTBE-
WERB SCHOTTISCHES ARCHITEKTUR-
UND DESIGNCENTER**

Edinburgh, 1995
L   Suki Sangha

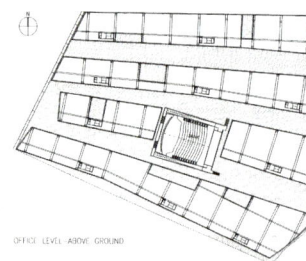

**MA 31 HEADQUARTERS BUILDING
BETRIEBSGEBÄUDE MA 31**

Wasserturm, Raxstraße, Wien 10, 1995
Competition 1st prize | Wettbewerb 1. Preis
L   Bernhard Moos

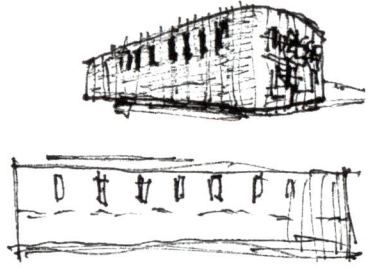

**ARCHITECTURAL EXPERT CONSULTANT
PROCESS | BAUKÜNSTLERISCHES
EXPERTENVERFAHREN**

Hauptplatz, Wiener Neustadt, 1995
2nd prize | 2. Preis
L   Karin Krummlauf

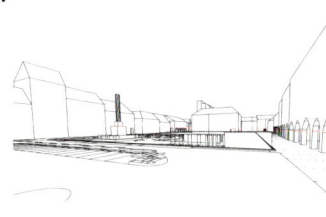

**SECONDARY SCHOOL | AHS ALLGEMEIN-
BILDENDE HÖHERE SCHULE
GENTZGASSE**

Wien 18, 1995
Development study | Bebauungsstudie
C   BIG Bundesimmobilien Gesellschaft Wien

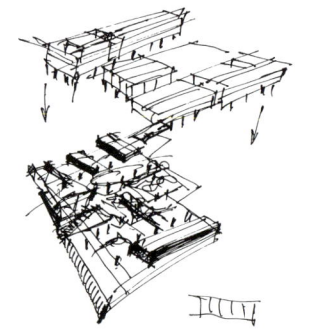

**DEVELOPMENT STUDY
BEBAUUNGSSTUDIE
HAWELGASSE 23**

Wien 18, 1995
C   Martin Schwanzer

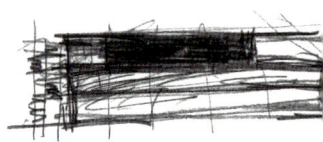

**SECONDARY SCHOOL COMPETITION
WETTBEWERB HAUPTSCHULE
CARLBERGERGASSE**

Wien 23, 1995
2nd prize | 2. Preis
L   Hannes Schild

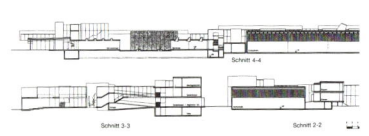

**URBAN DESIGN CONSULTANT
PROCESS | STÄDTEBAULICHES
EXPERTENVERFAHREN**

Thürnlhofstraße, Wien 11, 1995
2nd prize | 2. Preis
L   Agnes Stryjewska

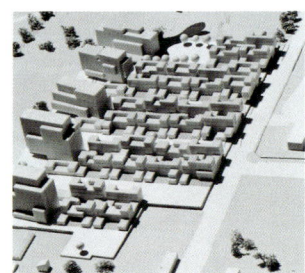

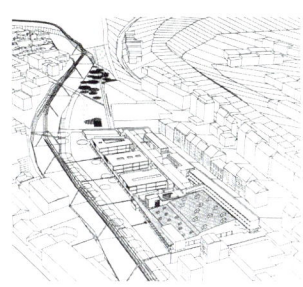

**REALISATION COMPETITION COMPREHENSIVE SCHOOL
REALISIERUNGSWETTBEWERB GESAMTSCHULE**

Wuppertal, 1995
3rd prize | 3. Preis
L Bernhard Moos

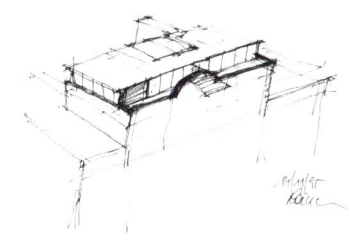

ROOF PAVILIONS | DACHPAVILLONS GYMNASIUM STUBENBASTEI

Stubenbastei 6–8, Wien 1
Project | Projekt 1996
A Werner Silbermayr
L Suki Sangha, Bernhard Moos
    Initiative Wolfgang Zinggl

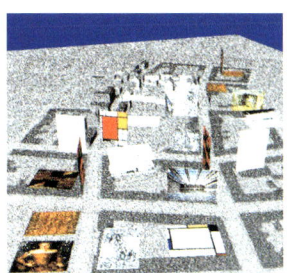

**RESEARCH PROJECT DESARTE
FORSCHUNGSPROJEKT DESARTE**

Computer supported Design of Artefacts: The emergence of new design practices and domains between art, technology and everyday culture
1995–2000
A Ina Wagner, TU Wien,
University of Lancaster, Aarhus University

SCHOOL COMPETITION | WETTBEWERB SCHULE VEITSHÖCHSHEIM

Germany | Deutschland, 1996

**AUSTRIAN EMBASSY COMPETITION
WETTBEWERB ÖSTERREICHISCHE BOTSCHAFT**

Berlin, 1996

**REALISATION COMPETITION SAXON FEDERAL & STATE LIBRARY
REALISIERUNGSWETTBEWERB SÄCHSISCHE LANDES- UND STAATS-BIBLIOTHEK**

Dresden, 1996
L Suki Sangha

**PRIMARY SCHOOL COMPETITION
WETTBEWERB VOLKSSCHULE PRANDAUGASSE**

Wien 22, 1996

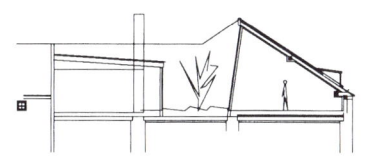

ROOFTOP EXTENSION | DACHAUSBAU ÖLZELTGASSE 4

Wien 3, 1996
L Michael Strobl
C Kosesnik-Wehrle

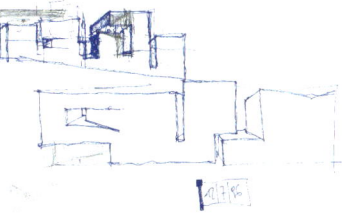

**DEVELOPMENT STUDY
BEBAUUNGSSTUDIE**

Martinstraße/Schopenhauerstraße
Wien 18, 1996
C Martin Schwanzer

**CONVERSION APARTMENT
UMBAU WOHNUNG R + M
UNGARGASSE 9**

Wien 3, 1996
L Edith Kissner

LIST OF PROJECTS | WERKVERZEICHNIS

MILLENNIUM WORKSHOP THE CONCRETE UTOPIA – STRUCTURAL ELEMENTS OF THE CITY | MILLENNIUMSWORKSHOP DIE KONKRETE UTOPIE – STRUKTURELEMENTE DER STADT

Wien, 1996
A Rudolf Kohoutek
L Karin Grausam
C MA 21B

FEDERAL SCHOOL CENTER COMPETITION WETTBEWERB BUNDESSCHULZENTRUM TAMSWEG

Tamsweg, Salzburg
1997

COMPETITION | WETTBEWERB SCHÖMER BAU-MAX

Schwechat, 1996
L Lorenzo Rossi, Michael Strobl
C Karl-Heinz Essl

FEDERAL SCHOOL CENTER COMPETITION WETTBEWERB BUNDESSCHULZENTRUM

Schärding, Oberösterreich
1997

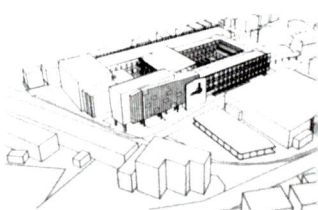

CONVERSION | UMBAU PALAIS EQUITABLE, MEZZANIN STOCK IM EISEN-PLATZ 3

Wien 1, 1996/97
A Werner Silbermayr
L Suki Sangha
C Herbert M. Liaunig/Auricon Holding

URBAN PLANNING STUDY STÄDTEBAULICHE STUDIE JÄGERSTRASSE

Wien 20, 1997
L Suki Sangha
C SEG

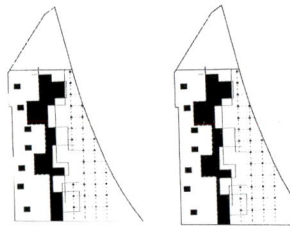

TABLE FOR AURICON | TISCH FÜR AURICON

Wien, 1997
C Herbert M. Liaunig

EXTENSION TO THE WIFI, ECONOMIC DEVELOPMENT INSTITUTE COMPETITION WETTBEWERB ERWEITERUNGSBAU WIFI WIRTSCHAFTSFÖRDERUNGSINSTITUT

St. Pölten, 1997
A Werner Silbermayr, Guido Welzl
L Suki Sangha, Michael Strobl
Co Roman Ivancsics, Jochen Käferhaus
    Helmuth Locher

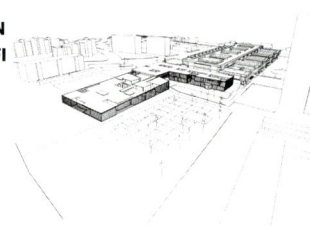

FREQUENTIS COMPETITION WETTBEWERB FREQUENTIS

Eibesbrunnergasse, Wien 10, 1997
1st prize | 1. Preis
A Werner Silbermayr
L Lorenzo Rossi, Michael Strobl

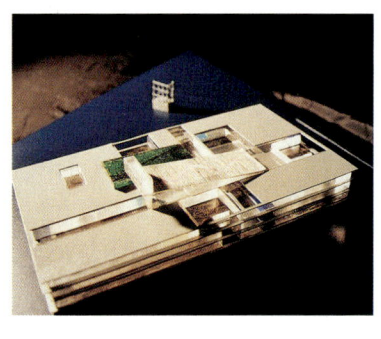

TOR | GATEWAY GYMNASIUM STUBENBASTEI

Stubenbastei 6–8, Wien 1, 1997
A Werner Silbermayr, Erich Monitzer
C BIG Bundesimmobilien Gesellschaft

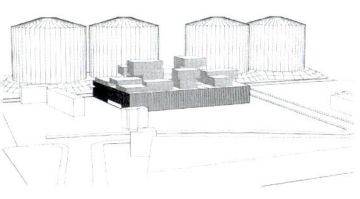

**DEVELOPMENT STUDY
BEBAUUNGSSTUDIE
PARAGONSTRASSE/GUGLGASSE**

Wien 3, 1997
L   Maria Siencnik
C   Zwerenz & Krause

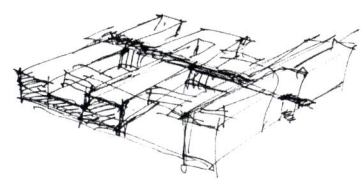

**FEDERAL STATE HOSPITAL COMPETITION
WETTBEWERB LANDESKRANKENHAUS**

Knittelfeld, Steiermark, 1998
A   Werner Silbermayr, Guido Welzl

**INSTITUTE BUILDING UNIVERSITY OF
TECHNOLOGY | INSTITUTSGEBÄUDE
TECHNISCHE UNIVERSITÄT**

Favoritenstraße 9–11
Wien 4, 1997–99
A   Werner Silbermayr, Guido Welzl
L   Maria Siencnik, Michael Lange
    Michael Pitsch
Co Helmuth Locher, Introplan
C   BIG Bundesimmobilien Gesellschaft

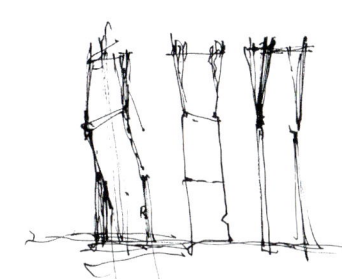

**STUDY FOR A SKYSCRAPER
STUDIE HOCHHAUS
FRIEDRICH ENGELS-PLATZ/HANDELS-
KAI**

Wien 20, 1998
L   Lorenzo Rossi, Claus Suttner
Co Helmuth Locher
C   Ernst Bosin

**EUROCITY CINEMA CENTER
KINO-CENTER
BAHNHOFSVORPLATZ, SALZBURG**

Competition 1st prize | Wettbewerb 1. Preis
1997–2001
A   Hannes Schild
L   Claus Suttner, Lorenzo Rossi, Klaus Leitner
Co Werner Rosinak, IBK-Reinhold Klestil
    TB-Alfred Eipeldauer
C   Konstruktiva/Projekta

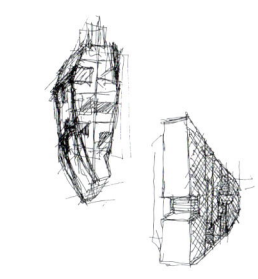

**ZMF COMPETITION CENTRAL MEDICAL
RESEARCH LABORATORY
WETTBEWERB ZMF ZENTRUM FÜR
MEDIZINISCHE GRUNDLAGEN-
FORSCHUNG**

Landeskrankenhaus Graz, 1998
A   Werner Silbermayr, Guido Welzl
L   Lorenzo Rossi, Michael Strobl, Claus Suttner
Co Helmuth Locher, ZFG-Projekt & TB
    Alfred Eipeldauer, Erich Monitzer

**JUGENDKULTUREN ´68 – ´98
STYRIAN FEDERAL STATE EXHIBITION
STEIRISCHE LANDESAUSSTELLUNG**

Bad Radkersburg, Steiermark
Exhibition conception | Ausstellungs-
konzeption 1998
A   Erich Monitzer, Werner Silbermayr
L   Michael Strobl
Co Norbert Chmel, Adolf Tögel

SUMMER HOUSE | SOMMERHAUS

Klosterneuburg, NÖ, 1998
L   Hannes Schild, Claus Suttner

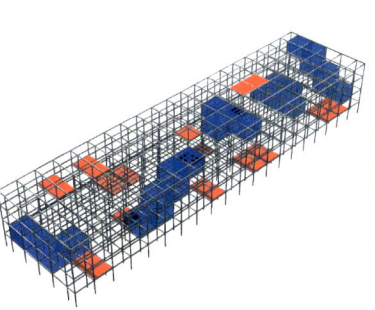

**BUILDING WITH WOOD
BAUEN MIT HOLZ
ALTMANNSDORFER ANGER**

Wien 12, 1998
Project | Projekt
L   Michael Pitsch, Lorenzo Rossi
    Hannes Schild
C   SEG, GPA Wohnbauvereinigung Wien

**PATHS OF IMPRESSIONISM
WEGE DES IMPRESSIONISMUS**

Landesmuseum Joanneum, Graz, 1998
Exhibition conception | Ausstellungs-
konzeption
A   Erich Monitzer, Werner Silbermayr
L   Michael Strobl
Co Norbert Chmel

LIST OF PROJECTS | WERKVERZEICHNIS

HOUSING DEVELOPMENT | WOHNBAU
FAVORITENSTRASSE 29–31

Wien 4, 1998
Project | Projekt
L Michael Strobl
C DIE ERSTE Bauträger AG

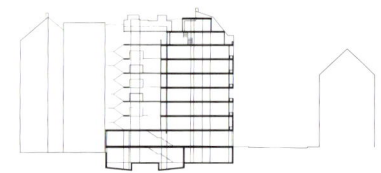

HOUSING DEVELOPMENT | WOHNBAU
TAUBSTUMMENGASSE 12

Wien 4, 1998–
A Werner Silbermayr, Guido Welzl
L Michael Lange, Isabel Brockdorff
C BIG Bundesimmobilien Gesellschaft

URBAN PLANNING DESIGN CONCEPT, AREA NORTH OF THE GASOMETERS
STÄDTEBAULICHES STRUKTURKONZEPT UMFELD NORD GASOMETER

Wien 3, 1998/99
A Rudolf Kohoutek
L Maria Siencnik, Michael Pitsch, Karin Grausam
Co Werner Rosinak, Kuzmich/Kleindienst
   Trafico/Snizek
C MA 21 A

PLEASURE DOME²
ENTERTAINMENT AND CINEMA CENTER
ENTERTAINMENT UND KINO-CENTER
PARAGONSTRASSE/GUGLGASSE

Wien 3, 1998–
L Lorenzo Rossi, Hannes Schild, Michael Strobl
Co Helmuth Locher, Werner Rosinak,
   ZFG-Projekt, TB-Alfred Eipeldauer
Projektentwicklung | Project development
   Günter Bischof
C Zwerenz & Krause

ROOFTOP EXTENSION | DACHAUFBAU
FAVORITENSTRASSE 27

Wien 4, 1998–
L Michael Strobl
Co Helmuth Locher
C Sigma-Bau Martin Schwanzer

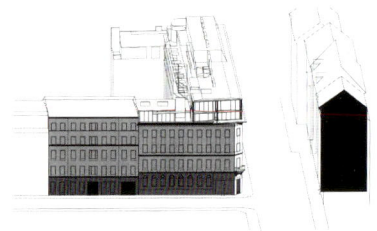

ARTPLACE/KARLSPLATZ COMPETITION
WETTBEWERB KUNSTPLATZ/KARLSPLATZ

Wien 1, 1999
L Josef Jakob, Holger Kurz
C K/Haus

HOUSING "THE HANGING GARDENS"
WOHNBAU „DIE HÄNGENDEN GÄRTEN"

Wiedner Hauptstraße/Schußwallgasse
Wien 4, 1998–
L Michael Strobl, Isabel Brockdorff
   Michael Lange
C Mischek Bau AG

COMPETENCE CENTER COMPETITION
WETTBEWERB KOMPETENZZENTRUM
FA. BLAHA

Korneuburg, 1999
C Blaha Büromöbel

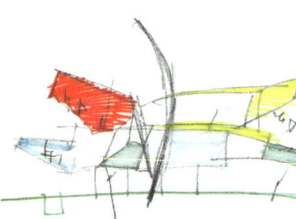

FUNCTIONS CENTER
VERANSTALTUNGSZENTRUM
KAISERBAHNHOF LAXENBURG

Laxenburg, 1998–
Competition 1st prize | Wettbewerb 1. Preis
A Werner Silbermayr
L Lorenzo Rossi, Michael Strobl
   Franz Bauernhofer
Co Helmuth Locher
C Gemeinde Laxenburg

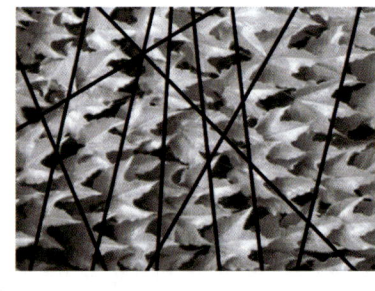

GALLERY OF RESEARCH – AULA, OLD UNIVERSITY | GALERIE DER FORSCHUNG – AULA, ALTE UNIVERSITÄT

Wien, 1999–2000
Exhibition conception | Ausstellungskonzeption
A Erich Monitzer, Werner Silbermayr
   Manfred Wolff-Plottegg
L Josef Jakob
Co Norbert Chmel, Rudolf Kohoutek
   Peter Weibel
C Österr. Akademie der Wissenschaften

Selection | Auswahl

1981 Housing. The Impact of Economy and Technology
Wien

1984 Tomorrow's Habitat
Grand Palais, Paris

1985 Projekte. Architektur
Rüdiger Lainer mit Gertraud Auer. Personale
Zentralvereinigung der Architekten Österreichs, Graz

Wiener Wohnbau. Wirklichkeiten
Künstlerhaus, Wien, Berlin

1986 Neuer Wiener Wohnbau/New Housing in Vienna
Wien. Internationale Wanderausstellung

1988 Visionäre Architektur Wien 1958/88
Internationale Wanderausstellung

1989 Peripherie. Direct Encounter
Haus der Architektur, Graz

Entwürfe für Wien. Architekturarbeiten zu aktuellen Stadtfragen
Ingenieur- und Architektenkammer, Wien

1990 Entwürfe für Wien. Städtischer Raum
Ingenieur- und Architektenkammer, Wien

175 Jahre TU Wien
Technische Universität, Wien

1991 Biennale di Venezia. 13 Austrian Positions
5th International Exhibition of Architecture
Giardini di Castello, Venezia

Neuer Wiener Wohnbau/New Housing in Vienna
Wien

Wien, Architektur. Der Stand der Dinge
Palazzo della Triennale, Milano

1992 Architecture in Styria
Buenos Aires

Möbel für sich. Ausgewählte Stücke österreichischer ArchitektInnen
Centroform, Wien

Architektur Wien zum Beispiel
Galerie und Architekturforum Aedes, Berlin

Participation in the exhibition at the Obalne Galerije Piran
Piran

Entwicklungsgebiete. Stand Oktober 1992
Wiener Planungswerkstatt, Wien

1993 Architecture as Commitment. Styrian Architecture 1986–1992
Architektur als Engagement. Architektur aus der Steiermark
Haus der Architektur, Graz

Vienna. State of the Art
University of Toronto, Toronto. Internationale Wanderausstellung

1993 Margherita Spiluttini: Neue Häuser, Architektur Fotografien
Architektur Zentrum Wien

1994 Neuer Wohnbau in Wien/Vienna Housing: Trends and Prototypes
Wiener Planungswerkstatt, Wien, UCLA, Los Angeles, UC Berkeley, Berkeley
Arizona State University, Tempe. Internationale Wanderausstellung

Wiener Städtebau
Architektur Zentrum Wien

Architektur zeigen
Österreich

1995 Wien, Architektur. Der Stand der Dinge
Wiener Planungswerkstatt, Wien. Internationale Wanderausstellung

Ein Raum für Fuenf
Altes AKH, Wien

80 Tage Wien. Architektur und Stadt
Architekturfestival und Ausstellung
Architektur Zentrum Wien

1995- Architektur im 20. Jahrhundert – Österreich
Deutsches Architekturmuseum Frankfurt/Main, Shedhalle, St. Pölten,
Centro Andaluz de Arte Contemporáneo, Sevilla, Ministerio de Fomento,
Galería de exposiciones del ministerio, Madrid. Intern. Wanderausstellung

1996 Biennale di Venezia. Sensing the future. The architect as seismograph
6th International Exhibition of Architecture
Giardini di Castello, Venezia

Kunst aus Österreich 1896–1996
Kunst- und Ausstellungshalle der Bundesrepublik Deutschland, Bonn,
Graphische Sammlung Albertina im Akademiehof, Wien

Baukultur in Österreich
Architekturstiftung Österreich, Parlament, Wien

1996- Innovative Austrian Architecture
Akademie der bildenden Künste, Wien, Thailand, Malaysia, Hongkong, Vietnam,
die Philippinen, Indonesien, Burma, Korea, Pakistan, Indien, Japan, Australien.
Internationale Wanderausstellung

1997 Architektur Wien. 500 Bauten
Wiener Planungswerkstatt, Wien

Architektur und Farbe
Architektenkammer Berlin

Das neue Schulhaus
Schüleruniversum und Stadtpartikel. Wien 1990–1996, Künstlerhaus, Wien

1999 Industrielle Wertschöpfung aus zeitgenössischer Architektur
Artware Edition Architektur, Haus der Industrie, Wien

Architektur Szene Österreich. Bauten Kritik Vermittlung
Ausstellungszentrum Ringturm, Wien

Rüdiger Lainer. Projekte
Künstlerhaus, Wien

EXHIBITIONS | AUSSTELLUNGEN

Biography | Biografie

1949	Born in Kaprun, Salzburg	Geboren in Kaprun, Salzburg
1968 – 71	Studied physics, sociology, painting in Vienna and Paris Studium der Physik, Soziologie, Malerei in Wien und Paris
1970 – 78	Study of architecture, University of Technology, Vienna, diploma	Studium der Architektur, Technische Universität, Wien, Diplom
1978 – 84	Theoretical works on the space/time complex Theoretische Arbeiten zum Raum-Zeitkomplex
1985 –	Self-employed architect	Freischaffender Architekt
1985	Visiting professor, Universidad de Buenos Aires, Argentina Gastprofessur, Universidad de Buenos Aires, Argentinien
1993	Summer Academy, Graz	Sommerakademie Graz
1995	Interim director of the Peichl master class / Visiting professor, Academy of Fine Arts, Vienna	Interimistische Leitung Meisterschule Peichl/Gastprofessur Akademie der bildenden Künste, Wien
1997–	Professor and director of the architecture master class at the Academy of Fine Arts, Vienna	Professor und Leiter der Meisterschule für Architektur, Akademie der bildenden Künste, Wien

Awards | Preise

1984	Tomorrow's Habitat, Paris
1989	Austrian State Prize for Experimental Tendencies in Architecture	Österreichischer Staatspreis für Experimentelle Tendenzen in der Architektur
1990	Major Austrian Housing Prize	Großer Österreichischer Wohnbaupreis
1991	Urban Renewal Prize, Vienna	Stadterneuerungspreis, Wien
	Prize of the Central Association of Architects in Austria Preis der Zentralvereinigung der Architekten Österreichs
1995	Prize of the Central Association of Architects in Austria Preis der Zentralvereinigung der Architekten Österreichs
	Architecture Congress, Piran, received award in recognition of his work	Architekturtage Piran, Anerkennungspreis
	American Institute of Architects/European Chapter- Excellence in Design Award
1997	Architecture Prize of the Austrian Cement Industry Architekturpreis der Österreichischen Zementindustrie

Selection | Auswahl

WOHNBAU ENGERTHSTRASSE, WIEN–LEOPOLDSTADT
Transposition, Superposition. Projet d'habitation, Engerthstraße, Vienne, AA L'Architecture d'Aujourd'hui, n⁰ 242. Paris 1985, pp. 36/37.
Wohnbebauung in Wien 2, Vorgartenstraße-Engerthstraße, Bauwelt, n⁰ 48. Berlin 1985, pp. 348/349.
Lainer, Rüdiger/Auer, Gertraud, Dekomponierte Idylle, Werk, Bauen + Wohnen, n⁰ 10/86. Zürich 1986, pp. 34/37.
Steiner, Dietmar, Urbanität & Understatement/Urbanity & Understatement, Neuer Wiener Wohnbau/New Housing in Vienna. Wien 1986, pp. 90, 95, 109, 126/127.
Arquitectura 'mambo'. Propuesta para una nueva zona residencial, A&V Monografías de Arquitectura y Vivienda, n⁰ 15. Madrid 1988, pp. 72–75.
Feuerstein, Günther, Neue Aspekte der achtziger Jahre, Visionäre Architektur. Wien 1958/1988. Berlin 1988, p. 172.

UMBAU HERMANNGASSE 29, WIEN–NEUBAU
Chramosta, Walter M., Der harte Gegensatz, Perspektiven, Heft 9. Wien 1989, p. 40.
– Freche Fragmente. Lainer & Auer retten mit scharfen Schnitten einen totgeglaubten Baukörper in der Wiener Vorstadt, Die Presse, 12./13. Mai. Wien 1990, p. XIII.
– Implantationen. R. Lainer und G. Auer veredeln ein Wiener Vorstadthaus, Architektur & Bauforum, n⁰ 138. Wien 1990, pp. 27–36.
Volumes en pièces. Réhabilitation de logement social à Vienne, Techniques & Architecture, n⁰ 393. Paris 1990/91, pp. 124–128.
Chramosta, Walter M., Biedermeier und Implantationen, archithese, n⁰ 2/91. Heiden 1991, pp. 12–16.
Lainer, Rüdiger/Auer, Gertraud, Umbau in Wien, Baumeister, n⁰ 3/91. München 1991, pp. 46–51.
Romanelli, Marco, Hermanngasse 29, Vienna, domus, n⁰ 724. Milano 1991, pp. 66–73.
Hermanngasse 29, Domestic Interiors, European Masters/3, n⁰ 5. Barcelona 1991, pp. 32–41.
Könnecke, Karl-Richard, Biedermeiers „Date" mit der Moderne, Häuser, n⁰ 1/92. Hamburg 1992, pp. 99, 114–119.
Lainer, Rüdiger, Der Gebrauch des Objektes, Möbel Raum Design, n⁰ 4/92. Wien 1992/Architektur & Bauforum, n⁰ 153. Wien 1992.
Redevelopment Project "Landed" Element, a+u Architecture and Urbanism, n⁰ 258. Tokyo 1992, pp. 52–59.
Reiners, Holger/Hoor, Dieter, Implantate schaffen Wohnqualität, Wohnen unterm Dach. Dachausbau. München 1992, pp. 130–133.
Lederer, Arno/Ragnarsdóttir, Jórunn, Sanierung/Rehabilitation, Wohnen Heute/Housing Today. Stuttgart/Zürich 1992, pp. 84–91.
Hermanngasse 29/Wien 7, Baujahre. Österreichische Architektur 1967–1991, Zentralvereinigung der Architekten Österreichs (Ed.). Wien 1992, pp. 208/209.
Ludwig, Karl/Weddige, Rüdiger, Ein Dachgarten für alle Hausbewohner, Dachgärten und Balkone. Ideen, Anlage, Beispiele. München 1993, pp. 148/149.
Porch/Windfang/Coupe-vent, A+D Architecture+Detail, n⁰ 1. Stuttgart 1993, pp. 58/59, 63.
Apartments, Hermanngasse: Wien, Austria, SD Space Design, n⁰ 26. Tokyo 1995, pp. 126–129, 167.
Gelandete Objekte. Umbau und Sanierung eines Biedermeierhauses mit Fabriktrakt, Neue Wohnräume unterm Dach, Gunda Dworschak/Alfred Wenke (Eds.). Augsburg 1995, pp. 13–26.
Dimster, Frank, Wohnkomplex Hermanngasse 29. Wien. 1990, Die neue österreichische Architektur. Stuttgart/Berlin/Köln 1995, pp. 148–151.

WOHNBAU WAIDHAUSENSTRASSE 24, WIEN–PENZING
Chramosta, Walter M., Scheiben/Schächte/Schichtungen/Sinnesschärfungen. Lainer & Auer finden auch im Selbstverständlichen das Spezifische, Architektur & Bauforum, n⁰ 145. Wien 1991, pp. 33–38.
Im lockeren Rhythmus der „Neustadt", Perspektiven, Heft 3. Wien 1991, pp. 8/9.
Zschokke, Walter, Was heißt da normal? Die zeitlose Behausungsfrage, von Lainer/Auer in Wien aktuell beantwortet, Die Presse, 2./3. März. Wien 1991, p. XI.
Wohnhausanlage Waidhausenstraße, Wien, 1991/Housing project Waidhausenstraße, Vienna, 1991, BauArt, Heft 3/Issue 3. Wien 1992, p. 72.
Margherita Spiluttini. Neue Häuser. Architektur Fotografien/New Houses. Architectural Photographs. Wien 1993, pp. 32.1–32.4.
Steiner, Dietmar, Architektur Beispiele Eternit. Ausgewählte Bauten, Architektur Beispiele Eternit. Kulturgeschichte eines Baustoffes. Wien 1994, pp. 204–207.
Dimster, Frank, Wohnkomplex Waidhausenstraße 24. Wien–Penzing. 1991, Die neue österreichische Architektur. Stuttgart/Berlin/Köln 1995, pp. 152–155.
Spezifische Selbstverständlichkeit, Neue Wohnexperimente, Gunda Dworschak/Alfred Wenke (Eds.). Augsburg 1997, pp. 57–66.

WOHNHAUSANLAGE SIEGESPLATZ 21/BENJOWSKIGASSE, WIEN–ASPERN
Chramosta, Walter M., 10 Ansätze im zeitgenössischen Wiener Wohnbau. Die vorstädtische Sequenz, Perspektiven, Heft 7/8. Wien 1988, pp. 55/56.
– Pars pro toto. Lainer/Auer bescheren der jungen Asperner Siedlungsfamilie ein typ(olog)isches Mitglied, Architektur & Bauforum, n⁰ 147. Wien 1991, pp. 27–33.
Waechter-Böhm, Liesbeth, Hört, hört! Am Asperner Siegesplatz steht eine Wohnanlage, die zu sprechen und zu schweigen weiß, Die Presse, 12./13. Oktober. Wien 1991, p. XI.
Walden, Gert, Eine Gestalt aus Romantik und Kalkül, Der Standard, 10. Oktober. Wien 1991 Architektur Wien zum Beispiel, Aedes, Galerie für Architektur und Raum (Ed.). Berlin 1992, pp. 12/13, 32–37.
Reveal. Laibung. Embrasure, A+D Architecture+Detail, n⁰ 2, Stuttgart 1994, pp. 62/63.
Global und lokal, Neue Wohnexperimente, Gunda Dworschak/Alfred Wenke (Eds.). Augsburg 1997, pp. 47–56.

WOHNHAUSANLAGE ROTHENBURGSTRASSE 2, WIEN–ALTMANNSDORF
Chramosta, Walter M., Bunte Steine aus dem Stadtbaukasten. Rüdiger Lainer & Gertraud Auer stärken das Situationistische in einer unsicheren Stadtfigur, Architektur & Bauforum, n⁰ 153. Wien 1992, pp. 123–127.

PENTHOUSE SEILERGASSE 16, WIEN–INNERE STADT
Walden, Gert, „Tabula rasa" über der Traufenkante, Architektur & Bauforum, n⁰ 174. Wien 1995, pp. 106–115.
Orben, Claudia, Wohnobjekt gelandet. Ein Dachaufbau in der Wiener Innenstadt, bausubstanz, Heft 10. Neustadt 1995, pp. 22–25.
Dungl, Leopold, Lichtblick im Chaos der Dächer über Wien. Rüdiger Lainer reüssiert in der City mit offen gestalteten Dachgeschossen auf historischem Bau, Kurier, 11. August. Wien 1995, p. 24.
Zschokke, Walter, Transparenz und Luftigkeit, Die Presse, 8. Juli. Wien 1995, p. IX.
– Attico a Vienna/Penthouse in Vienna, domus, n⁰ 781. Milano 1996, pp. 44–48.
Stock, Wolfgang Jean, Penthouse in Wien, Baumeister, n⁰ 5. München 1996, pp. 38–42.
Rodermond, Janny, Penthouse bekroont neo-Barok. Geslaagde transformatie naar ontwerp van Rüdiger Lainer, de Architect, n⁰ 62. 's-Gravenhage 1996, pp. 14–17.
Lerch, Helmut, Penthouseaufbau, Wohnhaus-Erweiterungen. Anbauten – Aufbauten – Ausbauten. Leinfelden-Echterdingen 1997, pp. 162–167.
Helsing Almaas, Ingerid, Penthouse Seilergasse, Vienna. Objects and Rituals. Architecture in Context. Köln/London 1997, pp. 8–23, 78.
Penthouse–Seilergasse 16–Vienna, International Architecture Yearbook, n⁰ 3. Victoria 1997, pp. 326/327.

UMBAU PALAIS EQUITABLE, MEZZANIN, WIEN–INNERE STADT
Waechter-Böhm, Liesbeth, Mondrian meets Ryman und andere/Mondrian meets Ryman and Others. Umbau im Mezzanin des Palais Equitable in Wien-Innenstadt, architektur aktuell, n⁰ 202. Wien 1997, pp. 39, 80–91.
Palais Equitable – Vienna 1, Stock im Eisen Platz 3, International Architecture Yearbook, n⁰ 4. Victoria 1997, pp. 106, 404.
Walden, Gert, Mit edler Blässe im Palais. Architekt Rüdiger Lainer plante einen Büroumbau im Wiener „Equitable", Der Standard, 14. Februar. Wien 1997, p. 12.
Séron-Pierre, Catherine, Aménagements tertiaires. Vienne, Autriche. Aménagement d'un étage de bureaux, le moniteur architecture amc, n⁰ 88. Paris 1998, pp. 84–89.

STÄDTEBAULICHES LEITPROJEKT ALTES FLUGFELD ASPERN
Lainer, Rüdiger/Kretschmer, Rudolf, Flugfeld Aspern – Die urbane Partitur/Flugfeld Aspern – Kooperatives Städtebauliches Expertenverfahren, Perspektiven, Heft 10. Wien 1992, pp. 62–64/65–70.
Stracke, Ferdinand/Schönfeld, Manfred, Bewegung und Raum/Flugfeld Aspern, Wien wächst. Bewegung. Beirat für die Stadtentwicklungsbereiche, Magistrat der Stadt Wien (Ed.). Wien 1993, pp. 12–15/22–25.
Lainer, Rüdiger/ Schönfeld, Manfred, Zwischenland-Zwischenstadt. Überlegungen vor der Landung am Alten Flugfeld/Was hat bis jetzt geklappt?, Wächst Wien? Raum, Zeit, Qualität, Magistrat der Stadt Wien (Ed.). Wien 1993, pp. 56–59.
– Intermediate Country/Intermediate Town. Considerations on the Altes Flugfeld, Vienna. To the year 2000 and beyond, Municipal Administration of the City of Vienna (Ed.). Wien 1993, pp. 37–39.
Urbane Partitur des neuen Donauwalzers. Altes Flugfeld Aspern, architektur aktuell, n⁰ 163/164. Wien 1993, pp. 49–54.
Kühn, Christian, Wohin mit dem fahrbaren Haus? Die Quadratur des Kreises: Zwei neue Mammutsiedlungen in Simmering und Aspern, Die Presse, 30. Jänner. Wien 1993, p. XI.
Lainer, Rüdiger, Altes Flugfeld Aspern, MA 21 C, Stadtteilplanung und Flächennutzung (Ed.). Wien 1994.

BIBLIOGRAPHY | BIBLIOGRAFIE

Lainer, Rüdiger, Die Regeln, die Vielfalt und der Gebrauch. Läßt sich die instrumentelle Phantasie wachküssen?, HdA Dokumente zur Architektur, Heft 2. Graz, pp. 38–43.
Klopf, Peter/Pirhofer, Gottfried/Schenekl, Manfred, Themenstädte: Nachrüstung der Peripherie, Bauwelt, n° 24. Berlin 1995, pp. 1384–1387.
Stock, Wolfgang Jean, Urbane Partitur, Baumeister, n° 12. München 1996, pp. 19–22.
Un nuovo modello urbano. Space and Movement, l'ARCA, n° 101. Milano 1996, p. 90.
Tilman, Harm, Weense ontwikkeling stagneert, de Architect, n° 62. 's-Gravenhage 1996, pp. 38–49.

STEIRISCHE LANDESAUSSTELLUNG 1998
Welcome to the pleasure dome. Steirische Landesausstellung '98 - Jugendkulturen '68 –'98. Ausstellungskatalog. 1998, pp. 20–23/Architektur & Bauforum, n° 195. Wien 1998, pp. 77–82.

HAUPTSCHULE ABSBERGGASSE 50, WIEN-FAVORITEN
Eiblmayr, Judith, Neubau einer 12-klassigen Ganztags-Hauptschule. Absberggasse. Wien X, Perspektiven, Heft 5. Wien 1993, pp. 32/33.
Zacek, Patricia, Le peintre, la pomme, Picasso. Schulen müssen keine Kunstwerke sein – seit neuestem sind sie es doch. Der Schulbau von Rüdiger Lainer in der Absberggasse, Architektur & Bauforum, n° 168. Wien 1994, pp. 50–60.
Zschokke, Walter, Wiener Schulbau-Frühling. Hauptschule in Wien-Favoriten, Leonardo, n° 6/94. Augsburg 1994, pp. 32–36.
– Kunst im Spiel, Unterricht in den Bäumen, Die Presse, 24. September. Wien 1994, p. XI.
– Hauptschule Wien 10, Absberggasse, Architektur zeigen, Zentralvereinigung der Architekten (Ed.). Wien 1994.
– Vom Buchstabenbild zum Buchstabenrätsel. Schriften an neueren Bauwerken in Österreich, archithese, n° 1–95. Sulgen 1995, pp. 34–36.
Schule in Wien, A+D Architecture + Detail, n° 5. Stuttgart 1995, pp. 8–13, 62.
Chramosta, Walter M., Aufforderung zum Schichtwechsel, Projekte und Konzepte. Hauptschule Absberggasse Wien 10, Heft 2, Stadtplanung Wien, Magistratsabteilung 19, Architektur und Stadtgestaltung (Ed.). Wien 1995.
– Aufforderung zum Schichtwechsel/Call to change shifts, Das neue Schulhaus. Schüleruniversum und Stadtpartikel/The New Schoolhouse. Schoolchild's Universe and Urban Particle. Wien/Berlin 1996, pp. 108–121, 246/247.
Lainer, Rüdiger, Schule als Innenstadt, Werk, Bauen+Wohnen, n° 5. Zürich 1996, pp. 56–59.
Eicher, Jürgen, Rhythmus und Relief. Hauptschule in Wien-Favoriten, db deutsche bauzeitung, n° 2/96. Stuttgart 1996, pp. 78–83, 166.
Rodermond, Janny, Neutrale structuur genuanceerd benut. Hauptschule Absberggasse van Lainer en Auer, de Architect, n° 62. 's-Gravenhage 1996, pp. 34–37.
Lang, Christian, Typologie-Raumqualität/Hauptschule Absberggasse – Wien 10, Schulbau in Österreich. Eine qualitative Bestandsaufnahme. Wien 1996, pp. 19–34, 160–165.
Steiner, Dietmar, „Konjunktur der Architektur" – von 1970 bis heute, Architektur aus Österreich. 1896–1996. München/New York 1996, pp. 87, 105.
Lainer, Rüdiger, Hauptschule Absberggasse, Wien-Favoriten 1994, Architektur und Farbe. Berlin 1997, pp. 34–37.
Highschool Absberggasse, International Architecture Yearbook, n° 3. Victoria 1997, pp. 84/85.
Kapfinger, Otto/Zschokke, Walter, Secondary school, Vienna/Hauptschule Absberggasse, Wien Favoriten, 1994, New Austrian Architecture/Architektur Szene Österreich. Constructions Critique Communication/Bauten Kritik Vermittlung. Salzburg/München 1999, pp. 46–49.

BETRIEBSGEBÄUDE AUSTRIA EMAIL, WIEN-FAVORITEN
Holletschek, Bernhard, Industriebau in Österreich: Zwei neue Ansätze. Fa. Austria Email AG, Wien, Industriebau. Radikale Umstrukturierung. Praxisreport. Basel 1995, pp.162/163
Gutachterverfahren: Austria Email AG, wettbewerbe, n° 150. Wien 1996, pp. 98–101.

EUROCITY KINO-CENTER, SALZBURG
Lainer, Rüdiger, Eurocity. Kino- und Einkaufszentrum Eurocity in Salzburg, Architektur & Bauforum, n° 191. Wien 1997, pp. 77–80.

PLEASURE DOME², WIEN-LANDSTRASSE
Walden, Gert, Welcome to the pleasuredome². Ein Urban Entertainment Center vor den Gasometern, Architektur & Bauforum, n° 199. Wien 1999, pp. 121–128.
– Architektur-Landschaft im Kinozentrum der Gasometer, Der Standard, 3. Februar. Wien 1999, p. 37.

GENERAL PUBLICATIONS | ALLGEMEINE PUBLIKATIONEN
Wiener Wohnbau. Wirklichkeiten, Magistrat der Stadt Wien, MA 19-Stadtgestaltung (Ed.). Wien 1985, pp. 238, 241, 282, 287.
Lainer, Rüdiger/Auer, Gertraud, Projekte 1981–1986, Transparent, n° 1/2, Günther Feuerstein (Ed.). Wien 1986, pp. 23–37.
Steiner, Dietmar, Going Backwards Towards the Future. Young Austrian Architecture, Ottagono, n° 88. Milano 1988, p. 32.
Die Kultur des Wohnens, Bd. 2, Dietmar Steiner (Ed.). Wien 1988, pp. 102/103, 162/163.
Zwei Antworten auf identische Grundfragen. Vernetzung und Labyrinth: Totalsanierung Wohnhaus Wien 14, Landung und Implantation: Totalsanierung Wohnhaus Wien 7, architektur aktuell, n° 130. Wien 1989, pp. 72–74.
Gleichzeitigkeiten/Altes und Neues, Entwürfe für Wien 1989, Ingenieur- und Architektenkammer für Wien, Niederösterreich und Burgenland (Ed.). Wien 1989, pp. 64/65.
Peripherie. Direct Encounter, Haus der Architektur Graz (Ed.). Graz 1989, pp. 30–33.
Chramosta, Walter M., In der Leere lockt die Spannung der Wechselfelder. Zur Architektur von Rüdiger Lainer und Gertraud Auer, Möbel Raum Design, n° 2/90. Wien 1990, pp. 19–31.
Rüdiger Lainer, Gertraud Auer. Wohnbebauung Engerthstraße/Umbau Gyrowetzgasse, SD Space Design, n° 306. Tokyo 1990, pp. 38–41.
Eine Mitte am Ende als neuer Anfang, Entwürfe für Wien 1990, Ingenieur- und Architektenkammer für Wien, Niederösterreich und Burgenland (Ed.). Wien 1990, pp. 66/67.
Fleck, Robert, Vivre. Milena Jesenská. Eine literarische Installation in szenischen Räumen, Wiener Festwochen 1990. Wien 1990, pp. 115–117.
Gentner, Monika, Dem Wort Raum geben. Die politisch-literarische Installation „Vivre! Milena Jesenská!" in neun Räumen, architektur aktuell, n° 137. Wien 1990, pp. 78–80.
Remodelling Hermanngasse, „Landed elements", Vienna, 13 Austrian Positions. Biennale di Venezia 1991. Klagenfurt 1991, pp. 80–85, 95.
Steiner, Dietmar, Urbanität & Understatement/Urbanity & Understatement, Neuer Wiener Wohnbau/New Housing in Vienna. Wien 1991, pp. 90, 95, 108, 166/167.
Kapfinger, Otto, Fragmentarische Inventur, Möbel für sich. Ausgewählte Stücke österreichischer Architektinnen/Architekten. Wien 1992, pp. 10/11, 13, 38/39.
– Möbel für sich. Ausgewählte Stücke österreichischer Architekten. Eine fragmentarische Inventur, Architektur & Bauforum, n° 151. Wien 1992, pp. 66–71.
Gelandete Elemente, Architektur & Bauforum, n° 152. Wien 1992, pp. 102–105.
Flos, Birgit, lo(o)sgelöst, lo(o)sgelöst, n° 0. Wien 1992, pp. 19–22.
Lainer, Rüdiger, Vielfalt, Ordnung und Gebrauch. Wohin führen Vorgaben – eine Teilansicht, Perspektiven, Heft 3. Wien 1993, pp. 33/34.
Experimentelle Tendenzen in der Architektur. Architektur & Bauforum, n° 157. Wien 1993.
Rüdiger Lainer, Sprechen über Architektur, Bene, Wien (Ed.). Wien 1993.
Klasmann, Jaan, Sparmeister am Reißbrett, a3 Bau, n° 10. Gießhübl 1994, pp. 26–29.
Delera, Anna, La sperimentazione ad Almere, Housing, n° 6. Milano 1994, pp. 18–27.
Bucher, Viktor, Zehn Fragen an zehn Architekten, Architektur & Bauforum, n° 173. Wien 1995, pp. 54–67.
Eiblmayr, Judith, Rüdiger Lainer. Wettbewerbe 1983–1995, Architektur & Bauforum, n° 176. Wien 1995, pp. 78–101.
Lainer, Rüdiger, Exit House. Learning from the Bosnian House, Architektur & Bauforum, n° 178. Wien 1995, pp. 44–51.
Architektur im 20. Jahrhundert – Österreich, Annette Becker/Dietmar Steiner/Wilfried Wang (Eds.). München/New York 1995, pp. 54/55, 110/111, 312/313, 339.
Wien, Architektur. Der Stand der Dinge/Vienna, Architecture. The State of the Art, Stadtplanung Wien, Magistratsabteilung 18 (Ed.). Wien 1995, pp. 9, 16–18, 28, 63–65.
Achleitner, Friedrich, Österreichische Architektur im 20. Jahrhundert, Bd III/2 Wien 13.–18. Bezirk. Salzburg/Wien 1995, pp. 75, 92, 98/99.
Helsing Almaas, Ingerid, Vienna. A guide to recent architecture. London 1995, pp. 152–155, 200/201, 288–291. Wien. Ein Führer zur zeitgenössischen Architektur. Köln 1996, pp. 152–155, 200/201, 288–291.
Wustlich, Reinhart, Heldenplatz: Neue Architektur in Österreich. Herausforderung durch das, was Architektur fordern könnte, Centrum. Jahrbuch Architektur und Stadt 1996. Braunschweig/Wiesbaden 1996, pp. 226, 230.
Delera, Anna, Flessibilité e autodeterminazione. Graz. Rüdiger Lainer, Strumenti, Le regole del progetto, n° 177. Rimini 1996, pp. 70–73.
M 1:333. Innovative Austrian Architecture, Ramesh Kumar Biswas (Ed.). Wien/New York 1996, pp. 52/53, 93, 108–111, 130, 204, 210, 212, 221.
Emerging voices. Rüdiger Lainer, 6th international architecture exhibition. Sensing the future. The architect as seismograph. La Biennale di Venezia 1996, pp. 206–209.
Bottero, Bianca, Citté del mercato – citté degli abitanti – citté sostenibile, Housing, n° 7/8. Milano 1997, pp. 26,29.
Lainers Architekturideen. Interview mit Gerfried Sperl, konstruktiv, n° 203. Wien1997, pp. 46–49.
Lainer, Rüdiger, Zwischen den Bäumen am Turm vorbei. Ingrid Zernig, Manfred Zernig, Architektur & Bauforum, n° 191. Wien 1997, pp. 137–139.
Lainer, Rüdiger/Wagner, Ina, Dezentrale Gesundheitseinrichtung Antonigasse, Architektur & Bauforum, n° 188. Wien 1997, pp. 77–80.

Architektur Wien. 500 Bauten, Stadtplanung Wien/MA 18/MA 19/Architektur Zentrum Wien (Eds.). Wien/New York 1997, pp. 50, 195, 223, 258, 344.
Walden, Gert, Neue Bilder einer Wohnung, Architektur & Bauforum, n° 188. Wien 1997, pp. 85–88.
– Die Thermobox im Stelzendorf, Der Standard, 14. August. Wien 1998, p. 62.
Wir produzieren Auslaufmodelle. Rüdiger Lainer über Chancen und Probleme des Baustoffs Beton. Interview mit Martin Fritzl und Alfred Bankhamer, Bau & Immobilien Report, n° 10. Klosterneuburg 1998, pp. 32–37.
Sarnitz, August, Vernetzung der österreichischen Architektur seit 1945. Rüdiger Lainer (1949), Bauen in Europa. Österreichische Architekten im Europa des 20. Jahrhunderts/Architectes autrichiens en Europe au Xxème siècle. Wien 1999, p. 118.

RESEARCH PAPERS | FORSCHUNGSSCHRIFTEN

Lainer, Rüdiger, Konkrete Utopien für Wien. Millenniumsworkshop – Strukturelemente der Stadt, architektur, Heft 5. Perchtoldsdorf 1996, pp. 12/13.
Die konkrete Utopie – Strukturelemente der Stadt, Arbeitsbericht Millenniumsworkshop 1996, Magistratsabteilung 21B (Ed.). Wien 1997.
Lainer, Rüdiger/Wagner, Ina, Die Wunderkammer. Zur computerunterstützten Konzeption von Objekten und Räumen, Architektur & Bauforum, n° 188. Wien 1997, pp. 57–62.
– Vienna Architecture Scenario. DESARTE First Phase Project Overview. Ina Wagner, Technische Universität Wien (Ed.). Wien 1997.
DESARTE. The Computer-Supported Design of Artefacts & Spaces in Architecture Landscape Architecture Industrial Design IT Design, Esprit LTR Project N° 21870. First Phase Final Report: Part 1, Ina Wagner, Technische Universität Wien (Ed.). Wien 1997.
Lainer, Rüdiger/Wagner, Ina/Tellioglu, Hilda, Flexible Standardisierung. Möglichkeiten der computerunterstützten Integration von Design und Produktion am Beispiel Architektur. Forschungsarbeiten der Abteilung für CSCW am Institut für Gestaltungs- und Wirkungsforschung der Technischen Universität Wien, n° 7. Wien 1997.
Lainer, Rüdiger/Wagner, Ina, Offenes Planen. Erweiterung der Lösungsräume für architektonisches Entwerfen, Architektur & Bauforum, n° 196. Wien 1998, pp. 145–148.
– Reichhaltige Erzählungen. Themenbezogenes Arbeiten und die Kommunikation von Qualitäten, Architektur & Bauforum, n° 197. Wien 1998, pp. 138–141.
Tellioglu, Hilda/Wagner, Ina/Lainer, Rüdiger, Open Design Methodologies. Exploring Architectural Practice for Systems Design. Proceedings of the Participatory Design Conference PDC '98, R. Chatfield/S. Kuhn/M. Muller (Eds.), November 12–14. Seattle 1998.
Lainer, Rüdiger/Wagner, Ina, Connecting Qualities of Social Use with Spatial Qualities, Cooperative Buildings. Integrating Information, Organization, and Architecture, Norbert A. Streitz/Shin'ichi Konomi/Heinz-Jürgen Burkhardt (Eds.), Lecture Notes in Computer Science, Vol. 1370. Berlin/Heidelberg 1998, pp. 191–203.
– Vernetzte Arbeitsräume: Orte, Zwischen-Räume, An-Orte, Work & Culture. Büro. Inszenierung von Arbeit, Herbert Lachmayer/Eleonora Louis (Eds.). Klagenfurt 1998, pp. 327–336.
Lainer, Rüdiger/Wagner, Ina, Offene Raumorganisation – schwebende Nutzungen, Architektur & Bauforum, n° 198. Wien 1999, pp. 130–133.
Büscher, Monika/Kompast, Martin/Lainer, Rüdiger/Wagner, Ina, The Architect's Wunderkammer: Aestethic Pleasure & Engagement in Electronic Spaces, Digital Creativity, Volume 10, n° 1. 1999, pp. 1–17.
– Space for Inspiration: Ethnography and User Involvement in Designing the Wunderkammer. Proceedings Workshop Ethnographic Studies in Real and Virtual Environments: Inhabited Information Spaces and Connected Communities, January 24–26. Edinburgh 1999.

MitarbeiterInnen 1997–99

Karin Grausam, Josef Jakob, Michael Lange, Klaus Leitner, Bernhard Moos-Seiller, Michael Pitsch, Lorenzo Rossi, Suki Sangha, Hannes Schild, Maria Christina Siencnik, Michael Strobl, Claus Suttner, Lisa Zentner • Midya Arif, Franz Bauernhofer, Isabel Brockdorff, Anna-Marija Dufils-Meniga, Heike Frohnapfel, Manuela Gerschwiler, Holger Kurz, Jörg Westphal

MitarbeiterInnen bis 1997

Inge Andritz, Wolfgang Arnezeder, Stephen Bidwell, Ramesh Biswas, Betül Bozkurt, Sigrid Brewka, Andreas Breiner, Henrike Cramer, Birgit Ecker, Robert Fritz, Roland Gasperl, Andreas Gasser, Karsten Gatke, Martina Grabensteiner-Kalteis, Rainer Grelle, Petra Gruber, Paul Grundei, Bernhard Grusch, Rosa Hilbe, Susanne Höhndorf, Barbara Höller, Konrad Hutter, Claudia Janisch, Claudia Jung, Michael Karassowitsch, Marina Kieser, Edith Kissner, Horst Konrad, Fritz Koszik, Tobias Kreissl, Karin Krummlauf, Peter Kusstatscher, Eva Langheiter, Uli Machold, Eva Madshus, Alexander Manolopoulos, Thomas Maresch, Richard Messner, Johann Moser, Richard Obermayr, Michaela Pammer, Irmtraud Peer, Josef Perner, Friedrich Pühringer, Otmar Pribitzer, Konrad Rautter, Klaus Safar, Ulrike Schartner, Johann Schindler, Florian Schmidhuber, Claudia Schrammel, Peter Seyffert, Jutta Steinfels, Martin Simmel, Gabriele Sinzinger, Markus Stöger, Agnes Stryjewska, Gabor Szabo, Elemer Szilassy, Markus Tomaselli, Peter Tremba, Dustin Tusnovics, Irmgard Wenzl